About the author

A former Sheffield steel worker and trade union convenor Mick Drewry graduated from Sheffield Hallam University in 1997. He worked as a volunteer and then paid worker for a local community group before moving to Barnsley Council as a Community Development Worker in 2002. He took early retirement in 2010. *Intimidation* is his third publication and second book as author.

Dedication

For my mum, *'the wind beneath my wings'*.

Mick Drewry

INTIMIDATION

The History, the Times
and the People of the Sheffield Outrages

'The Shooting of Linley',
from *Illustrated Police News*, June 29, 1867

AUSTIN MACAULEY PUBLISHERS™
LONDON • CAMBRIDGE • NEW YORK • SHARJAH

A CIP catalogue record for this title is available from the British Library.

ISBN 9781787106475 (Paperback)
ISBN 9781787106482 (E-Book)
www.austinmacauley.com

First Published (2017)
Austin Macauley Publishers™ Ltd.
25 Canada Square
Canary Wharf
London
E14 5LQ

Acknowledgements

My most grateful thanks to the following people who have helped me in various ways and means to produce this book:

Ron Clayton, friend and fellow advocate of the promotion of Sheffield's history and the preservation of its heritage: for his support in sourcing information and photographs.

Kathryn Hewson, my daughter and proof-reader.

David Sallery, for permission to reproduce photographs of historic Sheffield bricks on his excellent website on the subject.

Joan Unwin at the Company of Cutlers in Hallamshire: for permission to use images of the portraits of Wilson Overend and William Leng that hang in the Cutlers' Hall.

Chantelle Stackpool at the Walker Art Gallery: Liverpool, for the Gallery's permission to reproduce *Brickfields*.

Preface

Although I had been an active trade unionist in the Sheffield steel industry during the 1980s,[1] I didn't become aware of the Sheffield Outrages until studying for a diploma in Trade Union & Industrial Studies at Northern College, Barnsley, and then for my degree at Sheffield Hallam University in the 1990s. In becoming active in the trade union movement I took an interest in its history as any shop steward worth his/her salt would do, but the books I read focused on the historical battles with employers to increase pay and improve working conditions; the struggles with successive governments to gain legal status and in establishing and improving the employment rights of British workers. I learnt about the origins of trade unions beginning with the 1799

---

[1] I joined the Transport & General Workers Union on taking up employment with the British Steel Corporation at the Tinsley Park Works in 1973. In 1978 I was elected shop steward in the Billet Finishing Department. In 1980, at the start of the National Steel Strike, I became branch Chair and in 1981 I was elected to the office of works convenor for the T&GWU. In 1984 I was elected chair of the works' multi-union committee, a position I held until the works closed in 1985. Throughout my service as a lay official I served on the Sheffield District Committee of the T&GWU and was elected to four biennial delegate conferences: 1979; 1981; 1983 and 1985.

Combination Acts that set the scene for class conflict, to the deportation of the Tolpuddle Martyrs[2] in 1834; from the dock strikes of 1899 and the 'dockers' tanner' (minimum wage of 6d per hour), to the General Strike of 1926; and the rise of trade unionism through the mid-20th century. In all of this reading I didn't notice anything of significance that was specific to Sheffield. Books written on Sheffield's history include a paragraph or two at most on the 'trades unions' outrages'. It is as if, like the *'Great Sheffield Flood'* of 1864, the subject of my last book, the *'Sheffield Outrages'* is an aspect of the City's history that the powers that be would rather see forgotten about, despite it being a pivotal point in the development of trade unionism in Britain and a significant episode in Sheffield's history. The incidents of intimidation that occurred in Sheffield's trades throughout the 1850s and early 1860s, which resulted in a Royal Commission of Inquiry specific only to Sheffield, are given a paragraph at most in books on the acknowledged British trade union history reading list. Of course there were contemporary works covering the subject, including a novel by Charles Reade,[3] and numerous newspaper reports of the incidents as they occurred but most of the books, pamphlets and information leaflets that have been published on the subject, if not all, are out of print, and the only recent work specifically on the Sheffield Outrages published locally was

---

[2] Tolpuddle Martyrs: six farm labourers sentenced to 7 years transportation to Australia for swearing an illegal oath under the Mutiny Act of 1749 when organising a trade union; they spent many months incarcerated in a prison hull in Portsmouth harbour before sailing. After much public protest they were pardoned in 1836.
[3] Reade, Charles, *Put Yourself In His Place,* Chatto & Windus, Piccadilly, London, c1870

a 26 page booklet by Peter Machan in 2001.[4] I consider that the Sheffield Outrages deserve to be more than just another footnote in Sheffield's history and need to be revisited. Thus the motivation for this, my second book, is consistent with that of my first; to retell the history of an important and significant series of events of 19th century Sheffield. My intention is to raise the profile of the Sheffield Outrages focusing on the people affected by the incidents of intimidation and those who perpetrated them; some incidents that would be considered acts of terrorism in the modern world but which need to be understood in the context of the times when violence was a frequent means of settling disagreements.

---

[4] Machan, Peter, *Outrage – The Story of William Broadhead and the Trade Union Scandals of Victorian Sheffield,* (No. 3 in a series of Tales of Victorian Sheffield), Alistair Lofthouse Design & Print, 2001

CONVICTED OF FELONY,
And Transported for SEVEN YEARS

COUNTY OF DORSET,
Dorchester Division.

February 2nd. 1834.

C. B. WOLLASTON,
JAMES FRAMPTON,
WILLIAM ENGLAND,
THOS. DADE,
JNO. MORTON COLSON,

HENRY FRAMPTON,
RICHD. TUCKER STEWARD,
WILLIAM R. CHURCHILL,
AUGUSTUS FOSTER.

G. CLARK, PRINTER, CORNHILL, DORCHESTER.

THE MEN CONCERNED

Tolpuddle Martyrs, 1834

Contents

Introduction

The history of the Sheffield Outrages begins at around the turn of the 19th century when British trade was in the ascendancy during the period that is now known to us as the age of the first 'Industrial Revolution'. For Sheffield this was a period of an unprecedented growth of its industries and of its population. With this growth came new challenges for the people of Sheffield and for the local authorities. The inadequacies within the town's social structures and public facilities, in particular housing, sanitation and public health, made for a harsh existence. Life for the working classes in 19th century Sheffield, a dark and dismal place surrounded by some of England's finest countryside, was bleak, austere, and often short. For most people work was hard, hazardous and a threat to their health and personal well-being but the alternatives weren't worth contemplating; no work meant dire poverty that engendered starvation, a life of crime, begging or the dreaded workhouse. Thankfully such standards wouldn't be tolerated today; whilst poverty may still inexcusably exist in 21st century Britain it is incomparable with that of the 19th century. We can also be grateful that other aspects of life in the 19th century are no longer tolerated such as an unregulated food industry that often led to the adulteration of provisions, sometimes with highly toxic contaminants, motivated by the need or greed of shop keepers or suppliers; the inadequate supply of clean and pure water, and poor standards of sanitation; high levels of susceptibility to disease and infections with no systems of health care for anybody but the wealthy, which all too often led to an early grave; high levels of pollution that screened out the sun on the finest summer's day making Sheffield a dark, dire and dangerous place to live.

For many of the people that laboured in Sheffield's staple industries of cutlery, edge tool manufacture, iron and steel, etc, the only means of protection against employers who took advantage of them; unemployment; being too sick or injured to work; and the only means of obtaining and maintaining a wage that actually kept themselves and their families alive were the many trade unions that the workers had organised for themselves. Despite having no recognition in law the trade unions were successful in collecting enough revenue through their members' subscriptions to be able to pay sick pay; out of work pay; and strike pay when in dispute with employers. The ability to pay workers when they were on strike made for a powerful lever when negotiating prices (payment per product or process), which determined the level of their members' earnings and in turn, their standard of living. Being able to pay workers to keep them out of the labour market also gave the unions an element of control of the trade. Whenever the strength of the trade unions was threatened, or perceived to be threatened, it was only natural that they would defend their position. As there was no legal means of defence, trade unions and their members resorted to other, very often illegal means; those who became *'obnoxious to the trade'* inevitably faced some form of coercion. Wayward members who found themselves at odds with their union's rules or non-union workers who worked against the unions would find themselves a victim of *'rattening'*; the loss of their tools or the bands that drove their machines, which would disappear in the night. Only when the wrong was righted would their missing equipment be surreptitiously returned to them. Although not unique to Sheffield, such intimidation became part of its industrial culture and synonymous with the Sheffield trades. Whilst this form of coercion was somewhat tolerated, there were occasions when some trade union members took intimidation to a more ruthless level and a line was crossed when people were shot at and canisters of gunpowder were thrown into workshops and into workers' homes, endangering life as well as property. Although such instances were few and far between during the first half of the century, by the 1860s pressure was building for something to be done to put an end to the outrages that were now seen to be bringing the town into disrepute. In February 1860 a saw grinder called James Linley died from a wound he received after being shot the previous August for allegedly being *'obnoxious to the trade'*. In 1861 an innocent elderly woman was killed in her own home in Acorn Street by an exploding canister of gunpowder meant for her co-tenant who had made himself an enemy of the Fender Grinders' Union. Then in 1866 following another canister of gunpowder exploding in the cellar of a saw grinder's house in New Hereford Street, the alleged trade union violence in Sheffield became a national scandal when the proprietor of a local newspaper launched a national campaign that brought the issue to the attention of the government. The ensuing outcry engendered the establishment of a Royal Commission to look into the activities of trade unions nationally and

Sheffield was singled out and assigned its very own Royal Commission of Inquiry into what had now become known as the 'Sheffield Outrages'.

The Sheffield Commissioners, who sat between 3 June and 8 July 1867, had a remit to examine all incidents involving trade unions that had been brought to the attention of the local police and magistrates over the previous ten years within the town and its immediate neighbourhood. The court heard evidence from all interested parties, including victims; alleged perpetrators; local masters and employers; and local trade union leaders. Other witnesses were also called upon to be examined. Each statement, each question and each answer over the 25 days that the court sat were recorded verbatim in minutes of the proceedings which were later published. It is from these minutes that I have extracted the stories that form the greater part of the narrative of this book. It follows, therefore, that I am not telling the whole story of the Sheffield Outrages as this began earlier in the century, as we shall see. Although some previous incidents are touched upon, this account is primarily about the high profile incidents that occurred at the height of the Outrages between 1857 and 1867, which sparked the establishment of the Royal Commission and which were investigated by it.

The 'main event' of the story of the Sheffield Outrages is the nefarious activities of the Saw Grinders' Union and its dastardly secretary William Broadhead along with his chief henchmen Samuel Crookes and James Hallam. Their numerous victims included a saw grinder, who also ran the post office at Dore, who was shot and wounded and had his horse hamstrung; many of the saw grinders at Moses Eadon & Co.; the above mentioned James Linley; a saw grinder blown up at his grinding stone; and another saw grinder along with his family blown out of their beds as a canister of gunpowder exploded in his cellar. However, the Sheffield Outrages were not the sole preserve of the town's saw grinders and rattenings and outrages extended beyond the staple industries. At least two master brickmakers found themselves at odds with the Brickmakers' Union during the decade that the Commissioners inquired into, and beyond the town's boundary we find gunpowder attacks on nail makers at Thorpe Hesley and a sickle grinder at Dronfield. We also find incidents involving scissor forgers; scissor grinders; file grinders; pen and pocket blade grinders; and edge tool grinders. A member of the renowned Tyzack family was shot at and the persecution of a wood carving tool maker from London by the Edge Tool Forgers' Union was used as the subject for a contemporary novel. We also find instances where a number of trade unions joined together in the undertaking of rattenings and outrages, including the New Hereford Street outrage that sparked the national outcry which led to the appointment of the Royal Commission. Unruly strikes and rattenings continued long after the Commission but the threat of gunpowder attacks, thankfully, became history.

Running parallel with the Royal Commission in Sheffield was a national Commission held in London where leading figures from Britain's larger unions gave evidence with a more positive approach and in a more articulate manner than did their northern colleagues. They were also fortunate in there being two barristers who were sympathetic towards trade unions amongst the London Commissioners. The outcome of both Commissions was a Minority Report presented to government which led to changes in the law that would improve the legal status of trade unions; changes that were pivotal in the development of trade unions and led to them becoming the professional organisations we know today.

The story of the Sheffield Outrages is not just about the infamy of the secretary of the Sheffield Saw Grinders' Union; it is about a way of life in a period of Sheffield's history; it is about a time of struggle and strife for Sheffield's working classes; and it is about a time of transition for the British trade union movement. The story of the Sheffield Outrages is a significant and important aspect of Sheffield's history that has been understated for far too long. I offer the reader my contribution on the history, the times and the people of the Sheffield Outrages.

Notable Milestones in the Development of Sheffield 1801—1851

1801— Population **46,336** (23,154 male, 23,182 female)

1808—New Town Hall built

1815—Canal built into Sheffield from Tinsley

1818—Gas introduced

Sheffield Seal 1843

1823—Music Hall built in Surrey Street

1824—Mechanics and Apprentices' Library founded

1825—Free Grammar School built

1832—Mechanics' Institute founded

1832—Reform Act: Sheffield to elect 2 members of Parliament

1832-33—Cutlers Hall built

1835—Collegiate School, Broomhall established

1836—General Cemetery opened

1836—Botanical Gardens opened

1837—Wesley College, Glossop Road built

1838—Sheffield to Rotherham railway opened

Sheffield Town Hall 1808

1840—Midland Railway opened

1843—Sheffield incorporated as municipal borough: 9 wards governed by a Town Council consisting of a mayor, 14 aldermen and 42 councillors

1845—Sheffield to Manchester railway opened

1851—At the Great Exhibition in London Sheffield exhibitors awarded 60 Council or Prize medals

1851—Population **136,287** (68,045 male, 68,242 female)

Sheffield at the
Time of The Outrages

*'I passed through Sheffield, which is one of the foulest
towns in England in the most charming situation.'*[5]

The era of the Sheffield Outrages coincides with a period of
economic growth and expanding population in Britain
during the early to mid-19th century, although there were
periods of economic depression following the end of the
Napoleonic Wars in 1815, and again between 1839 and
1842.[6] Between 1800 and 1861 the population of Sheffield
grew from 45,000 to 185,000 and the town ranked 8th largest
in the UK behind London.[7] Nationally, the population grew
at an astonishing 16% per decade during the first half of the
century.[8] The greater portion of this increase occurred in the
towns and cities and by 1851 the urban population was for
the first time greater than that of the rural population; 54%

---

[5] Horace Walpole (1717-1797) quote from 1760
[6] Hopkins, Eric, *A Social History of the English Working
Classes 1815-1945,* Hodder & Stoughton, 2004, p.1
[7] Best, Geoffrey, *Mid-Victorian Britain 1851-75,* Fontana
press, 1971, p.29
[8] Wright, Christopher, *The Working Class,* B. T. Batsford Ltd,
London, 1972, p.19

of British people now lived in towns and cities.[9] In the same year there were 7.25 million industrial workers recorded compared to 1.79 million agricultural workers.[10] By 1861 Britain's urban population had further increased and was 58.7% of the total population.[11] Sheffield's population expanded with the growth of the cutlery and the iron and steel trades for which the town became world famous. The number of people working in the cutlery trades trebled between 1843 and 1873, and those working in heavy industry (iron and steel) quadrupled.[12] This economic expansion not only attracted labour from the outlying rural areas but also from as far as Ireland where the living conditions of the poor was far worse than in Britain, even before the potato famines of the 1840s.[13] However, despite the economic prosperity of the times, between one tenth and a third of Britain's working classes lived in poverty.[14]

Population of Sheffield pre-1801-1871[15]

Pre-1801	1801	1811	1821	1831	1841	1851	1861	1871
27,000	46,000	53,000	5,000	2,000	111,000	135,000	185,000	240,000

---

[9] 1851 census

[10] Ibid

[11] Op. Cit. Best, p.24

[12] Walton, Mary, *Sheffield Its Story and its Achievements,* The Sheffield Telegraph & Star Limited, 1948, pp.189-190

[13] In 1861 2.8% of British residents (806,000) were Irish-born: 1861 census.

[14] Thompson, F.M.L., *The Rise of Respectable Society – A Social History of Victorian Britain, 1830-1900,* Fontana Press, 1988, p.290

[15] Evans, Eric J., *The Forging of the Modern State – Early Industrial Britain 1783-1870,* Longman, London and New York, 1996, p.431

Education of the working classes at this time was sparse and mainly consisted of *'Dame'* schools provided on a voluntary basis by unqualified elderly women; hence the name. The classroom was usually the woman's living room and teaching was slotted in between domestic duties and any other job the *'Dame'* might undertake to earn a living. A Royal Commission led by the Duke of Newcastle found that less than one in eight children attended school in 1858.[16]

The Village School by Alfred Rankley (1819-1872) painted in 1855; an illustration of the archetypical 'Dame' school.
Wood Gallery, London

---

[16] Op. Cit. Hopkins, p.119

Sunday schools provided lessons in reading and writing, naturally of a Biblical nature, but church attendance in Sheffield amongst the working classes was below the national average of 54% returned in the Church census undertaken on Sunday 30 March 1851. It was reported in 1843 that *'not one family in twenty of artisans attended church or chapel in Sheffield.'*[17] A later survey in 1882 found that only 23% of the total population of Sheffield attended church or chapel.[18] The Church of England was perceived as being the church of the employer. Pew rents segregated the lower classes into the free pews at the back or around the sides of the church accentuating their inferiority to the middle and upper classes.[19] Few workers had a decent set of clothes that would be acceptable to wear to church and illiteracy was also a barrier to church attendance as people couldn't read the hymn books and prayer books. Despite all of this the Bible was the most popular book to be found in the Sheffield home and 121 lost or damaged copies were claimed for following the Great Flood of 1864.[20]

Life for the people of Sheffield during this period was rather bleak, particularly for those of the lower social order. House building did not keep pace with the population expansion, which resulted in overcrowding and its inevitable consequences on the health and wellbeing of the urban poor. There were no regulations to provide minimum building standards and the inferior houses built for the lower classes

---

[17] Ibid, p.82

[18] Ibid, p.131

[19] Ibid, p.82

[20] Drewry, Mick, Inundation – The History, the Times and the People of the Great Sheffield Flood of 1864, youbooks.co.uk, 2014, p.53

exacerbated their dreadful situation. Poor quality terraced and back-to-back houses often surrounded a common area or yard with shared privies and a communal water stand or pump. In 1864, the year that the Sheffield Corporation banned the building of any more, there were 38,000 back-to-back cottages in the town.[21] Many families kept pigs (often their biggest asset) and other animals. In these yards the filthy dung-heaps and mounds of rotting garbage added to the grime and stench of the undignified existence of the urban poor. At the beginning of Charles Reade's contemporaneous novel he describes the urban landscape of Sheffield where his story is set against a backdrop of the 'outrages':

Charles Reade

[21] Hey, David, *A History of Sheffield,* Carnegie Publishing, 1998, p.192

'All ups and downs and back slums. Not one of its wriggling, broken-backed streets has handsome shops in an unbroken row. Houses seem to have battled in the air, and stuck wherever they tumbled down dead out of the mêlée. But worst of all, the city is pockmarked with public-houses, and bristles with high round chimneys. These are not confined to a locality, but stuck all over the place like cloves in an orange. They defy the law, and belch forth massy volumes of black smoke, that hang like acres of crape over the place, and veil the sun and the blue sky even in the brightest day.'[22]

Postcard painting of mid-19th century Sheffield entitled *On a Very Clear Day*.

---

[22] Op. Cit. Reade, p.1

The blight and human squalor manifest of Sheffield's industry was set in some of the most picturesque countryside in the land. Charles Reade continues:

'This infernal city, whose water is blacking, and whose air is coal, lies in a basin of delight and beauty: noble slopes, broad valleys, watered by rivers and brooks of singular beauty, and fringed by fair woods in places.'

In September 1861 a description of Sheffield appeared in the trade publication *The Builder*, which graphically revealed the uninviting conditions of the town:

'... a thick pulverizing haze is spread out over the city [sic] which the sun, even in the dog days, is unable to penetrate, save by a lurid glaze which had the effect of imparting to the green hills and golden corn fields as of snow...The three rivers sluggishly flowing through the town, have made the conduits of all imaginable filth and at one particular spot ... positively run blood. These rivers are polluted with dirt, dust, dung and carrion, the embankments are ragged and ruined: here and there overhung with privies: and often the site of ash and offal heaps – most desolate and sickening objects.'[23]

In 1843 the average age of Sheffield people dying was just 24.[24] Astonishingly low as this might appear it wasn't the lowest in Britain; the average age at death of a Liverpool

---

[23] Drinkall, Margaret, *The Sheffield Book of Days,* The History Press, 2012, p.266
[24] Op. Cit. Walton, p.157

labourer in 1840 was just 15 years.[25] Infant mortality at this time was extremely high in towns like Sheffield with half of the children dying before they reached their fifth birthday when Victoria came to the throne in 1837.[26] An example of a young child having died came to light during the Commissioners' Inquiry from witness Mary Ann Needham, the wife of a convicted perpetrator of outrage, Thomas Needham, the engine tenter[27] at Messrs. Moss & Crookes and who was now in America. Whilst being questioned about her husband's criminal activities, and those of his associates, it was established that she lost a child aged 15 months in 1856. Child murder was also extraordinarily common in Victorian Britain and there was a *'supposed epidemic'* of infanticide across the country in the 1850s and 1860s.[28] Between 1837 and 1842 there were 11,944 deaths registered in Sheffield. Of these, 6,038 (a little over 50%) were children under 5 years old: 2,983 under 1 year; 1,511 aged 1 year; and 1,544 aged 2 to 4 years.[29] The death rate for babies under 12 months was 25%.

---

[25] Op. Cit. Wright, p.34

[26] Hart-Davis, Adam, *What the Victorians Did for Us,*
Headline Book Publishing, 2001, p.132

[27] Tenter: someone who tends to something, in this case an engine.

[28] Butcher, Emma, *A Most Barbarous and Revolting Murder,* article in *History Today, Vol. 65, Issue 8,* August 2015, p.3

[29] Thompson, E.P., *The Making of the English Working Class,* Pelican Books, 1968, p.361 Thompson's information is sourced from Dr. George Calvert Holland's *The Vital Statistics of Sheffield,* 1843

Causes of Death in Sheffield 1837-1842	
Recorded Cause of Death	**Number of Deaths**
Consumption	1,604
Convulsions	919
Inflammation of Lungs	874
Decay of Nature	800
Accidents (returned by Coroner)	618
Scarlet Fever	550
Debility	519
Dentition	426
Inflammation of Bowels	397
Inflammation of Brain	351
Decline	346
Measles	330
Small Pox	315
Whooping Cough	287
Inflammation not distinguished	280
Common Fever	255
Asthma	206
Croup	166
Paralysis	107
Disease of the Liver	106
Other deaths*	2,488
Total:	**11,944**

*Deaths from causes that numbered less than 100 recorded deaths.

Source: Op. Cit. Thompson, E.P., pp.359-361

This figure didn't improve a great deal during the rest of the 19th century and was still 20% as late as the 1890s.[30] The remaining 5,906 deaths covered all other age groups. Consumption was the biggest killer with 1,604 recorded deaths (see table on causes of death above). At the other end of the scale, just one death was registered as being caused by *'want of food'.* On this Dr. G Calvert Holland, physician at the General Infirmary and who collated these figures commented:

'The observation of any medical practitioner must indeed be very limited, that has not led him to the conclusion

---

[30] Mathers, Helen, and McIntosh, Tania, *Born in Sheffield – A History of the Women's Health Services 1864 – 2000,* Wharncliffe Books, 2000, p.12

that the deaths of hundreds in this town are to be traced to a deficiency of the necessaries of life. They may die of disease, but this is induced by poor living, conjoined with laborious exertion.[31]

This short life expectancy was mainly due to the poor hygiene that accompanied overcrowded housing, poor diet, inadequate sanitation, and contaminated water, which was a major factor that led to outbreaks of cholera, typhus and typhoid; a cholera epidemic claimed the lives of 402 Sheffield people in 1832,[32] including the Master Cutler, John Blake. In addition to bacteria, water was contaminated with cadmium, arsenic, copper oxide and other toxic chemicals used in industry, which had a particular effect on the poor who lived in the highly-populated industrial districts of cities and large towns, especially in centres like Sheffield. The working class had few clothes and those that they owned were of poor quality and generally made of cheap damp-retaining cotton material that exuded a musty odour. There was a ready market for second-hand, often stolen clothes, at various outlets such as market stalls, pawn shops and street traders. They would wear the same garments for long periods of time and they rarely took a bath. This meant they were sweaty, dirty, smelly and highly vulnerable to disease. The upper and middle classes were not as exposed to these factors as the wealthy tended to live on their country estates or large houses on the hills above the expanding riverside industries, which for many were the source of their wealth.

---

[31] Op. Cit. Thompson, E.P., p.360

[32] Op. Cit. Walton, p.157. By the time the epidemic was over a total of 1,347 Sheffield people had been afflicted; 945 recovered

Here the water was fresh and there was less chance of contamination. They wore quality clothes and their country house or urban villa would have at least one bathroom.

Examples of 19th century Sheffield working-class housing: Snow lane (left) and Mowbray Street (right). (Photographs by author, 2016).

Poor diet also impacted upon the health of the 19th century urban poor and their meagre rations were often adulterated by suppliers for financial gain. Copper oxide was used on rotten vegetables to enhance their colour, as was red lead on other foodstuffs; plaster of Paris or lime was used to add weight to flour; Yew leaves added to tea; contaminated water used to dilute milk. In 1850 five Sheffield butchers were charged with selling spoiled meat that was unfit for human consumption, and in 1869 pork butcher George Hillier of Percy Street, Neepsend Lane was sentenced to 6 months hard labour for adding horse meat from the knacker's yard to his sausages.[33] In 1856 Dr. Bingley, professor of chemistry at the Sheffield Medical School, reported to a committee set up to investigate food adulteration that:

'Amongst the lower class of druggists in the town he had found adulterated butter, and chicory that was mixed with peat dust. Within the past six months, he had found three cases of lime juice adulterated with pyroligneous acid.'[34]

Unemployment often meant having to go without food and for some the workhouse was the only option to literally starving to death. The lowest paid male worker was the unskilled labourer whose basic wage was generally fixed at subsistence level, which was about half of what a skilled craftsman would earn and women and children were generally paid below subsistence level.[35] For the unskilled labourer even a short spell of unemployment could force him and his dependents to the doors of the workhouse or to chance a life of crime or beggary. A trade recession lasting a

---

[33] Op. Cit. Drinkall, p.90 and p.280

[34] Ibid, p.123 Pyroligneous acid is an impure acetic acid obtained by the distillation of wood

[35] Hobsbawm, E.J., *Custom, Wages, and Work-load in Nineteenth-Century Industry,* in Briggs, Asa and Saville, John, (Eds), *Essays in Labour History,* Macmillan, 1967, p.115

few weeks brought desperate need to many workers.[36] This was an age of extreme wealth and extreme poverty.

The Drunken Man by Walter Geike (1795-1837);
note the young lad's bare feet.

Whilst decent food was in short supply for the poor and the lower working classes, there was no shortage of alcoholic beverage; ale, beer and gin formed part of their daily sustenance. Following the 1830 Beer Act, which allowed any ratepayer to sell beer on a two guineas annual license, and the abolition of the duty on beer in the budget of the same year made drinking cheaper and more accessible.[37] Drinking in excess may have its problems but in moderation

---

[36] Chesney, Kellow, *The Victorian Underworld,* Temple Smith, London, 1970, p.23
[37] Op. Cit. Thompson, p.309 Beer remained duty free until 1880

it was far safer than drinking the water although beer too was often adulterated with a variety of substances to give it taste and strength, including of all things sulphuric acid, which apparently gave it more of a 'bite'.[38] However, the nature of work in the cutlery and metal trades engendered a culture of frequent consumption of ale and beer, which led to a high level of drunkenness in Sheffield that alarmed the authorities. In 1852 the Borough Council appointed a committee to report on the incidence of drunkenness in the town and it concluded that it was *'in excess over that in other towns of similar size.'*[39] There were no less than 724 public houses in Sheffield and Rotherham listed in the 1854 Kelly's Directory and there were countless beer houses and other outlets, which were open all day and late into the night. An 1861 investigation into local death rates concluded that intemperance was a contributory factor in the level of early deaths and that in 1859 there were 1,303 *'drinking shops'* in Sheffield. In the same year 979 people were arrested for drunkenness (844 men and 135 women).[40] The Vicar and Rural Dean of Sheffield, Rev. Thomas Sale, expressed the view that the Sheffield grinder preferred a *'short life and a merry one'.*[41]

These excesses undoubtedly had an impact on the health of those who over-indulged, not to mention the effect on morality and the level of anti-social behaviour and crime; including murder.

---

[38] Op. Cit. Hopkins, p.27

[39] Op. Cit. Walton, p.187

[40] Op. Cit. Hey, pp.191-192

[41] Pollard, Sidney, *The Ethics of the Sheffield Outrages,* article in the *Transactions of the Hunter Archaeological Society,* 1954

Saw grinder Joseph Myers murders his wife Alice;
Illustrated Police News, 1864

Saw grinder Joseph Myers was reported as being a good-natured man when sober, but that wasn't very often. When drunk he regularly beat his wife, Alice[42], and was eventually jailed for his abuse of her. Despite her suffering, Alice successfully pleaded for Joseph's early release but he was back to his drunken ways within a matter of days and in a state of intoxicated frenzy he stabbed poor Alice to death with a pair of scissors gouging her in the face, neck, shoulder and breast. On seeing what he had done Myers unsuccessfully attempted suicide by trying to cut his own throat with a table knife. He was taken to hospital where he made another unsuccessful attempt at killing himself by trying to throw himself from a window. On pleading guilty to Alice's murder, blaming drink for the crime, he was sentenced to death at the West Riding Assizes at Leeds Town

[42] Also known as Nancy. For a full account of the murder, Myers' trial and execution see Bentley, David, *The Sheffield Hanged 1750-1864,* ALD Design & Print, 2002

Hall on 17 August 1864; the town's first ever murder trial. Joseph Myers was hanged on Saturday 10 September 1864 alongside Rotherham murderer James Sargisson; the one and only public hanging at Armley prison.[43]

The committee set up by the Borough Council to look into drunkenness in the town in 1852 made some radical recommendations including a ban on serving people under the age of 17; closing pubs at 11 o'clock; and banning the payment of wages in public houses. Typical of its approach to social problems at the time, the Council failed to act and the report was left to gather dust. The scale of the problem of drunkenness nationally became a focus for the Government who in 1863 introduced a Bill before Parliament to prevent public houses opening on Sundays. On 21 April of that year Sheffield's Mayor, John Brown, presided over a meeting at the Temperance Hall on Town Head Street to discuss the Bill following a petition signed by 1,045 local dignitaries. The *Sheffield Times* reported that the hall was packed to capacity with others being unable to get in and that the meeting was somewhat chaotic. A resolution in support of the Bill was defeated in a vote by show of hands.[44]

---

[43] www.truecrimelibrary.com/Victorianhangings. Also Op. Cit. Bentley, *Sheffield Hanged,* pp.ix and 155-165
[44] Op. Cit. Drinkall, p.114

A Study in Greys: postcard of 19th century Sheffield by 'Jotter'[45]

The labouring classes of Sheffield also had the effects of their working environment to contend with. The nature of many of the jobs in the cutlery, edge tools and metals trades had a particularly adverse effect on their health, especially grinding. Many jobs were physically strenuous and were undertaken in both hot and dusty (forge or rolling mill) or cold and damp (grinding mill) confines. Grinders were hunched over their wheels for hours upon end resulting in malformation of their legs and back, their shoulders would be rounded and their chests narrow as a result of their positioning at the horsing[46] and breathing in the dust and

---

[45] 'Jotter' was the signature of postcard painter Walter Hayward Young (1868-1920)
[46] Horsing: the seat or saddle upon which the grinder sits astride while at work

metal particles off the grinding stones caused a high death rate from bronchitis, tuberculosis and other diseases of the lung.[47] The increase in what became known as 'grinders' asthma' or 'grinders' disease' was brought about by the expansion of dry grinding and the introduction of steam driven wheels in the late 18th century and remained a major health issue until the industry was better regulated towards the end of the 19th and into the 20th century.[48] File cutters suffered disease and early death from lead poisoning due to the cutting process being undertaken on a bed of lead. Being constantly exposed to the lead it seeped through their pores and was consumed directly via dirty hands when they ate. Many other workers were exposed to highly toxic substances and welfare facilities in the work-place were non-existent, which meant they would eat their meagre lunches with poisoned hands.

Such working conditions were particularly harmful to children, especially the young boys who were often found working beside their fathers in the grinding mills at an early age. In 1857 around 37% of Sheffield grinders were boys (see table). A study in 1865 undertaken by J B White[49] at the Soho Grinding Wheel on Bridge Street, one of the largest wheels in Sheffield, revealed the circumstances of a number of children between the ages of 7 and 15 who were working there: *James Higgins* (7) worked at the wheel every day from noon until 4 or 5 o'clock wiping knives for his grandfather. James never went to school; *William Henry Widdicombe* (8)

---

[47] Op. Cit. Walton, p.157
[48] Johnson, M P, *The History of Grinders' Asthma in Sheffield.*
[49] Ibid, White wrote a section on grinding in the fourth Report of the Children's Employment Commission, 1865. Sheffield Town Council presented a counter report in 1866.

worked for his father at the Wheel glazing and grinding cast metal scissors on a dry wheel, regarded to be the unhealthiest kind of grinding, with no fan. William couldn't read and didn't know who Jesus Christ was.

Number of Sheffield Grinders, 1857

Number of Grinders	Men	Boys	Total
Forks	160	120	280
Spring Knives	685	600	1285
Razors	300	220	520
Scissors	300	200	500
Table Knives	800	250	1050
Edge Tools & Wool Shears	200	80	280
Saws	160	50	210
Surgeons' Instruments	15	12	27
Files	160	85	245
Sickles	50	20	70
Jobbing Grinders	280	210	490
Total	**3110**	**1847**	**4957**

At the time of his interview (late on a Wednesday afternoon) William's father was absent and believed to be drinking at a nearby tavern. White comments on William that *'His pale face and squalid dress show his body to be uncared for'*; *George Greaves* (15) had been grinding and glazing scissors for about five years and had begun working aged 8 putting scissors together. George had dropsy when he was 4 years old and was caught in the Flood of 1864, since when he had had a cough and not been well, complaining of chest pains (White described him as *'Puny; looks full 3 or 4 years younger'*).[50]

There were deaths and horrific injuries from accidents in the workplace. In 1853 11 year-old fork grinder George Needham, in the employ of John Sanderson at the Tower

---

[50] See www.straightrazorplace.com

Wheel (also known as the Castle Mills) was killed when his smock became entangled in the wheel drive shaft. Young George was working alongside 13-year-old Walter Burton and 11-year-old John Sanderson (the three lads were working unsupervised) when he climbed a wall to retrieve an old bladder (probably used as a football by the young lads). What happened next was reported in the *Sheffield Free Press*:

'Whilst the deceased stood upon the wall, the key became entangled in his smock and he was whirled around several times by the shaft. When all his clothes were torn off he fell upon the ground. His right leg was fractured and he was much injured about the chest. He was removed and taken to the infirmary immediately, but died at 6 a.m. on the morning of November 2nd of shock sustained from his injuries.' [51]

[51] Op. Cit. Drinkall, p.309

In a similar incident in January 1851 at Messrs. William & Henry Turner's fire iron manufactory in Bridge Street, William Blount was very lucky when his shirt was caught on a coupling of a drive shaft as he was greasing it. He was drawn twice around the shaft and then thrown into the air, hitting his head on the floor above, then landing on the floor naked save for his stockings and neckerchief as his poor quality clothes had been torn from his body and ripped to shreds around the shaft. The *Sheffield Independent* reported that:

'He had been dreadfully bruised on various parts of his body, particularly on his head, which struck against the floor of the room above. Had it been a bottom instead of a top shaft, it was thought that death would have been inevitable.'
[52]

When a grindstone broke under speed it would be as devastating as exploding shrapnel. Some masters would buy cheap imperfect stones that were more likely to shatter and endanger the unsuspecting grinder. The very buildings in which they worked often concealed further perils. They lacked decent light and ventilation, and many were ill-maintained. In 1854 a complete section of the Castle Mills at Blonk Street collapsed injuring eight workers. On August 11 that same year the boiler at Castle Mills exploded killing 4 men and a week later a similar incident at Hartford Steel Works, Wicker, claimed the lives of a 19 year-old man and a 12 year-old boy.[53]

Whilst accidents were the cause of most deaths at the place of work, the propensity to resort to physical violence in settling personal disputes also resulted in murder in the workplace on a number of occasions. In a quarrel at Gallimore's Wheel in Radford Street on 22 January 1833, grinder Henry Whiteley was stabbed in the stomach by 15 year-old William Smith. On 29 January the coroner's jury returned a verdict of manslaughter against Smith. He was found guilty at his trial on 9 March and sentenced to 7 years transportation.[54] In another incident on 17 March 1837,

---

[52] Ibid, p.23

[53] See www.sheffielddiary.blogspot.com

[54] Leader, Robert, *The Local Register and Chronological Account of Occurrences and Facts Connected with the Town*

basket maker Thomas Froggatt was attacked by fellow workman Thomas Williams at George Moore's factory in Silver Street Head; Williams cut him across the top of his head with a bill-hook. Froggatt died on 5 April in the General Infirmary. Williams was committed to York Assizes, found guilty and sentenced to death on 15 July. He was hanged at York on Saturday 12 August 1837.[55]

The history of Britain during the 18th and 19th centuries is dotted with riots and uprisings and Sheffield bore its fair share of both. In 1774 there was a riot in the town over a rise in the price of coal. One man died after being struck by a policeman and troops fired over the heads of a mob in Fargate. On 27 July 1791 there was a riot over the Enclosures Act.

Broom Hall, the house of Rev Wilkinson in 1791.

and Neighbourhood of Sheffield, 1830 with continuations to 1857, 1833 pp.250-251
[55] Op. Cit. Bentley, pp.115-118

Windows were smashed at the town gaol in King's Street, as were those at Broom Hall, the house of Rev. Wilkinson, and the home of Vincent Eyre, the Duke of Norfolk's land agent. Rev. Wilkinson's library was set on fire, furniture was damaged and his haystack was set alight. The Light Dragoons had arrived from Nottingham the previous day as trouble was anticipated, and more soldiers were called in from York the following day to help bring things under control. Five rioters were arrested and committed to York Assizes. Four were acquitted but one; John Bennett[56], was found guilty of arson and was hanged on 7 September.[57] The Duke of Norfolk's and Rev. Wilkinson's losses were reimbursed by the County: £54-5s-8d and £190-5s-1d respectively. A gentleman named Mr Wheat was also compensated being paid £185-14s-5d for his losses during the rampage.[58]

In 1795 Colonel Athorpe, who had taken command of the troops in the 1791 Enclosures Act riots, read the *Riot Act* in Sheffield again, only this time the disturbance was between the military and the militia; a fight between the privates of a new regiment under the command of Colonel Cameron, and the Sheffield Independent Volunteers resulted in two people being shot in Norfolk Street.[59] On 22 April 1800 there was a riot in Queen's Street over the price of food. Things had not improved in 1812 when the *Riot Act* was read in different parts of the town to crowds protesting once more over the price of provisions. In 1820 there were riots over unemployment and John Blacker, known as *'King of the*

---

[56] Ibid, pp.52-63

[57] Op. Cit. Drinkall, p.210

[58] Op. Cit. Leader, 1791 and 1792, pp.68-69

[59] Op. Cit. Leader, 1795, p.79

Gallery', was committed to York for *'collecting mobs to excite unemployed workers'*.[60] There were election riots in 1832[61] and the Eyre Street medical school was attacked by a mob in 1835 over alleged illegal dissection.[62] There were Chartist riots in Sheffield in 1839 and 1842. In July 1844 the militia was called out again in a trade dispute at the Sheffield Coal Company's Soap House Pit in the Park area when strike breakers were attacked by a mob. William Mason, George Taylor and Richard Winker were committed to York Assizes charged with riot and assault. All three were found guilty and sentenced to 15 years transportation.[63] In August 1855 James Burke and Cormack Dunlevy were committed to York Assizes for the murder of a policeman named William Beardshaw following *'an affray with an Irish mob'*.[64] Burke was found guilty of manslaughter and sentenced to 15 years transportation. Dunlevy and a number of others engaged in the riot were sentenced to 12 months with hard labour. All of these instances have one thing in common: they were violent actions to address issues for which the people saw no remedy by other means. As the statesman Edmund Burke (1729-1797) told the House of Commons in the late 18th century *'The people would not look for illegal means of redress if they had legal ones'*.[65] This argument would be a significant feature of the trade unions' case at the

---

[60] Op. Cit. Leader, 1820, p.161

[61] Ibid

[62] Op. Cit. Drewry, p.130

[63] Op. Cit. Leader, 1844, p.399

[64] Ibid, 1855, p.539 Irish immigrants were often blamed for social and economic problems

[65] Gilmour, Ian, *Riot, Risings and Revolution – Governance and Violence in Eighteenth-century England,* Pimlico, 1992, p.20

Commission of Inquiry. Interestingly, despite Sheffield being perceived a hotbed for trade disputes the Luddite outbreaks of machine breaking between 1811 and 1817 that occurred in other parts of Yorkshire, Lancashire and Nottinghamshire appear to have missed the town completely.

Although there were some large scale manufacturers in Sheffield during the time of the outrages, e.g. James Dixon & Sons; Naylor Vickers & Co; Charles Cammel & Co.; Arthur Linley & Co.; John Brown & Co., most skilled craftsmen and industrial workers either worked for themselves or for one of the many small-scale employers such as, for example, the 67 edge tool makers; 106 scissor makers; 116 cutlery makers; and 171 file makers listed in the 1854 Kelly's Directory of Sheffield; it is here that the trades unions had their power. The jobbing grinder would hire a grinding trough at one of the various mills on or near one of Sheffield's five rivers, or work for one of the many small scale masters who either owned a mill or who rented a number of troughs from one or more local mill owners. In 1866 there were 164 wheels in and around Sheffield: 32 water-powered and 132 steam-powered.[66] Collectively the highly skilled craftsmen working in small workshops became known as *'little masters'* and latterly, *'little mesters'*. These small scale masters were little better off than

---

[66] Dr. J C Hall, *The Trades of Sheffield as Influencing Life and Health – More Particularly File Cutters and Grinders,* Longman, Green and Co., London, read before the National Association for the Promotion of Social Science, 5 October 1865, p.11 Of the water-powered wheels Hall tells us that there were 8 on the River Sheaf, 2 on the Don, 7 on the Porter, 6 on the Loxley, 8 on the Rivelin and 1 at Whirlow (if this is Whirlow Wheel then this is also on the River Sheaf).

the men who worked for them and many would themselves be dependent upon the unions to safeguard trade prices and their earnings. Many were themselves union members and some union committees were in the main made up of masters.[67] The masters who didn't join a union or refused work to union members were likely to be the ones who would take advantage of the labour market at lean times and be more inclined to exploit their workers and apprentices by paying less than the union rates; as many would have done, or tried to do, at the height of the outrages in 1858 when the unemployment rate was 11.9%.[68]

Trade unions in England emerged generally amongst the journeymen[69] craftsmen in the early 18th century although craft guilds, whose highly skilled members included masters and workers, were formed even earlier to protect their trades. The first recorded trade union in Sheffield was formed by its tailors in 1720. Although it was primarily a 'sick club' one of its objects was the limitation of labour to 12 hours per day.[70] Similar societies were formed by cutlers in 1732 and by the Sheffield grinders in 1748.[71] At this time such societies were unlawful under various Acts of Parliament that had been introduced from as early as 1305. By 1799 there had been around 30 pieces of legislation that prohibited the combination of specific groups of workers. Twenty of

---

[67] Op. Cit. Pollard

[68] Op. Cit. Best, p.148

[69] Journeyman: artisan, craftsman, mechanic, etc, who worked for others on a daily basis, not unlike the controversial 'zero hours' contracts of today. From the Old French *jornee:* day.

[70] Derry, John, *The Story of Sheffield,* S.R. Publishers Limited, 1971 (reprint), p.147 This book was originally published c1915

[71] Ibid

these Acts were introduced between 1720 and 1799.[72] Employers would use the combinations and conspiracies laws as part of their armoury to smash any new trade union and they acted promptly to prevent them getting off the ground. As Trygve Tholfsen points out:

'When an employer confronted a newly established trade union, he set out to smash it as soon as possible and wasted no 'civility' in the process: lock-outs, victimisation, legal repression, blacklegs and blacklists were the order of the day'.[73]

Some of the master manufacturers formed their own societies. In 1790 Sheffield's master scissors smiths paradoxically combined to raise funds to prosecute scissors grinders for being in breach of the combination laws. Despite their own combination being unlawful they succeeded in their quest and four grinders were gaoled for 3 months and another gaoled for 1 month.[74] In 1814 400 Sheffield merchants and manufacturers came together to form the Sheffield Mercantile and Manufacturing Union. One of this organisation's rules barred its members from employing any person *'who had discontinued his work for an advance in wages.'* Any member found to have contravened this ruling faced a fine of £100. The group also assisted the import of foreign labour to replace striking workers and lobbied the overseers of the poor to deny relief to any man *'holding out*

---

[72] Fraser, W Hamish, *A History of British Trade Unionism 1700-1998,* Macmillan Press Ltd, 1999, p.8

[73] Tholfsen, Trygve R, *Working Class Radicalism in Mid-Victorian England,* Croom Helm, London, 1976, p.268

[74] Op. Cit. Derry, p.148

for higher wages.' The Sheffield Mercantile and Manufacturing Union were also able to lean on magistrates (some would be members of the Union) to enforce the combinations and conspiracies laws and many workers were prosecuted.[75] On 28 March 1814 13 Sheffield grinders were sentenced to 3 months in prison for *'combining together for the purpose of obtaining an advance in wages'.*[76] In 1844 a number of masters formed the Manufacturers' and Tradesmen's Protection Society; a society for their mutual defence against the 'intolerant dictation' of the workmen.[77] Members of the Protection Society would undertake their own investigations into incidents of intimidation with a view to bringing the perpetrators to justice. The Society would also put up rewards for information leading to a conviction. Ironically this led to the trades unions becoming more organised and to a call for the unions to form alliances of their own for their own protection against organised manufacturers.[78]

Such were the living and working conditions of the labouring classes during the period that cultivated the 'Sheffield Outrages'. Despite being generally a period of relative prosperity, little was done by employers to improve working conditions and the workers themselves were reluctant to accept changes that they saw as interference with trade. Whilst the trade unions voiced their concerns about working conditions, particularly in the grinding branches, they were primarily concerned with controlling trade and defending their members from exploitation. A trade union's

---

[75] Ibid

[76] Op. Cit. Leader, 1814, p.140

[77] *Whites General Directory 1845,* p.10

[78] Op. Cit. Leader, 1845, p.409

funds were needed to pay its members when they couldn't work due to sickness; when work was scarce and they were laid off; and when they were called out on strike. In some instances union funds were used to provide employment by way of social projects such as that of the Edge Tool Grinders' Union which took on a farm at Wincobank in 1848 to give their unemployed members some paid work. Similar projects were undertaken by the Britannia metal smiths' and file hardeners' unions.[79] Trade unions also undertook a social role in that they would often discipline and fine their members if they were persistent drunkards or if they misbehaved in public. Trade union members were also proud of their skills and their reputation for good workmanship and idlers and sub-standard workers were regularly reprimanded; the unions would censure inferior goods and any infringement of trade marks.[80] In contrast the masters' prime considerations were subservience and profits, and they viewed trade unionism as a threat to the proper order of things:

'Trade Unions constituted an improper, if not immoral, interference with the free play of the market in labour.'[81]

Union leaders and active union members knew that living standards for the workers and their families would only improve through organisation and struggle; the 1850s and 1860s were turbulent times and industrial conflict in England was rife.[82] The workers who refused to join a union;

---

[79] Ibid, 1848, p.453
[80] Op. Cit. Pollard
[81] Op. Cit. Tholfsen, p.270
[82] Ibid, p.269

those who laboured for less than the union rates; and those who flouted the rules of the trades, undermined the trade union movement and the workers' struggle to maintain a living, let alone economic and social elevation. To the committed union members such workers were betraying their class and were no better, if not worse than, the ruthless masters who exploited them. To coin the phrase used by Charles Reade for the title of his contemporary and subjective novel, 'put yourself in their place' and consider how you would deal with those who were betraying you, your beliefs and your principles; those who took the food out of your family's mouths; those who were holding you back from improving your life and that of your family; those who were working with the masters to counter the work of the trade unions and whose actions perpetuated the struggle? The unions were disadvantaged by the fact that they had no legal rights. They had to meet in secret, often in the back room of a public house, where very usually the landlord was a prominent union officer, and they had no legal redress for any financial losses that may arise from fraud or embezzlement. They could not legally make their members pay their subscriptions regularly, or at all. Wayward members; non-union members; anti-trade union workers and hostile employers had to be dealt with and some form of persuasion was deemed necessary if they were to maintain some control of their trade; some form of intimidation!

Sheffield, looking down Castle Gate towards Lady's Bridge
in the 1860s

Intimidation in
the Sheffield Trades

*'No state of society that I ever heard of could exist together
without regulations, and more or less of coercion made use
of to enforce them; and trades' unions need them in
particular...* [83]

On 23 May 1867, three Commissioners were appointed by
Act of Parliament to undertake an investigation into the
violent intimidation of employers and workers in Sheffield
at the hands of the many trade unions that existed at the time.
This investigation revealed a systemic regime of
intimidation within the Sheffield trades that had extended to
acts of bombing and murder in what became known as the
'Sheffield Outrages'. William Overend QC[84] had headed the

---

[83] From a letter written by Henry Cutts, secretary of the File
Smiths' Union, to the *Sheffield Independent*, 8 April 1862 in
Sidney Pollard's introduction to *The Sheffield Outrages –
Report Presented to the Trades Unions Commissioners in
1867,* Adams & Dart, 1971. p.x
[84] William Overend QC (1809-1884): son of Sheffield
surgeon, Hall Overend (1772-1831), considered one of the
leading barristers of his day, called to the bar in 1837 and
appointed QC in 1855, Op. Cit. Bentley, *Sheffield Hanged,* p.x
and p.129. William Overend stood as a Tory candidate in the
1852 and 1857 Parliamentary elections for one of the two
Sheffield seats, nominated by Mr. W F Dixon and Mr. M H

Commission that oversaw the compensation claims made against the Sheffield Waterworks Company following the Great Sheffield Flood on the night of 11/12 March 1864.[85] He found his services were required once more in leading the three-man Trades Unions Commission: Sheffield Outrages Inquiry determined by the Trades Union Commission Act, 1867; he was joined by Thomas Irwin Barstow and George Chance, both Barristers-at-Law. A third Barrister-at-Law, John Edward Barker, was appointed secretary to the Commission.

The three Commissioners met for the first time at the Council Hall on 3 June 1867 and their inquiry lasted a little over a month, closing on 7 July.

William Overend

Atkin in 1852 and by Mr. W F Dixon and Mr. E Vickers in 1857. On both occasions the Sheffield seats were won by John Arthur Roebuck and George Hadfield. He was elected MP for Pontefract in April 1859 but resigned his seat in less than a year. William Overend was also President of the People's College. He never married.
[85] Op. Cit. Drewry, p.134

During this time, the Commissioners examined witnesses from all parties with the employers being represented by solicitor John Chambers, and the trade unions by solicitor Hubert Henri Sugg. In his evidence given to the Inquiry Sugg stated that he represented 41 trade unions with a membership of around 9,000 men.[86] The Commission's remit was to inquire into some 209 cases of violence recorded by employers and the police but their inquiry was limited to cases that had occurred only in Sheffield and its neighbourhoods and specifically during the previous ten years. The most significant power bestowed upon the Commission was the power to grant certificates of indemnity to any lawbreaker adjudged to have made *'a full and truthful confession'.*[87] Almost unprecedented in British law, this allowed self-confessed murderers to walk free and it became a matter of great controversy. It would appear that the Government was determined to ascertain the truth of the allegations at any cost and as things turned out it is evident that the end justified the means, although it wasn't generally appreciated at the time.

The Commissioners' Report at the end of their inquiry covered a number of incidents over the preceding ten years, roughly in chronological order, and involved the actions of just 14 Sheffield trades unions. Whilst we are familiar with large national trade unions today – unions that have evolved generally through amalgamation over the years – the trades in mid-Victorian Sheffield had many demarcation lines and the production of a single product involved workers from different unions allied to, and in control of, specific

---

[86] Ibid, TUC minute number 23,208.
[87] Ibid, p.vii. All further references from the TUC Report shall be a minute number.

processes such as forging; blade-making; grinding; handle-making, etc. The different products would also have their own associated unions: Saw Grinders' Union; Fork Grinders' Union; Sickle Grinders' Union; Scissor Grinders' Union, etc. Some unions formed alliances with each other for mutual benefit in maintaining prices and for support in times of disputes, as did for example the File Smiths' Union with the File Grinders' Union. All told there were about 60 autonomous trade unions in Sheffield at this time, although only 12 were indicted by the Commissioners.[88] A survey undertaken by the National Association for the Promotion of Social Science in 1859 found that there were then 56 trade unions in Sheffield and that most of these were in the cutlery trade. Some of them had a very small membership: 14 in the Corn Grinders' Union; 50 in the Plate, Spoon and Fork Filers' Union; 55 in the Scythe Makers' Union.[89]

The most prolific form of intimidation against union dissenters was 'rattening'; the stealing of workmen's tools or the bands that drove their machines, such as those that drove grinding wheels; the word derived from the notion that imaginary 'rats' had been in the night and taken them. Once the dispute between the offender and his union was settled, his tools or bands would be surreptitiously returned. These disputes could be about non-payment of union subscriptions; the unofficial employment of hands, particularly apprentices who were seen to undermine prices; working for non-union employers; working under price; refusing to strike, etc. Rattening, although a form of blackmail and illegal, had been custom and practice in Sheffield - an accepted and tolerated means for sustaining trade unions and for the control of trade

---

[88] Op. Cit. Walton, p.198
[89] Op. Cit. Evans, p.174

- for a number of years, which first assumed public notoriety as early as 1820.[90]

Most cases of rattening remained undetected but a number of 'ratteners' were brought before the courts. On 1 April 1829 Samuel Green and Lionel Bun were tried at the York Assizes on a charge of *'rattening'* and firing a loaded pistol at a watchman called Thomas Frost. The pair was found guilty and sentenced to death but this was later commuted to transportation.[91] On 28 January 1845 the Member of Parliament Henry George Ward[92] chaired a public meeting at the Cutlers' Hall where union leaders and masters debated issues of intimidation and 44 separate incidents of violence were highlighted.[93]

---

[90] Ibid, p.196

[91] Op. Cit. Leader, 1829, p.203

[92] Sir Henry George Ward (1797-1860): colonial governor; attaché to Stockholme, 1816; The Hague, 1818; Madrid, 1819; Minister to Mexico, 1823-27; Liberal MP for St. Albans, 1832-37; Sheffield, 1837-49. *The Concise Dictionary of National Biography, Volume III N-Z,* Oxford University Press, 1994, p.3125

[93] Op. Cit. Leader, 1845, p.405 also Op. Cit. Derry, p.151

On 3 July 1845 razor grinder Alexander Heathcote was committed to York Assizes on a charge of rattening at the Castle Mills Wheel. He was tried and acquitted on 19 July.[94] However, Alexander and his brother Thomas Heathcote, also a razor grinder, were charged with rattening at the Union Wheel on 17 July 1847, along with another razor grinder named Henry Sykes. Sykes was acquitted but the Heathcotes

---

[94] Ibid, 1845, p.410

were found guilty and got 3 months in gaol.[95] On release from gaol they soon found themselves in trouble again and were charged with rattening at the Kelham Wheel on 29 November 1847. On 21 December 1847 they each received a sentence of 7 years transportation, which was later commuted to 18 months in gaol.[96] The Heathcotes gave evidence that led to the secretary of the Razor Grinders' Union, John Drury, and three members of the union committee, William Marsden; William Hall; and T Bulloss, being charged with having employed the brothers to destroy property belonging to one Peter Bradshaw. On 22 March 1848 they were all found guilty and sentenced to 10 years transportation. This was later commuted to 7 years as legally that was the maximum sentence allowed for the offence.[97] Fork grinders John Smith and H Holmes Vaughan were committed to York Assizes on a charge of rattening on 16 April 1856. They were found guilty and sentenced to 1 year in gaol.[98]

The use of gunpowder as a means of intimidation also predates the period covered by the Royal Commission. On 2 March 1826 there was an attempt to blow up Messrs. Chadburn and Wright's steam-engine wheel in the Nursery.[99] However, it was during the early 1840s that the use of gunpowder to blow up mills and wheels became more prevalent. There was also an explosion at the Globe Works, Neepsend, on 30 September 1843 after an iron pipe charged with gunpowder had been put through a window under the

---

[95] Ibid, 1847, p.442

[96] Ibid, p.448

[97] Ibid, 1848, pp.450-451

[98] Ibid, 1856, .582

[99] Ibid, 1826, p.185

warehouse and fired by a fuse.[100] In a similar incident on 5 January 1844, at the hardening shop of Mr Kitchen at Union Lane, a piece of iron pipe charged with gunpowder failed to go off as the fuse went out before reaching the powder.[101]

William Christopher Leng
Portrait by Barnsley-born artist Ernest Moore, (1865-1940).
(Courtesy of the Company of Cutlers in Hallamshire)

The use of gunpowder was not solely used to damage commercial property; it was also used in attacks upon people in their homes. On 31 March 1850 there was an attempt to throw a can of gunpowder through a bedroom window at the home of file manufacturer William Butcher at Five Oakes, Glossop Road.[102] William and his brother Samuel, had works at Eyre Lane, Furnival Street and Philadelphia. They were in dispute with the Edge Tool Grinders' Union at the time. The 'infernal machine', as the improvised bomb was described in one account, struck the window frame breaking

[100] Ibid, 1843, p.389
[101] Ibid, 1844, p.391
[102] Ibid, 1850, p.476

just one pane of glass and didn't actually go through the window. It landed on the balcony over the dining room below where it exploded breaking just one more pane of window glass.[103] William Bailey and Daniel Ensor were committed to York on 6 April charged with the offence.

They were tried on 12 July 1850 and found guilty of that attack and were sentenced to 7 years transportation.By the 1860s, the alleged violent intimidation by a small number of trade unions, or at least by their members, which included shootings and bombings, was considered as having gone far enough. A campaign to bring trade unions to account which had long been taken up by the part proprietor and editor of the *Sheffield Daily Telegraph*, William Christopher Leng[104] eventually brought the issue to the attention of the national press and the government following an incident that became known as the *'Hereford Street Outrage'*. The 'Sheffield Outrages' became a national scandal and led to the establishment of the Royal Commission of 1867.

During the ten-year period covered by the Inquiry 166 cases of rattening and 12 cases of unspecified intimidation were reported to the police and magistrates but many were dropped or failed a conviction due to lack of evidence. In the opinion of the clerk to the borough magistrates, Thomas Thorpe, there were a 'great many more' which never came

---

[103] Op. Cit. www.sheffielddiary.blogspot.com

[104] Sir William Christopher Leng (1825-1902); journalist; contributed to *Dundee Advertiser* from 1859; managing editor and owner of *Sheffield Daily Telegraph* (1864), which became a powerful Conservative organ; first to set up linotype machines. Knighted in 1887. *The Concise Dictionary of National Biography, Volume II G-M,* Oxford University Press, 1994 p.1768. Leng is portrayed in Charles Reade's novel by 'Mr. Holdfast' editor of the *Liberal,* Op. Cit. Reade, p.74

before the magistrates or the police.[105] There were 22 cases of threatening letters reported and 20 'outrages'; cases of explosions and shootings that in some instances resulted in murder.

Not all instances of intimidation were directly at the hands of trade unions. It was often the case that union members took action against non-union men without the authorization of their union's committee. In some cases union officials were themselves the victims of intimidation. In March 1864 Henry Cutts, the secretary of the File Smiths' Union, had a brick thrown through his window and received a death threat in the form of a letter bearing a crude drawing of a pistol and a coffin with the inscription 'In memory of Cutts'. The letter ran: 'Death is sure and time is short'.[106] One of the File Smiths' Union committee members was also assaulted. This occurred at a time when the union was in dispute with file manufacturer William Torr over his paying below the union rate and who was rattened on a number of occasions. Cutts maintained that the rattening was not authorized by the File Smiths' Union committee and must have been perpetrated by workers of their own accord.

From the evidence given at the Commissioners' Inquiry we get a picture of what life was like for the working men of mid-19th century Sheffield, particularly those who worked in the metal and cutlery trades, and an understanding of the relationships between men and masters; men and their trade unions; the interaction between union and non-union members; and the very nature of industrial relations at the time. However, I would emphasise that the most extreme and violent incidents that occurred were perpetrated by a

---

[105] Op. Cit. TUC, 22,473
[106] Op. Cit. TUC, 15,818

minority and were not condoned by the wider trade union movement. On the contrary, national union leaders at the time recognised that the nature of these local incidents could have an adverse impact upon the institution of trade unionism nationally:

'The respectable leaders in London and elsewhere were naturally very anxious to persuade the public that what had happened in Sheffield had nothing to do with them, and perhaps nothing to do with trade unionism at all'[107]

Even in Sheffield the trades unions had always publicly condemned violent intimidation. At a meeting of Sheffield trades unions on 24 February 1841, called to vindicate their right to combine, the men also protested against being supposed to approve such actions as one that had recently taken place at Ashton-Under-Lyne, where a man had been murdered for violating the rules of the Sawyers' Union.[108]

Whilst the incidents that occurred in Sheffield were widely condemned, and would be even more so today, we must not make moral judgements about them by present day standards but consider them in the context of the violent social standards of the times; as did the Commissioners. These were times when the State was pretty liberal in dispensing capital[109] and corporal punishments and the gentry still resorted to violence in settling their own

---

[107] Pelling, Henry, *A History of British Trade Unionism,* Penguin Books, 1992, p.54

[108] Op. Cit. Leader, 1841, p.350

[109] Prior to 1837 there were over 200 capital offences on the statute book before they were then reduced to 15. They were further reduced to just 4 in 1861.

differences; duelling persisted well into the 19th century. The social reformer Edwin Chadwick[110] reported in the 1830s that 11,000 Britons per year (30 per day) died from acts of violence.[111] Using an average population for the 1830s of 25 million, this equates to 0.044% of the population of Britain.

A similar Commission in London ran parallel with the Sheffield Inquiry but this was a more orderly undertaking with evidence being more skilfully presented by national union leaders who welcomed the inquiries as much as the masters did. It was an opportunity for them to make the case for the recognition of trade unions, to establish their rights and for the protection of their funds in law. This was something that was long overdue and it came at a crucial time for the unions who were reeling from the Hornby v Close legal decision of January 1866 following the Leeds branch of the United Order of Boilermakers and Iron Shipbuilders taking action against its treasurer (Close) for embezzling £24 from its funds under the Friendly Societies Act of 1855. The Lord Chief Justice and three other judges declared that trade unions were not covered by the Act (which offered legal protection to registered friendly societies) as trade unions acted in restraint of trade, which was illegal.[112]

---

[110] Edwin Chadwick (1800-1890): assistant commissioner for poor law, 1832; chief commissioner, 1833; commissioner to investigate conditions of factory children, 1833; secretary to poor law commission, 1834-46; Sanitary Commission, 1839 and 1844; Board of Health, 1848-54; knighted 1889. *The Concise Dictionary of National Biography, Volume I A-F,* Oxford University Press, 1994, p.511
[111] Op. Cit. Chesney, p.93
[112] Op. Cit. Pelling, pp.54-55, also Op. Cit. Fraser, p.42

The two Royal Commissions would greatly influence the future development of British trade unionism and radically reshape the relationship between the employer and the worker.

THE ROAD TO SHEFFIELD.

Satire on the Sheffield Outrages from Punch, July 6 1867 Caption reads: Punch A 1. *"Now then, stop that, I say! We'll have no intimidation here."*

**The many serious outrages and acts of intimidation practised by Trades Unionists in Sheffield had necessitated inquiry by a special Commission

The Case of the
Whiteley Brothers

1847

Whilst the climax of the Sheffield Outrages occurred in the 1860s, the practice of rattening had been around since at least the 1820s, if not earlier. Few ratteners came before the courts, principally because they would have to have been caught in the act or have been witnessed by someone willing to give evidence against them; the prospect of detection was very remote. As they undertook their criminal activities in the dead of night the chances of the ratteners being caught red handed were slight. However, in October 1847 brothers John and Thomas Whiteley, both table blade grinders, found themselves before the controversial Sheffield magistrate Wilson Overend,[113] an elder brother of William Overend

---

[113] Wilson Overend (1806-1865) was one of seven children of Sheffield surgeon Hall Overend (1772-1831) and Ruth Wilson (1776-1845). He was elected to the office of surgeon to the General Infirmary in March 1830; elected one of four Vice Presidents of the Literary & Philosophical Society in January 1838; added to the Commission of the Peace for the West Riding, 11 December 1841; elected councillor for the St. Phillip's Ward in municipal election, 1 November 1844; ex-officio Guardian for the Sheffield Union Workhouse, 4 April 1846; laid foundation stone of farm building on land at Hollow

who would chair the Royal Commission on the Sheffield Outrages in 1867, on charges of aiding and abetting the attempted murder of fellow table blade grinder Samuel Warburton during a rattening sortie.[114]

Wilson Overend
Portrait by Gerge Frederick Watts, RA (1817-1904)
(Courtesy of the Company of Cutlers in Hallamshire)

Wilson Overend, who was also a surgeon and who lived at 39 Church Street, had to endure votes of confidence at the Town Council, the Town Trustees, the Cutlers' Company and the Church Burgesses following a public meeting that called for a petition to Parliament over his magisterial conduct. The petition, signed by 17,000 people[115], was

Meadows for the employment of the able poor of the Sheffield Union, 10 July 1848: Op. Cit. Leader
[114] *Sheffield Independent,* 16 October 1847
[115] This was around 12.5% of the population of Sheffield at this time

presented by Mr. Thomas Duncombe MP[116] on 13 May 1847. The alleged misconduct was in respect of Overend's convictions of workmen under the Combination Act since 1842, most of which had been overturned on appeal. The petition called for an enquiry into Overend's rulings in such cases.[117] The Government agreed to look into his return of convictions for *'threatening and intimidation at Sheffield'* and was *'desirous of the fullest enquiry'* of Wilson Overend.[118] The enquiry found that of ten convictions, involving twenty-five people, only one was confirmed on appeal and that six out of the ten were overturned.[119] Overend also found himself at odds with the Coroner on a number of occasions when he ruled that prisoners accused of murder and manslaughter could not attend the Coroner's inquests of the victims. In one such case in 1847 the Coroner wrote to the Home Secretary to complain about Overend's ruling.[120] However, Wilson Overend survived all of the votes of confidence and he continued to practice undeterred and often still controversially. The petition did nothing to hinder his magisterial career and in 1853 he received a commission as one of the Deputy Lieutenants of the West Riding. However, he was later referred to the Lord Chancellor over his conduct in another case in June 1855. The case in question involved a charge of assault against a man named Ralph Carr, who was alleged to have assaulted one John Halford. Wilson Overend found in favour of Halford and

---

[116] Thomas Duncombe was a County Member of Parliament and a Chartist

[117] Op. Cit. Leader, 3 May 1847, p.439

[118] Ibid, 19 May 1847, p.140

[119] Ibid

[120] Drinkall, Margaret, *Murder & Crime Sheffield,* The History Press, 2009, p.49

fined Carr £5.[121] Whatever the reason for him being referred to the Lord Chancellor, once more Overend was vindicated and in 1856 he was given another vote of confidence, this time as chairman of the West Riding Magistrates.[122]

Twenty-six year-old Samuel Warburton was one of five table blade grinders who worked at one of two hulls at the Swallow Wheel on the River Rivelin near to Belle Hag. The other four table blade grinders that worked there were his father, Thomas Warburton;[123] his brother, Thomas junior; George Howe; and a man named Stokes. The second hull at the Swallow Wheel was used by razor grinders. On Thursday 7 October 1847 Thomas Warburton senior had heard through the trade grapevine that they were to be rattened that very night. The Warburtons had no idea why they should be a target but they decided to keep watch at the Wheel. At nine o'clock that night the three Warburtons, Thomas junior armed with a gun, and George Howe arrived at the Wheel and entered the razor grinders' hull, which still had the remains of a fire burning from the day's working. They stoked up the embers and added more coal to keep them warm as they kept their vigil. The two hulls each had its own entrance door from the outside but there was a

---

[121] Op. Cit. Leader, 13 June 1855

[122] Ibid, 7 February 1857

[123] Fifty-one year-old Thomas Warburton lived at Reservoir View, Crookes with his wife Mary, aged 46 (1847). The 1841 census lists four of their children living with them at that time: James, aged 20; Thomas, 15; Joseph, 7; and Robert, 5. Samuel also lived at Reservoir View (separate house) with his wife Hannah, who is recorded as being aged 15 (the age of consent at this time was 13; it was raised to 16 in 1885). Samuel and James were of the same age and were possibly twins. James was also a grinder.

communicating door between the two. From the razor grinders' hull they could observe their own hull through the cracks in this communicating door. As the same applied in reverse they hung an old leather apron up to the door to cover the cracks, preventing anyone the other side seeing into the razor grinders' hull. They worked out a plan of what they would do should the information Thomas had received prove to be correct. On the ratteners' arrival they would wait until the perpetrators had time to remove the bands from the grinding wheels, then Samuel, Thomas senior and George Howe would leave by the outer door and go around to the door of the other hull and confront the ratteners, barring their escape. Meanwhile, Thomas junior would remain in the razor grinders' hull with the loaded gun and enter through the communicating door once the others had entered the other hull, thus capturing the ratteners in a pincer movement.

Satisfied with their plan they waited quietly until they were alerted by footsteps approaching the Wheel at around midnight. Next they heard the door to their hull opening and through the cracks in the communicating door Samuel Warburton could make out a number of figures in the darkness. One of the men struck a match and lit a candle that he had pulled from his pocket. In the candlelight Samuel saw that there were six men, all with blackened faces, some were wearing their coats inside out. He also saw that one of them carried a gun. One of the intruders removed the band from the drive wheel of George Howe's grindstone. He rolled it up and put it into a large pocket of one of the other men's coat. One of them then removed a band belonging to the man named Stokes and threw it onto the floor; it was an old band that had little life left in it.

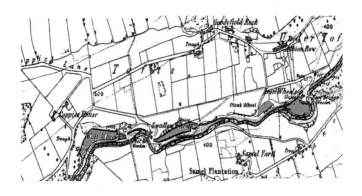

The Swallow Wheel on the River Rivelin

Samuel thought it was now time to make their move before they did any damage to the tools or the grindstones and silently signalled to the others to put their plan into action. Samuel, Thomas senior and George Howe crept out of the door and around the Wheel to the other door where they paused for a moment before Samuel opened it. As he entered one of the men, who was on guard immediately behind the door, threw a punch at him but missed. Samuel threw a punch at the man in turn but it too missed the mark and the man was able to push past the three wily table blade grinders and run off across the Wheel yard. Samuel Warburton gave chase but soon realised that he too was being pursued by three of the other ratteners; one of them was the man with the gun. To his horror the man raised his gun and took aim at him from about five or six yards and fired. Although the cap went off, the gun misfired. The three men then disappeared into the night as Samuel, horror-struck after looking death in the face, recovered his composure then made his way back to the Wheel.

Meanwhile, Thomas Warburton junior had entered their hull through the communicating door just as George Howe closed the outer door trapping the two men left inside; one was the man holding the candle. The other took hold of a hammer to use on Thomas but soon thought better of it when his captor raised the gun and pointed it at him. He immediately dropped the hammer and the two of them pleaded for their lives to be spared. Young Thomas told them not to move and to be quiet or *'he would blow their brains out!'*[124] Within a few moments Samuel, Thomas senior, and George Howe returned to the hull and although the two captives had blackened faces Howe was able to recognise them by their voices. He knew them to be John and Thomas Whiteley; two brothers who had lived in the same neighbourhood as Howe and were also working for the same master, John Walters of Carver Street.[125] The two were searched and on John Whiteley was found a broken chair leg that he had obviously brought to use as a weapon should the need arise. Being taken by surprise he didn't get the chance to wield the chair leg before being confronted by Thomas Warburton's gun.

---

[124] Op. Cit. Leader, 7 February 1857

[125] John Walters & Co. was listed as table, palette, and plated and German silver dessert and fruit knife manufacturers at 7 Carver Street. John Walters lived at Wilkinson Street. Ibid

Table blade grinding

Thus far the Warburtons' plan had partly succeeded with two of the six ratteners having been apprehended; now they had to decide what to do with their captives. George Howe asked the pair why the Swallow Wheel had been targeted. John Whiteley told him that they had heard that they had been grinding blades under statement price (union rate). He also told him that they knew Howe had been doing work for Mr. Pitt who had been *'put on the shelf'.*[126] Howe denied both of these accusations. After quizzing the brothers they decided that they would escort them to Crookes, where they all lived, and hand them over to the local watchman. On the

---

[126] *'Put on the shelf'* probably meant Mr. Pitt was blacked by the union. The only Pitts found in the Directories at this time are John and Charles Pitts, both razor manufacturers at Chester Street.

way they allowed the pair to wash their blackened faces at a spot on the river that they had apparently called at on their way to the Swallow Wheel to prepare for the raid. Here a bag of soot was found that they had used. It appears that they had planned getting washed here on their return from the raid as one of them produced a bar of soap from his pocket for that very purpose. On reaching Crookes they were unable to locate the watchman so they knocked up the landlord of a public house and asked him to take their captives in. The landlord refused and wouldn't allow any of them in, probably suspecting they were all up to no good. This left them with a dilemma; what were they to do with the ratteners? As they were both known to them and that they knew where they lived they decided to let them go and to take out a warrant against them the following day. The Whiteley brothers were later apprehended on the warrant and brought before Wilson Overend on the following Tuesday, 12 October.

The three Warburtons and George Howe all attended the magistrates' court to give evidence against John and Thomas Whiteley and they were represented by solicitor Mr. Anthony Clarke Branson of 4½ Fargate.[127] The Whiteleys were represented by Mr. Joseph John Eyre of 18 Bank Street. It is curious that the Whiteleys were solely charged with aiding and abetting the attempted murder of Samuel Warburton and not also for the rattening, for which they would have surely been convicted by the anti-trade union magistrate. Perhaps the sheer horror of the experience of facing a loaded gun disposed Samuel Warburton to rather seek revenge for his ordeal than for the failed rattening,

---

[127] 4½ Fargate seems a strange address but that is the address listed in *Whites General Directory*, 1849

despite the unknown identity of the gunman. After all, had the gun not misfired he could well now be dead.

Joseph John Eyre cross-examined the witnesses at some length but was unable to put their story into any doubt and a gaff by one of the accused confirmed that they had been party to the raid. When Samuel Warburton described the scene of the Whiteleys washing their faces and finding the bag of soot one of them blurted out *'you could not see what we had put in there. You were twenty yards from us when we washed our faces!'*[128] However, Eyre was able to establish that the Whiteley brothers did not actually witness the shooting incident and submitted that there was no charge to answer. Eyre insisted that it could not be proved that the gun was loaded and therefore it could not be proved that there had been an attempted murder: *'If the gun was not loaded, the mere pulling of the trigger and firing of a cap could not be construed into an attempt at murder.'*[129] Wilson Overend stated that he needed to look into a legal point upon which he wasn't clear and adjourned the hearing until the following Friday. John and Thomas Whiteley were bailed.

On Friday 15 October 1847 the Whiteley brothers appeared again before Wilson Overend to hear his judgement. In a short hearing Overend told the pair that *'you have brought yourselves into a very awkward predicament. However, I have weighed all the circumstances of the case, in all its details, and as it stands at present I shall neither commit you for trial nor discharge you.'* He ordered that they enter into their own recognizance[130] of £40 each and that

---

[128] *Sheffield Independent,* 16 October 1847
[129] Ibid
[130] Recognizance: Bond by which person engages before a court or magistrate to observe some condition, in this case to

they find two sureties of £20 each to appear again when called upon.[131] John and Thomas Whiteley were able to find the sureties (probably through the Table Blade Grinders' Union) and were subsequently discharged.

I have been unable to find anything further on this case but according to the *Sheffield Local Register* George Howe was rattened again at the Swallow Wheel in 1850. We can only assume that the Whiteleys and the other four men who rattened the Swallow Wheel were members of the Table Blade Grinders' Union, a trade union that didn't figure in the Commissioners' investigations in 1867. This union suffered some turbulent times during the 1840s having broken up on a number of occasions, as it did again towards the end of 1847 and efforts were at that time being made to reorganise it. The incident at the Swallow Wheel may have been partly due to these prevailing issues. We know that the union existed in 1828 as it was reported in the *Sheffield Local Register* on 31 January that year that the table blade grinders *'struck work'*. From the same source we find that in July 1847 a number of table blade grinders were held on bail to appear at the York Assizes charged with riot at Sykes' Wheel.[132] We also know that the union existed in 1849 as eight of its members were tried at York on charges of conspiracy and riot when trying to force two wayward table

---

appear before the magistrates if called upon should further evidence come to light in respect of the charge that they faced.
[131] *Sheffield Independent,* 16 October 1847
[132] This was possibly Endcliffe Wheel on the River Porter tenanted by William Sykes in the 1790s. See Crossley, David; Cass, Jean; Flavell, Neville; and Turner, Colin, (Eds), *Water Power on the Sheffield Rivers,* Sheffield Trades Historical Society and University of Sheffield Division of Continuing Education joint publication, 1989, p.79

blade grinders to pay into the union's funds. The eight pleaded guilty and entered into their own recognizance to appear for judgement when called upon.[133] I have found no record of what that judgement actually was. Also in 1849 a report in the *Sheffield Local Register* on 17 February informs us that the table blade grinders obtained an advance in wages.[134]

Another point of interest from my research is that in addition to the Table Blade Grinders' Union I found references to the Table Knife Grinders' Union. However, I have not found references to both of these trade unions in any one same year, which suggests that they may well be one and the same and that there was a name change for a period during the 1830s. The references I have found on the Table Knife Grinders' Union, which had a membership of around 800 in 1841,[135] were all reports on the amounts of money that the union paid to its unemployed members between 1830 and 1842. This in itself is most interesting as it gives us an idea of how trade was performing during this time (see table below). The figures suggest a slump during the years 1831-32 and again in 1837-42. They also suggest that trade was good in the years 1835-36. The total amount paid by the union to its unemployed members during this 12 year period was £20,650; a huge amount for the time.

As for Wilson Overend, he appears to have survived the controversies that dogged his career as a magistrate pretty well and he maintained the respect of his peers. Wilson Overend moved in influential circles; being anti-trade union would have helped him in this regard. He made a lucrative

---

[133] Op. Cit. Leader, 1849, p.472

[134] Ibid, p.462

[135] Ibid, 10 July 1841, p.370

living as a private surgeon from his Church Street surgery and at the General Infirmary where he was elected to the *Office of Surgeon to the General Infirmary* on 24 March 1830, a position he held until resigning the post on 27 April 1853.[136]

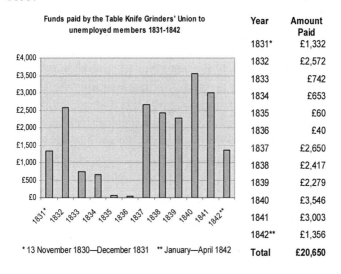

Funds paid by the Table Knife Grinders' Union to unemployed members 1831-1842	Year	Amount Paid
	1831*	£1,332
	1832	£2,572
	1833	£742
	1834	£653
	1835	£60
	1836	£40
	1837	£2,650
	1838	£2,417
	1839	£2,279
	1840	£3,546
	1841	£3,003
	1842**	£1,356
* 13 November 1830—December 1831 ** January—April 1842	Total	£20,650

He took over his father's private surgery at 21 Church Street after his death in 1831, and he practiced there up to at least 1837. By 1849 he had gone into partnership with Jonathan Barber and moved the surgery to 41 Church Street next door to where Overend was living at number 39. By 1855 Overend & Barber had moved their surgery to Cadman's Lane but Wilson continued to live at Church Street.[137] In the following year their surgery moved to 85 Norfolk Street.[138] By 1862 Wilson Overend had moved to 10

---

[136] Ibid, 1830 and 1853
[137] *Slater's Directory,* 1855
[138] *Whites Directory,* 1856

St. James Street and was practicing alone; Jonathan Barber had set up his own surgery at 5 Eyre Street.[139]

In 1861 we find Wilson Overend and his wife Mary (nee Swettenham), whom he had married on 29 April 1830, living at Sharrow Head Cottage with their 20 year-old daughter Alice. A second daughter, 26 year-old Mary Isabel, was probably now married and had moved out of the family home. The Overends appear to have had a comfortable lifestyle, being looked after by an overabundance of domestic staff. From the 1861 census returns we find the family of three were taken care of by a cook, Mary Ashmore (aged 25); a waiting maid, Eliza Ogley (31); a house maid, Amelia Morley (27); a lady's maid, Elizabeth Kellam (19); and a stable boy, William Richardson (17). How the other half live!

Wilson Overend didn't live to see his younger brother oversee the Sheffield Outrages Royal Commission as he died in 1865 aged 58.

---

[139] *Whites Directory,* 1862

A 19th century Sheffield blade forge.

The Trials and
Tribulations of Elisha Parker

*'To be a Sheffield Grinder it is no easy trade
There's more than you'd imagine in the grinding of a blade
The strongest man amongst us is old at thirty-two
For there's few who brave such hardships as we poor
grinders do'*[140]

1853-1865

Although limited by the Trades Unions Commission Act
1867 to investigating occurrences of intimidation in the
preceding 10 years, the earliest incident that came under
investigation by the Sheffield Commissioners actually
occurred in 1853. For this to happen, a written sanction was
granted by the Home Secretary, Spencer Horatio Walpole.

---

[140] Opening verse of *The Sheffield Grinder* (Horn), recorded
by Tony Tapstick-Carlton Main/Frickley Colliery Band,
Dingles Records Ltd, 1981

Post card sketch of Newbould's Bridgefield Works[141]

The case in question was that of the Saw Grinders' Union and 47 year-old Elisha Parker, who lived at Dore and kept the local post office but also worked as a saw grinder for Samuel Newbould at the Bridgefield Works, Sheffield Moor.[142]

---

[141] Sheffield Local Studies Library: Picture Sheffield s09773
[142] According to the 1854 edition of Kelly's Post Office Directory of Sheffield the Dore Post Office was run by Mrs. Francis Swift. However, recorded in the 1851 Census returns for Dore, the Swift household consisted of shoemaker Samuel Swift, his wife Francis, 29 year-old saw grinder Alick Parker, and his 27 year-old wife Martha. A search for Elisha Parker in the 1851 Census drew a blank. It may well be that Alick and Elisha Parker are one and the same, and that Francis Swift was his mother-in-law. In White's Directory for 1871, Elisha Parker is recorded as a farmer, shopkeeper & Post Office at Dore. Evidence given by Parker to the Commissioners in 1867 indicate that he ran the Dore Post Office during the whole of this period

William '*Smite 'em*' Broadhead,
Secretary of the Saw Grinders' Union[143]

Elisha Parker had served his apprenticeship and been a member of the Saw Grinders' Union from being 14 years-old, becoming a fully-fledged saw grinder in 1841 when 80% of English saw makers worked in Sheffield.[144] His altercation with the Saw Grinders' Union began in 1853 following a 21 weeks strike after the company gave their grinders a month notice for refusing to work at 10% reduced rates. During the strike Parker had received 8s-6d per week from the Union. The strike ended when the company offered the grinders a return to work on the full original rates.

On their return, Samuel Newbould took on two grinders who did not belong to the union. Within days of going back to

[143]Sheffield Local Studies Library: Picture Sheffield s08365
[144]Op. Cit. Hey, p.124

work, Elisha Parker had a midnight visit at home from William Broadhead, secretary of the Saw Grinders' Union, and Edwin Machin, a member of the union committee. Broadhead, who was also known as *'Smite 'em'*, informed Parker that following a meeting of the union committee about the non-union grinders employed by Samuel Newbould he must ask him and his brother George, who also worked for Newbould, not to continue their work there. Having been on strike for 21 weeks, Parker would have felt reluctant to put himself out of work again so soon and told Broadhead that he would continue to work but would make his usual contributions to the Union. Broadhead and Machin spent about half an hour trying to persuade Parker to comply but to no avail. The following morning they visited Parker's brother making the same request. A few days later Parker and his fellow grinders received a visit at work from another saw grinder called Benjamin Roebuck who reiterated Broadhead's request and said that the *'trade would find money for them if they were to go'*. Having given them a couple of days to consider the request, Roebuck returned but Parker stood his ground and continued to work for Samuel Newbould and stopped paying his union subs. It isn't clear whether all of the grinders at Newbould's continued to work or if any of them complied with the Union.

There is no evidence of malice in these early exchanges between Parker and the Saw Grinders' Union but things were soon to take a turn for the worse. Broadhead upped the ante when, in July 1853, he sent three of his henchmen to hamstring Parker's horse, which he used for daily transport to and from his work at Sheffield Moor. Elijah Smith, John

Taylor and Phineas Dean[145] attacked the horse as it grazed in a field near Dore Moor Inn, about half a mile from Parker's house, cutting its hind leg above the hocks to the bone.[146] The horse, which Parker valued at £20, had to be put down. The incident was reported in the *Sheffield and Rotherham Independent* on 23 July 1853. There is no recorded account of the incident from the perpetrators as Smith, Taylor and Dean had all died by the time the Commissioners took their evidence.[147]

Following the incident with the horse there appears to have been a lull in the intimidation of Elisha Parker despite him continuing to work for Samuel Newbould and refusing to pay his *'natty money'*[148] until he was compensated for the loss of his horse. Then on the night of 8 March 1854, a second and more disturbing incident occurred at the Parker household. It had been a rainy day and Elisha had got soaked on his way home from work and most of the family had gone to bed early; all except his mother-in-law, who stayed up to dry some clothes. Alerted by a pungent odour, she went to the kitchen door and on opening it found a man laying gunpowder up to the door step. She ran upstairs and raised Elisha but before he could get downstairs there was a mighty explosion outside which shook the kitchen door in its jamb. All that remained outside the door when Elisha opened it was

---

[145] Phineas Dean is recorded in the 1851 Census as a 37 year-old saw grinder and living at Infirmary Lane, St. Philip's with his wife Jane, also 37 years old. In 1834, a 20 year-old Phineas Dean was charged with manslaughter but later acquitted. I am sure this is the same Phineas Dean. He died on 1 August 1862 and is buried in Burngreave Cemetery.

[146] Op. Cit. TUC 12,610.

[147] Ibid, 12,616

[148] 'Natty' or 'Natty money': union subscriptions

the remnants of the fuse used to light the improvised bomb. Soon after returning indoors, another explosion was heard but some way off; this turned out to be a similar incident at the house of a scythe maker named Thomas Bishop. It is likely that both incidents had been perpetrated by men hired by Broadhead. Thomas Bishop's son had just taken up an apprenticeship in the saw handle making trade, which may have been in breach of prevailing union rules (apprenticeships were often the reserve of the sons of trade union members), although no evidence came to light to indicate that this was actually the case.

Grinders at their troughs[149]

Following the gunpowder incident Elisha Parker borrowed a double-barrelled shotgun from his master, Samuel Newbould, and took to keeping a vigilant watch at night in case of further attacks. One can imagine the Parker

[149] Sheffield Local Studies Library: Picture Sheffield y02464

family's fears engendered by these incidents and it wasn't long before their fears were realised. On Whit Sunday, 4 June 1854, Elisha was alerted by stones being thrown onto the roof of the house sometime just after midnight. He took the shotgun and his dog and went outside to investigate. No sooner had he ventured out a shot was fired from about 20 yards away from the plantation across the road, then another shot was fired from the opposite direction, again from across the road and about 20 to 30 yards away. No figures were seen in the dark, only the flashes from the guns. The second shot caught Elisha Parker on his right arm, scattering pellets up to his neck and on his chin. He crossed the road towards where the shots had been fired and came across a man with a gun. He raised his shotgun to fire at the figure but was struck a blow on his left arm knocking him down and causing his gun to go off, harmlessly hitting a wall. The shots had aroused people in the neighbourhood and one of Parker's neighbours came to help his wife carry him back into the house and the local doctor was sent for. The doctor decided that the injury was severe enough to have Elisha taken to the infirmary where he was hospitalised for 11 weeks. At one point it was thought that he would lose his arm and although it was saved, the injury rendered Elisha Parker partially disabled and unable to work for about 12 months.

Sheffield General Infirmary[150]

Parker could not recognise any of his attackers but he was sure they were acting on behalf of William Broadhead and the Saw Grinders' Union; there was no other plausible explanation. Interestingly, whilst Parker was in its care, the Saw Grinders' Union donated £20 to the Infirmary. It was thought by some that this donation was to cover the cost of Parker's treatment and as such an admission of guilt but trade union donations to the Infirmary were not uncommon. For example, on 7 August 1846 the file trade voted £100 to the Infirmary and £50 to the dispensary.[151] There was no direct contact between Broadhead and Parker at any time.

It transpired from the evidence given to the Commissioners that William Broadhead had acquired the help of one of Parker's neighbours, George Peace, *'a stout,*

[150] Taylor, John (Ed), *The Illustrated Guide to Sheffield and the Surrounding District*, Pawson and Brailsford, Sheffield, 1879, p.161

[151] Op. Cit. Leader, 1846, p.425

ruddy, grey-haired man, of respectable middle-class appearance, [152] who hired a third party to undertake the laying of the gunpowder and the shooting; one John Hall. Hall had done occasional work for Peace, who owned a colliery at the time and was also a farmer and a saw grinder. Peace claimed that Broadhead had been asking him for a number of months to find someone to give Parker a fright; it is clear that Broadhead kept himself distanced from the dirty deeds. The intimidation of Elisha Parker was instigated by Broadhead but always carried out by third parties, as were the making of payments to the culprits. Peace maintained that Hall was hired to simply frighten Parker and not to do him any serious bodily harm. [153] Payment was made to Hall by leaving the money under a stone in Peace's yard. There is a suggestion in the minutes of the Commissioners' Inquiry that Hall's accomplice in the shooting was Elijah Smith, one of the men responsible for hamstringing Parker's horse, but as he was now dead, it couldn't be proven. Whether Parker's shooting was intended to harm him or not, Broadhead felt it would be safer to get Hall out of reach of the police and he paid £13 for his transport to America; Peace accompanied John Hall to Liverpool to ensure he got on the ship.

Elisha Parker next found himself at odds with William Broadhead and the Saw Grinders' Union in April 1859, along with his brother George and a number of other saw grinders in the employ of Samuel Newbould, when a dispute arose between the company and the Saw Makers' Union. The company had taken on two men and a boy at its Abbey Dale works who were not union members and the company's

---

[152] *Sheffield Telegraph,* Op. Cit. Pollard
[153] Op. Cit. TUC 13,871

saw makers went on strike.[154] As was the custom, the Saw Grinders' Union called on their members at the company to support the saw makers, offering those who complied 24/- per week *'play wages'.*[155] There were nine saw grinders who worked for Samuel Newbould at three different wheels on the River Sheaf: Abbey Dale; Warp Mill and Broadway Wheel.[156] The saw grinders in question were Elisha and George Parker; John Taylor; Henry Taylor; John Thorpe; Samuel Dungworth; George Crookes; Joseph Daws; and George Frith. Elisha Parker and John Taylor both gave evidence to the Commissioners. Having not responded to the union's call, all of the men found that their bands were missing when they turned up for work one Monday morning. On his horsing, John Taylor found a note that read:

'When the blood is in an impure state, brimstone and treacle is applied as a mild purgative, etc. We have taken the bands as a mild remedy. This is the brimstone and treacle; but should the seat of the disease be not reached we shall administer something stronger; we shall take away the treacle and shall add thereto a necessary quantity of charcoal and saltpetre.' [Signed] *'Tantia Topee'*[157]

---

[154] This was not the first 'outrage' to occur at Abbey Dale; the grinding shop was blown up by members of the grinders' union in 1842. Op. Cit. Crossley et al, p.98

[155] Play wages: strike pay.

[156] These named works are taken from the minutes of the Trades Union Commission Inquiry 1867. Samuel Newbould actually leased work space at Abbeydale Works; Walk Mill and Bradway Mill. The company also owned the Broomhall Wheel on the River Porter at this time. Op. Cit. Crossley et al, pp. 98-99, 95-96, 83-84

[157] Op. Cit. TUC 9803

This was a clear and unambiguous warning that the removal of his bands was only an opening gambit and that should he continue to ignore the union, much worse was to come. John Taylor and a number of the others went to see William Broadhead to find out why their bands had been taken when there was no dispute involving the saw grinders. Broadhead told them that it was down to the saw-makers' issue and that they would be paid while they were out of work; Taylor received £1 19s per week for himself and an apprentice. At this time Taylor and his lad were earning around £3 per week, making the strike pay 65% of earnings, which compares well with what striking workers can expect today.

Elisha Parker got the same letter from *'Tantia Topee'*[158] but a few days later he received another note addressed to him personally and obviously with a view to reminding him of his previous experiences:

'To Elisha Parker. Dear Sir, I take the liberty of addressing you on the subject of making yourself such a busy tool in the hands of Messrs. New bold Brothers. Let me tell you that your conduct is closely watched, and if you refuse to act with the men I would advise you not to act against them by running about to find men to fill their places. It is a filthy job, and I am sure if you act wisely for your own interest's sake, you will keep out of it. There is an abundance of means of paying you back with interest for all the mischief you are capable of doing in this case. The truth of this your past experience ought to teach you. Messrs. New bold cannot compensate you for the consequences you are surely

---

[158] Tantia Topee: one of a number of signatures used in threatening letters by William Broadhead

bringing upon yourself. It is out of mortal power to do so. Be advised ere it is too late.' (Signed) *'A Grinder'*[159]

The strike lasted five or six weeks and ended after a joint meeting of the saw makers and grinders decided to send a deputation to negotiate with Newbould. The meeting was prompted by a note delivered to all the saw grinders from the company saying that new bands had been bought and that if they were not to return to work next day they would be summoned before the magistrates.[160] The threat of legal redress probably changed Broadhead's position as the saw grinders were not directly in dispute with Messrs. Newbould & Co, but turning out in support of the saw makers. The Saw Grinders' Union faced being sued for taking action in restraint of trade. The following day the grinders received a note to tell them where their original bands were to be found; Broadhead had called off the strike. It isn't clear whether the saw makers had resolved their dispute as, according to the evidence given by John Taylor, some were reluctant to return to work.[161]

One Friday in May 1865 Elisha Parker's and John Taylor's bands went missing again, along with those of two other saw grinders (a man named Joseph Martin had taken them and was paid 5s for the job by William Broadhead, 5s being the going rate for rattening at the time[162]). This followed the disappearance of the *'cart book'*; the book that contained a record of the work done by Newbould's men. The Saw Grinders' Union had 'borrowed' the book to check

---

[159] Op. Cit. TUC 10,228
[160] Ibid, 9,846
[161] Ibid, 9,859
[162] Ibid, 12,538

that the union subscriptions paid by the men tallied with their earnings; their *'natty'* money was based on a percentage of their earnings. It was reported at a general meeting of the union (not the Committee) that money was owed by Parker and Taylor as they had falsely accounted their work. They calculated that Taylor had earned £15-14s-6d more than what was recorded and Parker £7-5s-3d.[163] The day after the bands went missing Taylor and Parker went to see William Broadhead at the Royal George public house in Carver Street where he was the landlord, to find out why their bands had gone. Broadhead told them that the Committee had decided that they were in arrears with their *'natty'* and that Taylor should pay 19s and Parker £2; both were also to pay 10s each for *'Mary Ann'*[164] to cover the union's expenses in the matter. They rejected the claim of false accounting of their work and refused to pay anything. The two of them went back to Broadhead a number of times over the next week to try to reach a compromise and at one point the *'Mary Ann'* had increased to 50s. Finally, on the following Monday, Broadhead told them that the Committee would settle for 15s each for *'Mary Ann'*, 19s *'natty'* for Taylor and £2 *'natty'* for Parker. They both paid up although Parker was 5s short for *'Mary Ann'*. They got their bands back the following day. In addition to the arrears and the fine that they paid, Taylor and his lad lost between £3 and £4 in wages whilst his bands were missing.[165] We can assume that Parker's lost earnings were about the same.

---

[163] Ibid, 9,891

[164] Mary Ann: another signature to threatening letters but in this instance another name for a fine.

[165] Op. Cit. TUC minute 9.998

This was the last incident of intimidation that Elisha Parker reported to the Commissioners.

Old Smite 'em's pub, The Royal George, Carver Street (pencil drawing by the author)

Moses Eadon & Co. and the Saw Grinders' Union

'If the law would give them (trades unions) *some power, if there was a law created to give them some power to recover contributions without having recourse to such measures there would be no more heard of them.'*[166]

1859-1866

Grinders at Moses Eadon & Co, saw manufacturers of Saville Street East in Sheffield, experienced a number of incidents of rattening between 1859 and 1866; all due to some or all of their saw grinders being in arrears with their union subscriptions. In 1859, the bands of two saw grinders, Henry Taylor and Henry Bollington, were taken. Taylor and Bollington were members of the Saw Grinders' Union and when they found their bands missing they went to see William Broadhead. They paid their arrears and a sum to cover expenses incurred by the union in taking the bands. The bands were found a couple of days later after the men received a note telling them where they had been secreted. Despite the bands actually belonging to the company, and costing about £2-10s each to replace, Moses Eadon & Co

---

[166] William Broadhead giving evidence to the Commissioners, Op. Cit. TUC, 13,241

took no action as it was a *'trade matter'* and when asked by the Commissioners if the theft was reported to the police, the company's representative at the hearing, Robert Thomas Eadon, said that it was not reported *'because the police in my opinion would have been useless in the matter'*.[167] Nor did he approach Broadhead or anyone else from the union; Eadon was of the opinion that the bands would be returned quicker via the men sorting things out with the union themselves rather than involving the police or by the company making any representation.

Not only were the saw grinders' bands the property of the company, so were their tools. It was against union rules for the men to own their own tools as this would engender competition between those with and those without their own equipment, which was liable to drive down prices. However, the union owned its own tools and often acted the master by taking on work itself but only at the going price and all profits were added to the union's funds.[168]

In 1860 Moses Eadon & Co experienced another incident of rattening and this time Robert Thomas Eadon did approach William Broadhead, not to complain about a missing band but to recover the cost of repairing a door that was damaged by the person who took it. One of the saw grinders called Charles Challenger had lapsed into arrears with his *'natty money'*. A band was taken by Abraham Green,[169] a fellow saw grinder at Eadon's, but it turned out to be the band of another grinder, Christopher Taylor, with

---

[167] Ibid, 709.

[168] Ibid, 895 - 902

[169] Ibid, 12,173. Green had died prior to the Inquiry but Broadhead told the Commissioners of his involvement, being one of the few men he had actually employed to ratten.

whom the union had no grievance; Green, who was rattening under instruction from William Broadhead, had taken the wrong man's band. Broadhead denied all knowledge of the missing band but later sent the 2s-6d that Eadon had claimed for the repair to the door via Christopher Taylor as *'he didn't want any unpleasantness; but his paying the 2s-6d must not be construed into the fact of the trade* (the union) *knowing anything at all about it'.*[170] A few days later Taylor's band was returned following a visit made to Broadhead by a former secretary of the Saw Grinders' Union, John Staniforth, who was also in the employ of Moses Eadon & Co. It was thought that Staniforth may have some influence with Broadhead. At this meeting at the Royal George a bit of a farce took place when amidst their discussion Broadhead suddenly turned towards the fire and pointed to a piece of paper lodged in the fender and exclaimed *'What have we here?'* Written on the paper was the location of Taylor's band.[171] The absurd nature of this scenario was not wasted on Charles Reade, who appears to have researched the minutes of the Royal Commission and included this ridiculous drama, and other incidents given in the evidence, to embellish his story. [172] Perhaps Reade even attended the court in session and took notes from the public gallery.

---

[170] Ibid, 742
[171] Ibid, 753 - 757
[172] Op. Cit. Reade, p.274

Sheffield saw grinders at their wheels[173]

In November 1864 three saw grinders at Eadon's works, Henry Taylor, Joshua Barton and Henry Bollington, were the victims of another rattening incident when their bands disappeared due to their being in arrears; Taylor and Bollington for the second time. However, this time one of the perpetrators was accosted by a policeman as he stole through the night with one of the bands in his possession. The man in question was a saw grinder called Joseph Bradshaw, who was prosecuted and sentenced to six months in jail for the theft of the band. Although Bradshaw must have had an accomplice as he was in possession of only one band when two had gone missing, he denied this under oath at the Commissioners Inquiry. He also stated that this

---

[173] Illustrates London News 1864

incident was the only rattening expedition that he had ever undertaken.[174] He had served his time for the crime so a certificate of indemnity would be of little interest to Bradshaw. Although it was clear that the union was behind Bradshaw's rattening expedition, no prosecution against William Broadhead or the union was made.

Further incidents occurred at Eadon's works in November 1865 and September 1866 and in both cases the same grinders as before had again fallen into arrears with their union subscriptions. In both cases the outcome was a repeat of the previous incidents; the bands were covertly returned after the arrears were paid. Having been the same grinders falling behind with their *'natty'*, one would assume that Robert Eadon would have tried to instil a little discipline and encourage his men to pay their money to the union on time, but throughout he remained at a distance and left things to take their customary course. His only interventions in these matters were to employ a policeman on two occasions to keep watch on the works when rattening was expected, and in one instance to lend Henry Bollington 25s to pay off his arrears. William Broadhead must have also been inclined to think that Eadon should try to remedy this consistently disruptive pattern by putting pressure on the men to keep up with their union subscriptions and to this end, sometime between the 1865 and 1866 incidents, he sent Edwin Machin to talk to Robert Eadon with a view to persuading him to induce the men to regularly pay their 'natty'. During the discussion Machin inferred that other masters had taken steps in this regard so as to avoid trouble but he didn't indicate exactly what action they had taken. Eadon's response was to maintain his distance telling Machin *'We*

---

[174] Op. Cit. TUC 13,405 – 13,414

(the company) *should take no steps in the matter'.*[175] The check-off system[176] employed by many unionised companies today was a long way off in 1866. The Saw Grinders' Union subscriptions at this time were based on a percentage of their earnings and averaged around 5s per week.

The cost to the men in lost earnings due to rattening, and William Broadhead's harsh approach to 'trade matters' engendered considerable dissatisfaction within the Saw Grinders' Union and by the time of the 1866 incident at Eadon's most of their saw grinders had left and formed their own union, which was known as the Little Grinders' Union. The Commissioners wondered why these men wanted to be members of a trade union at all considering the trouble that there had been over the years and William Overend put the point to John Taylor, the saw grinder who had given evidence in the Elisha Parker inquiry and had also worked for Eadons:

William Overend: *'What made you join the Union and keep in it?'*

John Taylor: *'At the first commencement when I joined the trade had been broken up for about six months.'*

William Overend: *'Did you join it for the purpose of securing assistance when you were out of work for the benefits it would give you as a member of the trade?'*

John Taylor: *'There were two ways; one was at the time that they had shut up the box for about six months, and some*

---

[175] Ibid, 872

[176] Check-off: trade union subscriptions are deducted from wages by the employer and paid straight to the employee's trade union.

of the masters were taking such great advantage that the men were all willing to join.'

William Overend: *'What were the kind of advantages that the masters had taken at that time which induced you to join the Union?'*

John Taylor: *'At that time I worked for Moses Eadon and Sons and they took, I believe, 15 per cent off at that time. It was either 10 or 15 per cent at that time. I will not say which. They took off 10 or 15 per cent discount.'*

William Overend: *'Discount of what?'*

John Taylor: *'Off the saws when we had done them.'*

William Overend: *'Off the price they had to pay?'*

John Taylor: *'Yes; off the week's wages.'*[177]

Whatever the saw grinders thought about William Broadhead and his methods they knew that without joining together the masters would take advantage of each and every one of them. They had learnt the now familiar trade union motto; *'United we stand, divided we fall'.* Despite dissatisfaction amongst the ranks and the desertion of a number of its members to the new union, at the time of the Commissioners' Inquiry in 1867 membership of Broadhead's Saw Grinders' Union stood at about 190.[178]

---

[177] Op. Cit. TUC 9,939 – 9,947
[178] Ibid, 12,010

Sheffield knife blade grinding[179]

---

[179] Op. Cit. Longmate, p.31

James Robinson and the
Brickmakers' Union

1858-1866

Intimidation and rattening were not solely the preserve of the Sheffield metal trades and incidents occurred in all industries where trade unions had been formed, which by the mid-1860s was almost all. Rattening in the brick making trade took the form of spoiling tools and trampling the soft clay bricks before they were fired. It also took a more sinister form when pins and needles were added to the clay so as to injure the brickmakers as they moulded the bricks. In a similar fashion to the disputes with the Saw Grinders' Union, the use of more violent intimidation developed and the Commissioners looked into the case of master brickmaker James Robinson, who lived at Park View House, Intake Road[180]. Fifty-three year-old James Robinson had been a journeyman brickmaker before joining his father in the brick manufacturing business and had been in the trade for the whole of his working life; around 40 years. His two brothers, Joseph and Francis, were partners in the business until it was dissolved in 1851 after which time James took sole control

---

[180] Intake Road was renamed City Road in 1898; Sheffield had become a city in 1893, the 50th anniversary of its incorporation as a Municipal Borough.

(Joseph died in 1861 and Francis died in 1867).[181] The 1861 census records him as being a master brickmaker employing 50 men and 10 boys. By 1871 he was employing 50 men and 17 boys.[182] As a journeyman he was a member of the union but withdrew upon taking up the business. He reported to the Commissioners on incidents of rattening going back to 1854 and 1855 but they concerned themselves only with the incidents that had occurred during the previous ten years in line with the Act, despite Robinson's experiences being similar to those of Elisha Parker.

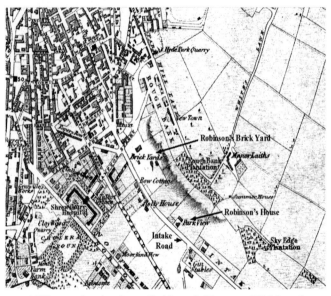

1863 map showing James Robinson's House and Brickyard, Intake Road

---

[181] Information from Geoff Lilleker, James Robinson's 3X great grandson.
[182] 1871 census returns

Much can be learnt from contemporary art and literature and the men who worked for Robinson were epitomised by a character in Charles Dickens' novel *Bleak House.* Based on his personal observations of the brickfield communities, Dickens' fictitious brickmaker is visited at home by Mrs Pardiggle, a sanctimonious philanthropist determined to improve his social standing and moral order. As Mrs Pardiggle's party entered the brickmaker's house, *'one of a cluster of wretched hovels in a brickfield, with pigsties close to broken windows, and miserable little gardens before the doors, growing nothing but stagnant pools',*[183] the scene is described by her companion, Esther Summerson:

'Besides ourselves, there were in this damp offensive room –a woman with a black eye, nursing a poor little gasping baby by the fire; a man, all stained with clay and mud, and looking very dissipated, lying at full length on the ground, smoking a pipe; a powerful young man, fastening a collar on a dog; and a bold girl, doing some kind of washing in very dirty water.'

There were no greetings for the party and despite Mrs Pardiggle's pleasantries it is clear that the brickmaker resents the intrusion and he cuts her short by answering the questions he anticipated she had come to ask:

---

[183] Dickens, Charles, *Bleak House,* Centennial Edition, Edito-Service S A, Geneva, originally published in 1853, pp.129-135 (Charles Dickens visited Sheffield in December 1855 and undertook a reading of his story *A Christmas Carol* at the Mechanics Institute. See Op. Cit. Drinkall, *Book of Days,* p.359)

'I wants a end of these liberties took with my place. I wants a end of being drawed like a badger. Now you're a-going to poll-pry and question according to custom – I know what you're a-going to be up to. Well! You haven't got no occasion to be up to it. I'll save you the trouble. Is my daughter a-washin? Yes, she is a-washin. Look at the water. Smell it! That's what we drinks. How do you like it, and what do you think of gin instead! An't my place dirty? Yes, it is dirty – it's nat'rally dirty, and it's nat'rally onwholesome; and we've had five dirty and onwholesome children, as is all dead infants, and so much the better for them, and for us besides. Have I read the little book wot you left? No, I an't read the little book that you left. There an't nobody here as knows how to read it; and if there wos, it wouldn't be suitable to me. It's a book fit for a babby, and I'm not a babby. If you was to leave me a doll, I shouldn't nuss it. How have I been conducting of myself? Why, I've been drunk for three days; and I'd a been drunk four, if I'd a had the money. Don't I never mean for to go to church? No, I don't never mean for to go to church. I shouldn't be expected there, if I did; the beadle's too gen-teel for me. And how did my wife get that black eye? Why, I giv' it her; and if she says I didn't, she's a lie!'[184]

The life of this brickmaker is almost summed up in his declarations, which typifies the lifestyle of the lower working classes and the poverty-stricken people of 19th century Britain. He is dirty, caked in the clay and mud of his trade; he is a habitual drunkard; he beats his wife who has borne five children that have died in infancy, as did the gasping baby that she was nursing immediately after Mrs

---

[184] Ibid

Pardiggle left the house; the water that the brickmaker's daughter was washing the clothes in, and that which the family had to drink, was contaminated; no-one in the house could read; and no-one went to church. Such was the way of life for many of Sheffield's poor.

The one thing that is perhaps exceptional about Robinson's brickmakers is that they were all male. It was not uncommon at this time for women and young girls to work in the brickfields alongside the men and boys. Their working conditions were most degrading and all traces of their femininity disappeared. One factory inspector observed in 1865:

'I consider that in brickyards the degradation of the female character is most complete…I have seen females of all ages, nineteen or twenty together (some of them mothers of families), undistinguishable from men, excepting by the occasional peeping out of earring, sparsely clad, up to the bare knees in clay splashes, and evidently without a vestige of womanly delicacy, thus employed, until it makes one feel for the honour of a country that there should be such a condition of human labour existing in it.'[185]

The depth of degradation in the women's appearance was matched by their attitude and behaviour. A master brickmaker in the midlands who employed fifty workers, half of whom were women and children, told the same factory inspector of his experiences:

---

[185] Hibbert, Christopher, *The English – A Social History 1066 – 1945,* Guild Publishing, London, 1987, p.589. See also Op. Cit. Hopkins, pp.103-104.

'A flippancy and familiarity of manners with boys and men grows daily in the young girls. Then, the want of respect and delicacy towards females exhibits itself in every act, word, and look; for the lads are so precocious and the girls so coarse in their language and they sing unblushingly before all, whilst at work, the lewdest and most disgusting songs. The overtime work is still more objectionable, because boys and girls, men and women, are not then so much under the watchful eye of the master, nor looked upon by the eye of day. All these things, the immorality, levity and coarse pleasures, awful oaths, lewd gestures, and conduct of the adults and youths, exercise a terrible influence for evil on the young children.'[186]

Such working conditions would inevitably engender a high level of promiscuity with the consequential pregnancies and illegitimate children amongst the women in the brickfields.

Whilst women and girls worked in the Sheffield paper mills and large manufactories at this time, they appear to have been excluded from, and spared the indignity of the Sheffield brickfields; the Sheffield Brickmakers' Union almost certainly kept women out of the trade.

The catalogue of acts of intimidation made against Robinson within the timeline of the Inquiry begins in 1858 when he fell foul of the Brickmakers' Union's rules relating to the employment of non-union men when their paid-up members were out of work; employers were expected to give work to union members in preference to non-union men. The nature of the brick making trade at this time was somewhat seasonal as the summer months were generally the busiest

---

[186] Ibid, p.590

time and work was harder to find in the winter when men often found themselves without work. Robinson had invested in a shed, machinery and a mortar mill driven by an 18 horse power engine that allowed work to continue all year round. The union objected to this machinery but there were no attacks upon it. The fact that Robinson employed some non-union men wasn't an issue when there was plenty of work to go around, as long as they each paid ½d in the shilling of their earnings to the union; they got no other benefit from the union such as sick pay or strike pay, but were simply allowed to work in the trade. The union rates at the time were 4s-6d for 10 hours labour or 3s-6d for 9 hours.[187] Although trade was good in 1858, four union brickmakers turned up at Robinson's one day stating that the union committee had determined they should be given work in place of four non-union members in his employ. Robinson refused to go along with this and sent them packing. The committee's response to this was to call out their members at Robinson's brick yard but they continued to work. At this, the union imposed fines of 30s on some, and £2 on others, but after confiding in Robinson and on his advice, they all refused to pay.[188] It was not long after this altercation that Robinson found himself a victim of rattening.

---

[187] Op. Cit, TUC 22,527
[188] Ibid, 21,735

A 19th century brickfield[189]

It was later in the year that Robinson was returning home late one night when he spotted some young boys playing around the brick fires and he chased them off. He also saw two men walk past the gates of the brickyard who he later established were Emanuel Elms and Abraham Glaves, two union brickmakers; Emanuel Elms was a member of the Brickmakers' Union committee. Robinson thought nothing of it at the time and after ensuring all was well in the yard and the brickfield, he continued his journey home. The next morning he found that some 15,000 to 16,000 bricks drying in the field had been trampled. From the extent of the damage

---

[189] Op. Cit. Hibbert, opposite p. 626, *Brickfields*, Liverpool, British School, Walker Art Gallery, Liverpool.

it was believed that this was the work of some four or five men. The identity of the perpetrators could not be proved but suspicion lay at the door of the union. In his evidence to the Commissioners Robinson revealed that he was a member of a *'protection society'* (probably the Manufacturers' and Tradesmen's Protection Society) and that this association's investigation of the incident proved fruitless despite the offer of a reward for information.[190] He reclaimed as much of the damaged bricks as he could and he estimated that the incident caused him losses of about £5. Robinson maintained his resolve and continued to discourage his men's involvement with the union. With the exception of the odd trading of insults between the union and non-union brickmakers, things quietened down until the following year.

As was commonplace at the time, the working classes of Sheffield, which was still a semi-rural town despite the expansion of its industry and urbanisation, supplemented their income by growing vegetables and keeping livestock; Robinson was no exception. To provide the family with fresh milk he kept two or three cows that grazed in a field opposite his house and brickyard. One morning in 1859 his men found one of Robinson's cows had been attacked and lay dying in the field; it had been stabbed and mutilated so as to expose its entrails. Robinson was alerted and a policeman was fetched. The policeman, who was also a butcher, advised that he must sell the cow before it died so as to save the carcase. This he did. As with the trampling of the bricks the previous year, the identity of the attackers could not be determined but as Robinson had no quarrel with anyone except the Brickmakers' Union, he concluded that it must be behind the attack.

---

[190] Op. Cit. TUC, 21,748

Up until now, the attacks on James Robinson, presumed to be at the hands of the Brickmakers' Union, had been on his property. In October 1859 it became personal and the next incident put his life, and the lives of his wife and children, in serious danger.

According to his evidence at the Inquiry, James Robinson lived with his wife Elizabeth, who was 40 years old in 1859, a son and four daughters.[191] However, the 1861 census records the household as being James, head of the family aged 47; wife Elizabeth, aged 42; daughter Ann, aged 20; son James M, aged 10; and daughters Mary H; Clara E; and Lily aged 6; 2; and 11 months respectively. Lily hadn't been born in 1859 so there would only have been three girls in the house unless there was another child that had died between 1859 and 1861. I can't imagine that he got the number of his children wrong at the time but it is possible that he got the year wrong and it was actually 1860 when this incident occurred; there were other statements in his evidence that suggests he wasn't always sure of the year that certain events occurred. Whichever year it was, at about 3am one October morning James Robinson was woken by *'a tremendous crash'.* This was followed by another two similar noises coming from either another room in the house or from immediately outside. Although he was unsure of what he had heard he instinctively knew that something was amiss. He quickly put on his slippers and ventured out of the bedroom and into an adjoining room, which appeared to be on fire; it was filling with smoke and he caught a glimpse of a small but lively flame. On closer inspection he found the light was coming from a fuse that lay sputtering upon the floor. He stood on the fuse to try and put it out and he felt

---

[191] Ibid, 21,794

the neck of a broken bottle underfoot. All around him there began small explosions made by *'bits of powder like squibs, one igniting the other'.[192]* He raised the alarm and told his wife to get the children out of the house fearing that it was about to be blown up.

What James Robinson had found was an improvised bomb that had been thrown through the window, consisting of gunpowder and hobnails in a stone ginger beer bottle with a fuse through its neck. Fortunately for the Robinson family, the bottle had smashed on impact and its contents had scattered across the floor. Although some of the powder had ignited it created nothing more than a few flashes; like poor quality fireworks. However, had the bottle remained intact the resulting explosion would have done significant damage and anyone in its blast would have been seriously injured or possibly killed.

Two further bottle bombs had been thrown at the house but they had hit the wall inches short of the window and smashed scattering their contents of gunpowder and hobnails in the grass below; powder marks could be seen where they had hit the wall. The perpetrators would have been well aware that their actions that night put the lives of the Robinson family in mortal danger and that had events taken that course, they would face the noose if they were caught. The police were fetched and three detectives named Sills, Airey, and Brayshaw, were put on the case but no-one was brought to book. Although it could not be proven, Robinson was in no doubt that this attack was the work of the Brickmakers' Union.

In November 1860, Robinson and his family came under attack once more. Sometime between 7 and 8 o'clock one

---

[192] Ibid, 21,797

Sunday morning, Ann Robinson went to milk the cows as usual but found something rather unusual. Upon the nearby haystack that James Robinson had built that year to feed his animals over the winter, which was valued and insured at between £100 and £150,[193] lay lengths of cloth. At first Ann thought that her mother had put some washing out to dry but on closer inspection she found that the material was in long lengths and had been pegged into the hay. She also noticed that there was a peculiar smell about the haystack. She returned to the house and called her father, who was still in bed. James Robinson got up, quickly dressed, and went out to examine the haystack, which stood about 15 yards from the house and about 10 yards from the stables. As Ann had told him, the stack was part-covered with lengths of what appeared to be new calico but it was soaked in naphtha and turpentine; that was the peculiar smell that Ann had reported. At one end of the stack was a pile of matches; the contents of 11 boxes that had been emptied and discarded nearby. Running from the matches was a length of calico wrapped with paper to form a taper that was about 5 feet long. This too was soaked in naphtha and had been set alight at the other end but it had burnt out after about 18 inches. Clearly this was an improvised fuse designed to slowly burn along its length until it reached and ignited the matches, which in turn would set the haystack ablaze, thus allowing the guilty party plenty of time to flee the scene before the stack went up in flames. Being a dank November night, there was probably enough moisture in the air to dampen the taper and douse the flame. Had the perpetrators been successful in setting the stack alight, depending on the direction of the wind, either the house or the stables would also have been in danger of

---

[193] Ibid, 21,849

being set alight. Despite a reward being offered by Robinson's insurers, the identity of the culprits was never established. However, as he stated at the Inquiry, James Robinson was convinced that the Brickmakers' Union was behind the attack; he had no quarrel with anyone else.

In August 1861, it was alleged that the Brickmakers' Union struck again whilst James Robinson was holidaying with his family in Cleethorpes, a popular holiday destination of the working classes. One Saturday morning his men turned up at the brickyard to find that one of his horses had suffered a similar fate to that of his cow and was lying dead in the field; it had been stabbed between the ribs and hind quarters. The incident was referred to the detectives who had investigated the bottle bomb attack but once more they failed to find the culprits.

In October 1861 James Robinson had a visit from William Henry Owen and John Jarrett of the Brickmakers' Union (Owen would later become secretary of the union and give evidence at the Inquiry). They had been directed by the then secretary of the union, John Mawson, to make peace with Robinson but they made it clear that they were doing so reluctantly, even though Owen was a personal friend of Robinson and had previously worked for him. Mawson thought that Robinson was more likely to listen to Owen and be persuaded to agree to the union's proposals. Owen was unaware of the alleged intimidation that Robinson had endured at the hands of the union, and on learning of the incidents he expressed dismay if it should prove to be the case that the union was behind them (he would put an end to all such activities once he became secretary himself). Over the next few days Owen and Jarrett negotiated with Robinson at a number of meetings. The union committee sought to put their differences with Robinson behind them and asked if he would agree to his men rejoining the union. To this Robinson said he had no objections but he made it clear that conditions would apply. The union wanted a payment to compensate for the mill that Robinson had installed but this he refused outright. Robinson suggested a method of arbitration be established to resolve any future disputes that arose and proposed an arbitrating party of 12 men; 6 chosen by the union and 6 chosen by him. Following a further meeting of the union committee these terms were accepted and Robinson's men would be allowed back into the union on payment of the normal entrance fee of £1-1s-6d; all arrears owed by any of the men would be written off. Those who couldn't find the money for the entrance fee, and some that the union would not take back, would be allowed to continue working subject to them paying ½d in the shilling of their earnings to the union. Around one third of Robinson's men rejoined the Brickmakers' Union on this basis; the rest paid their ½d in the shilling. The Commissioners asked Robinson why there were some men that the union would not take back. He told them that he had heard from the men that these brickmakers were known as 'Robinson's b-------- '[194]; we must use our imagination as to what the 'b' stood for but these were undoubtedly men who had consistently opposed the union and were consequently blacked.

---

[194] Ibid, 21,946 Words deemed offensive were expunged from the minutes but the inclusion of the letter that the word began with gives us a clue as to what it was.

One of James Robinson's bricks[195]

Following this agreement between Robinson and the union there was a period of peace between the parties until the agreement was put to the test in 1865. William Owen invited Robinson to a meeting of bricklayers at a public house on Snig Hill.[196] The purpose of the meeting was to discuss support for the trade in times of dispute with master builders and/or contractors. Master brickmakers had been invited so as to seek their support should the bricklayers be in dispute. Robinson and other master brickmakers were asked not to supply bricks to any master builder at odds with the trade. Not surprisingly Robinson declined his support.

---

[195] From the Frank Lawson collection, see
www.penmorfa.com/bricks/england19.html
[196] Robinson was uncertain of the name of the pub saying first it was the Nag's Head and then the King's Head. However no pubic house of either name has existed on Snig Hill. Kelly's Directory of 1854 lists four public houses on Snig Hill: Black Swan; Black Lion; Castle Inn; and Traveller's Inn. However, there was a King's Head in nearby Change Alley.

About six weeks later he was invited to attend a meeting of master brickmakers and the Brickmakers' Union committee where William Owen proposed that Robinson, and any other master brickmaker with a clay grinding mill, should make a payment of 4s-6d per man, per day for each of his men working the mill. At this time Robinson had 11 men working in his grinding mill which meant he would have to pay £2-9s-6d per day to the union. The reasoning behind this proposal was to raise money to pay the union brickmakers who found themselves out of work during the winter and were *'on the box'* (being paid unemployment benefit from union funds). Again Robinson rejected this proposal but to settle the matter he sought arbitration in line with the agreement made with the union in 1861:

'You will recollect, your agreement with me was to decide by arbitration, and I demand the arbitration now.'[197]

There was some discussion amongst the committee men and one or two were inclined to go along with arbitration but ultimately the committee decided against it and Robinson left the meeting with nothing resolved. Within the week Robinson had a visit from Owen and two bricklayers who asked him to reconsider his position but he told them he would only accept a decision through arbitration. The following day his men were called out by the union. Most of the union members came out, the exceptions being Robinson's manager and his sons who were under contract and although they were union members, they could face legal action for breach of contract if they refused to work and

---

[197] Op. Cit. TUC, 21,985

the possibility of a 3 months prison sentence. Some non-union members also continued to work.

The strike was to last 2½ weeks with the union men being paid 18s per week by the union, plus 1s-6d for each wife and child. Some were found work elsewhere. Half way through the third week a deputation of four men from the union committee came to Robinson with news of an alteration to their rules which could resolve their dispute; one of them was Emmanuel Elms, one of the men seen at the time of the brick trampling in 1858. Instead of paying the 4s-6d per man in the mill, he should pay a levy of ½d per thousand bricks to the union. They argued for about half an hour but Robinson made it clear that he would not pay one penny to the union ever again. It would appear that by now the union were keener to resolve the dispute than Robinson as finally they indicated that Robinson need only agree to the proposition and not necessarily make payment; it was a face saving exercise. Robinson too was under pressure to resolve things as the strike was costing him money. In addition to this he was under pressure from his wife and other members of his family as they feared a return to the violent attacks and that the house might be bombed again or that James Robinson may be shot; there had been a number of cases of murder and bombings alleged to be the work of trade unions in the press. Despite his resolve for arbitration, the inducement offered meant that he could play the union at their own game and as they had reneged on the arbitration agreement, he would do likewise with the ½d per thousand bricks. He signed a paper of agreement to the ½d and the men returned to work but we learn from his evidence to the Inquiry that he never made a payment to the union.[198]

---

[198] Ibid, 22,016

Robinson wasn't pressed for the ½d per 1,000 bricks payment for about 8 months and then in July 1866 he received another deputation, which included Owen, asking him if he would now make payment to the union. Robinson referred them to the previous agreement and once more insisted on arbitration. He would go along with whatever decision was made by arbitration, even if it was decided that he should pay more. The deputation wasn't in a position to agree this demand and left with Robinson once more refusing to pay anything.

It was at around this time that William Broadhead of the Saw Grinders' Union was steering a move for the amalgamation of a number of unions and there was a little uncertainty in the air as to how these negations would pan out. From the dialogue at the Inquiry we learn that the Brickmakers' Union were one of the unions involved. Using this as a pretext for another possible change to the union's rules, Robinson sent one of his men to ask if the ½d issue could *'stand over'* till the end of the year, when things might be more clear and the issue could then be settled. Surprisingly the union agreed.

At the end of the year a further deputation arrived at Robinson's door, including Owen and Elms, asking for the ½d per 1,000 payments but they faced another stalemate with Robinson once more demanding arbitration:

'You agreed with me for arbitration, therefore I claim the arbitration.........If you let me have a fair arbitration, I am decided by it either for or against me, even if they charge more'.[199]

---

[199] Ibid, 22,038

Once more the deputation left empty-handed but the next day Robinson's men were called out again. Robinson struggled to maintain his business up until Christmas 1866 as he couldn't find the workers to fire his bricks. Those who remained in his employ were threatened with physical violence and there were many others who were deterred from working for him in fear of *'being shot or disabled'*.[200] It is also clear from the evidence given to the Commissioners that some of his men had taken strike action under threat of physical violence, although as usual this wasn't proven. For a number of weeks there were pickets on the gates that prevented bricks leaving the yard. However, as news of the forthcoming Inquiry into the Sheffield Outrages got around the level of intimidation diminished and gradually Robinson was able to take on more men and by the time the Commission sat in July 1867 about half of his men had returned to work and the business was recovering.

In giving evidence to the Commissioners William Owen, now secretary of the Brickmakers' Union, admitted to removing pages from the Union's books that would indicate payments for the outrages against Robinson, although they would not name the perpetrators of the acts.[201] He also maintained that Robinson had made *'a great many falsehoods'* when giving his evidence and that he was apt to take advantage of his workers being the only master in the town who did not agree to pay the union rates.[202] Owen believed that this was the main reason behind the outrages.

---

[200] Ibid, 22,055
[201] Ibid, 22,484
[202] Ibid, 22,527

The Commissioners' investigation concluded that *'the thing was clearly brought home to the union'.* [203]

James Robinson died in 1885 and an obituary published the day after his funeral made strong reference to his tribulations with the Brickmakers' Union:

'The Late Mr. JAMES ROBINSON – The funeral of the late Mr. James Robinson, brick manufacturer, Intake Road, took place yesterday in the churchyard of St. John's, Sheffield Park. Deceased rose from humble circumstances to a position of considerable affluence through twin virtues of perseverance and thrift. At one time he suffered a great deal from rattening during the dark days of Broadheadism, having to live for many years with the windows of his house guarded with wire screens and iron bars to prevent explosive missiles being thrown into his dwelling. He, however, survived those troublesome times, and has for many years pursued his calling undisturbed by "the Trade," whose antipathy towards him was owing to his spirited introduction of machinery.' [204]

---

[203] Ibid, 22,530

[204] Provided on a Sheffield history web-blog by Geoff Lilleker, James Robinson's 3X great grandson.

Early Morning on the Don, Sheffield, 19th century postcard
by 'Jotter':

Henry Bridges' Broken Bricks

1861

James Robinson wasn't the only master brickmaker to fall victim of the union. On the night of Saturday 21 April 1861 Henry Bridges[205] had between 40,000 and 50,000 bricks destroyed; 25,000 pressed bricks ready for the kiln, the rest stock bricks. Five or six barrows and a pressing machine were also smashed. Bridges went to the police and an officer was sent to inspect the damage. From the number of hobnail boot prints and the extent of the damage the officer suggested that it was the work of 5 or 6 men. Bridges estimated the cost of this destruction to be in the region of £40; the equivalent of over £20,000 by modern values. Although he couldn't think of any reason as to how he could

---

[205] By the time Henry Bridges gave evidence at the Inquiry he had become a publican and was recorded as such in the 1871 census at the Lord Nelson Inn 184 Greystock Street. Although he was a brickmaker in April 1861, in the census returns he is recorded as a beer house keeper at Norroy Street (off Saville Street). White's Directory 1862 also lists him as a beer house keeper and brickmaker at Norroy Street. The beer house would supplement his income from the brickyard in the summer and maintain an income when the brickyard was idle in the winter months.

have upset the union he was convinced that it was a *'trade affair'*.

On the following Monday night he went to see the Brickmakers' Union committee to ascertain why he had been attacked. He met with 8 members of the committee, including John Baxter, Frederick Peach and Samuel Kaye. When he asked why his bricks had been spoilt John Baxter[206] told him that it was due to him being insulted by one of his men, one Thomas Poole[207]. It transpired that on the Saturday previous to the attack Poole and Baxter had a falling out about the amount of *'outworking money'[208]* that Poole had paid. Baxter thought he should have paid more and the verbal exchange between the two over the matter resulted in Baxter taking offence. At this Bridges exclaimed *'If my men insult you, am I to stand the loss of having my bricks spoiled?'[209]* Baxter gave no answer but suggested he came to the union's general meeting, which was to take place on the following

---

[206] Thirty-eight year-old John Baxter was boarding with a woman called Ruth Wilcock at Court 1 Allen Street at the time of the 1861 census.

[207] At the time of the 1861 census Thomas Poole was 26 years-old and lived in Princess Street with his 25 year-old wife Eliza and his three children, Thomas, aged 7; Sarah Ann, aged 5; and 2 year-old George. In 1871 he had a 1 year-old daughter called Sarah Ann and there was no 15 year-old Sarah Ann, which suggests his first daughter had died sometime between 1861- 1870 and her name was given to his second daughter; this seems to have been a regular practice in such circumstances at the time.

[208] To be able to work in the brickyards, men who were not members of the union had to pay a fee of ½d in the shilling of their earnings. This was known as *'outworking money'*. However, they were not entitled to any of the union's benefits.

[209] Op. Cit. TUC, 23,123

Monday, and he would see what could be done. Bridges didn't go to the general meeting but some of his men attended and they were told that Bridges would get nothing.

The extent of damage done in the attack on Bridges' brickyard would appear to be an extreme measure if it was simply in retaliation for a member of the union's committee being insulted by one of his men. Surely the offending man, Thomas Poole, would have been the target, not his master. As the union refused to compensate Bridges for his losses, something it would have done had the loss not been due to a *'trade affair',* this suggests that Bridges was the real target and that it was regarding a transgression of his and not Poole's. It emerged that two months previous to the attack Bridges was approached by Samuel Kaye and another committee man by the name of White, who asked that he paid the union 1s per week when the yard was working; brick making being seasonal meant that there would be periods when no work was undertaken in the yards. Bridges refused to pay and nothing further was said about the matter. However, despite Baxter stating that it was Poole's insults that triggered the attack, Bridges' refusal to pay the 1s levy was the most likely reason behind it.

One of Henry Bridges' bricks[210]

Despite his differences with the union Bridges, along with a number of other master brickmakers, joined the Brickmakers' Union a year or two after the attack following a decision by the committee to allow the masters in. He paid £1-1s-6d to join and subscriptions of 4d per week in the summer, and 2d per week in the winter. When asked by William Overend at the Inquiry why he had joined, Bridges replied *'To keep quiet and peaceable, and to go on quietly if we could.'[211]*

[210] From the Graham Hague (Sheffield) collection, see www.penmorfa.com/bricks/england19.html
[211] Op. Cit. TUC, 23,148

George Gillott and the File Grinders' Union

1857-1867

George Gillott was a file grinder living in a terraced house on Bramber Street, Tomcross Lane, at the top of Spital Hill with his wife, two children and two apprentices.

Sheffield file making

He worked at the Castle grinding mill in Sheffield, which was also known as the Tower mill and owned by Messrs. Wm. Parker & Co. The Castle mill was considered one of the more secure mills in the district, having lockable gates and three watchmen residing on the premises. It would be most difficult for rattening to be undertaken here. Although somewhat protected from intimidation at work, George Gillott found himself a target at home when it was thought that he was working under price and that he had more than the permitted number of apprentices working for him contrary to the rules of the union, although at this time he was no longer a member. At around 12.30 in the morning of 25 April 1857, George was in bed when he heard the clanking of his cellar grate being dropped and his two pointer dogs in the kitchen begin to bark. He also heard the soft footfall of someone running away and across the road. He considered that the person was wearing slippers or was in stocking feet; this was not the sound of boots or shoes. Discarding shoes as a method of avoiding being heard is illustrated by evidence given by John Clarke, a convicted rattener who was apprehended by the police one night in Cornish Place in possession of a jemmy and without shoes.[212] It is also possible that the person heard by Gillott had wrapped their feet in cloth to muffle the sound of their footsteps. Within a couple of minutes it became clear that whoever it was had lifted the grate and deposited an improvised bomb into his cellar as there was an almighty explosion that rocked the house. Gillott went down the stairs to find all the windows and doors had been blown out and a partition wall had been demolished. Much of the furniture downstairs was destroyed or damaged and it was evident that should anyone have been in this part of the house they would have suffered severe injury or possibly killed; there is no reference to the fate of Gillott's dogs. It is most likely that the damage suffered to the house made it uninhabitable and that the Gillotts had to move out, at least until it was repaired.

---

[212] Ibid, 7,720. See later chapter on William Darwin and the Scissor Forgers' Society.

The Gillotts may have moved out permanently after the attack as at the time of the inquiry the family were living in Rockingham Street.

The first man on the scene was a file cutter called Sam Brammer who lived in the neighbourhood and was on his way home from the casino.[213] But it wasn't long before all the neighbours were out in the street and a policeman had arrived. Gillott's family were taken safely out of the house and the officer inspected the cellar, where he found the remains of a canister that had been filled with gunpowder. He then questioned Gillott about the explosion and he told him of the soft footsteps he had heard and that he thought the perpetrator had crossed the street to the house of a man named Royston, a fellow file grinder. Royston had threatened Gillott over his not being a union member about a year previously and had said *'Thou hast been blown up once and thou will be blown up again if thou doesn't* (join the union). *'[214]* It transpired from his evidence that Gillott had been the victim of a similar incident in 1846[215] which he maintained was the work of the File Grinders' Union although as often was the case, it couldn't be proven. On 10 October the same year one of the engines at the Castle Mills

---

[213] Ibid, 16,214. The casino was probably the Old Surrey Theatre on West Bar which burnt down in 1865. See Op. Cit. Hey, p.201

[214] Ibid, 16,233

[215] According to the *Sheffield Local Register* this incident actually occurred on 16 March 1844. A tin case charged with gunpowder and with a lighted fuse was thrown through Gillott's bedroom window at 197 Granville Street. George Gillott, his wife and child escaped from the room before the explosion, which shattered the house: Op. Cit. Leader, 1844, p.395

was blown up. The watchman, William Ibbotson, was apprehended on suspicion but was later released.[216] As these incidents were outside of the timescale of the Commissioners' remit they weren't investigated. Royston was questioned by the police but he wasn't charged with the offence; nor was anyone else.

Castle grinding mill, also known as Tower mill[217]

Despite his house being blown up for a second time, allegedly at the hands of the File Grinders Union, Gillott eventually rejoined the union after finding himself isolated within the file making fraternity. He was approached by the secretary of the union, Joseph Rolley, in the spring of 1864 after most of the file makers, cutters, hardeners and grinders that Gillott worked with had now joined. This was not the

[216] Ibid, 10 October 1846, p.428
[217] Sketch from the Illustrated London News, 1860s

end of his problems however as on a number of occasions between 1864 and 1867 he found his bands missing, despite his working in the secure confines of the Castle mill. Rolley and the Union denied all knowledge of what had happened to Gillott's bands and even offered a reward for their return. It is plausible that they were simply stolen but it was no coincidence that Gillott had fallen into arrears with his *'natty'* at the times that his bands disappeared. Nevertheless, Rolley denied any attempt by himself or the union to remove Gillott's bands when questioned by the Commissioners under oath and in full knowledge that he wouldn't be punished for any crime he should admit to. Of course this doesn't mean that Gillott wasn't rattened; any member of the union could have taken the issue into their own hands without the authorization of the union, and very often they did.

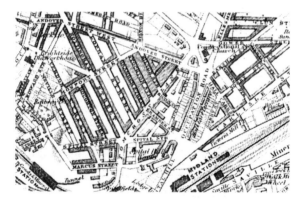

1863 map of Tomcross Lane area at the top of Spital Hill showing streets of terraced housing. By 1873 Tomcross Lane had become Brunswick Road, which still exists today. Bramber Street, where George Gillott lived, has been lost to subsequent development.

131

The Old Surrey Theatre on West Bar consumed by fire in 1865,
Illustrated London News

Ruins of the Surrey Theatre on Tuesday, the morning after the fire,
Illustrated London News

The Murder of James Linley

'He is dead and gone, but Linley wasn't a pleasant sort of man, poor fellow. Not a just man by a long way. He might have done well - as well as I am doing. But he was kind of greedy, you see, and thought that he might be getting something out of somebody else's labour as well as his own.'[218]

1857-1860

One of the most notorious Sheffield Outrages was the killing of saw grinder James Linley. Linley first came under the scrutiny of William Broadhead and the Saw Grinders' Union in 1857 when, having previously earned his living as a scissor grinder, he turned his hands to saw grinding as there was more money to be earned in the saw trade due to the influence of the Saw Grinders' Union. In setting up his new business he joined the Saw Grinders' Union and took on six apprentices, more than the union rules allowed, and worked below the union price. This was brought to Broadhead's attention by Samuel Crookes, one of the union's members and a former apprentice to Linley, who offered to deal with

---

[218] From an article by journalist James Greenwood on the shooting of James Linley in the *Sheffield Independent,* 18 September, 1867. See Op Cit. TUC, p.xv

him for £20. A similar approach was made by another of Linley's former apprentices, James Hallam who considered that Linley was *'doing us a great deal of injury'*.[219] Broadhead agreed and was of a mind that Linley was not only in defiance of the union's rules but if he was not dealt with he would totally undermine the union's work and in his words *'ruin the trade'*.[220] Linley's high turnover of apprentices was flooding the saw grinding labour market with more hands than it had work for and was increasing the number of union men *'on the box'*. In addition to this the lads were poorly trained and Linley's work was cheap and of an inferior standard. His apprentices had to chase him for their money on pay day yet he liked to be seen in a pub during working hours, arrogantly rattling money in his pocket in front of saw grinders *'on the box'*, thrown out of work by his apprentices.[221] It is fair to say that Linley was disliked across the trade. Hallam approached Broadhead again whilst he was collecting subscriptions at the Eagle Works at Neepsend, saying that Linley *'could be done for £15'*. Broadhead told him that he would think it over. William Broadhead didn't trust Hallam but after some deliberation over several days, Broadhead offered Samuel Crookes £15 for the pair of them to deal with Linley; to shoot him but not to kill him.[222]

On hearing of Broadhead's offer James Hallam bought a revolver for 50s at Sarah Cutler's pawnbroker[223] shop at the

---

[219] Ibid, 11,350

[220] Ibid, 12,070-12,075

[221] Op. Cit. Pollard

[222] Op. Cit. TUC, 12,079

[223] There would be many pawnbrokers in Sheffield at this time; always an indication of high levels of poverty. The number of pawn shops in Britain increased by 130% between 1851 and 1871. Op. Cit. Chesney, p.192

corner of Bank Street and Paradise Square with the intention of using it to shoot Linley, although he told Crookes, who went into the shop to buy it on his behalf, that he wanted it for his own protection. Samuel Crookes was already in possession of an air gun that he had a licence for, having previously bought it at Naylor's gun & pistol dealers at 37 Snig Hill. He used it to shoot rabbits and grouse in Ecclesall Wood. Of the two, Crookes considered he was the better shot and he was determined to do the actual shooting of Linley so as to ensure he wasn't killed.

Crookes and Hallam stalked Linley for several weeks before they found an opportunity to take a shot at him. A chance eventually came on 12 November 1857 when Crookes followed him to a house at Colliers' Row in Nursery Street. It was sometime between 7:00 and 8:00 in the evening and Crookes could see Linley silhouetted in the window against the lights inside. He was sat on a table with his back to the window. Crookes took aim from about 4 or 5 yards and shot Linley in the back with his air gun. To limit the damage he had not pumped the air in the gun, which must have been of the 'multi-pump' type, to its maximum, just enough to cause a slight wound at that distance; he had no intention of doing Linley serious injury. The shot hit Linley in the side but didn't penetrate the skin; he was left with just bruising and swelling. To confuse any investigation Crookes left a pistol in the street so as to give the appearance that it was the weapon used and not his air gun.[224]

It is not clear whether the shooting had the desired effect on Linley but he must have been aware that it was the union that was behind the attack. Perhaps it did for a while as there were no other attacks during the next twelve months, but

---

[224] Ibid, 13,523

Crookes was responsible for a further attack on Linley in January 1859, again paid for by Broadhead. This time he used the now familiar practice of dropping a canister of powder down the cellar grate of the butcher's shop that Linley was living over at 64 Wicker. According to the evidence given by Crookes and William Broadhead the butcher in question was named Samuel Poole and he was Linley's brother-in-law. Early in the morning of 11 January 1859 Samuel Crookes lit the fuse attached to a can of gunpowder and lifted the cellar grate of the butcher's shop, which wasn't under the wall of the building but at some distance away from the shop in the pavement. To achieve the desired impact he had to lower the canister down the grate in his hand and then throw it into the cellar underground. The improvised bomb exploded but caused little damage and no-one was injured. Linley escaped this second attack unscathed. He wasn't to be so lucky next time.

A 19th century air gun. Although this is a Swiss model from 1870 it is likely to be similar to the one used by Crookes

After trailing James Linley for between five and six weeks, on the evening of 1 August 1859 Samuel Crookes and James Hallam followed him from the American Stores public house at 36 West Bar Green to the Crown Inn at 31 Scotland Street. After Linley entered the Crown Hallam went around the back and Crookes stayed in the street in case he came back out. In the back yard of the Crown, Hallam observed Linley through the window of the back room talking with other drinkers. He went back and beckoned Crookes to join him in the back yard where they both watched Linley through the window. Hallam insisted that this was the opportunity they had been waiting for and urged Crookes to shoot Linley there and then. Crookes was a little hesitant as there were a number of people in the pub and he didn't want to accidentally shoot somebody else. The confines of the back yard offered little by way of an escape route once the deed was done; there was only one exit along a narrow passageway and there were other people walking about in the street. Hallam said that he would do it but Crookes couldn't risk that; he was the better shot and he couldn't let Hallam make the attempt. Despite his reluctance he decided to take a shot and raising his air gun he took aim at Linley's shoulder. He fired but as he did so Linley leant forward and the pellet struck him at the side of his temple. Unaware of the outcome of the shot, Crookes and Hallam ran off down the alleyway, Hallam brushing against a man and a woman in the entry. They entered Pea Croft then sped off in the direction of Crookes were they split up and made their escape into the night.

The next day Crookes and Hallam met up at the Old No.12 public house, known as *'Wylie's'* after the landlady, Mrs Anna Wylie, in Haymarket. The papers were full of the previous night's shooting in Scotland Street and they soon learned that Linley had been hit in the head. Yet, he was still alive and Crookes was satisfied that he had done what he had set out to achieve and what William Broadhead had paid him to do; to put Linley out of action, but not to kill him. Time would prove that Crookes was premature in this assumption.

Sketches of the shooting of James Linley published during the Commissioners' Inquiry[225]

The initial suspect for the crime was a local furniture broker and bailiff by the name of Richard Brown, who lived at 37 Pea Croft and who had been drinking in the Crown with his wife and Linley shortly before the shooting. A witness by the name of Mrs Smith, whose house shared the backyard of the Crown, had been sat sewing by her door and had looked out after hearing the shot. She said that she saw a man matching Brown's description run down the passageway at the side of the pub and into Scotland Street. Another witness,

[225] From *The Illustrated Police News, Law Courts and Weekly Record*, Saturday June 29 1867

one Mrs Dewsnap, who was walking down Scotland Street at the time, also saw the man come out of the passageway and run off down Scotland Street but she hadn't heard the shot. From newspaper reports we learn that Richard Brown's possible motive for the attack was due to an altercation regarding his wife's association with Linley. With a possible motive and the collaborating witness statements, the police apprehended Brown and further investigation uncovered a pair of pistols at his house that, in the opinion of the custody officer, Sgt, Christopher Whytell, had been recently fired. Brown was brought before the magistrates' court but Mr William Smith esquire, who heard the case, decided that there wasn't sufficient evidence to justify his committal and he was freed.

Although Linley initially survived the shooting, the injury was serious and he eventually died of the wound in February 1860. At the following inquest the Coroner recorded a verdict of *'murder by person or persons unknown'*.

The full account of the shooting of James Linley was revealed at the Inquiry where Crookes, Hallam and Broadhead eventually gave full confessions, although only after Hallam was jailed for 6 weeks by William Overend for contempt of court for refusing to reveal his accomplice in the shooting, and in other actions of intimidation. It was at this point that the canny Chief Constable played a significant card in the unfolding game between the trades unions and justice. John Jackson persuaded William Overend to allow him to keep Hallam at the Sheffield Police Office rather than sending him to the Wakefield House of Correction. Jackson kept Hallam in solitary confinement and allowed no-one to see him but himself, personally attending to all of his needs.

We may never know what passed between Jackson and Hallam during his spell in isolation but in the end Hallam agreed to confess all to the court on condition that John Jackson remained at his side to shield him from attack; he fully believed that there would be an attempt on his life. Hallam was back before the Commissioners after 6 days showing remorse for his conduct and now being prepared to tell all, subject to him getting his certificate of indemnity. During this second spell in the witness box, where John Jackson stood by his side throughout, Hallam fainted and had to be removed from the court; he must have been overwhelmed by fear of the consequences of incriminating Broadhead and the union. Taken to an adjoining room, he came round and made a desperate attempt at self-strangulation. In a short while he returned to the stand, pale and trembling, and crouching behind the Chief Constable, he confessed all to the Commissioners, incriminating Broadhead and Crookes. This was a pivotal moment of the proceedings. John Jackson's diligence was acknowledged by the Commissioners who were *'in no small degree indebted* [to him] *for whatever success has attended our inquiry.'* [226] He was also rewarded by the town's leading manufacturers and civic dignitaries who presented him with a silver salver and £700 in recognition of his services. [227] A portrait of Jackson was also commissioned that is now displayed in the reception area of the National Emergency Services Museum on West Bar, Sheffield.

It is worth considering at this point how the payments made to Crookes and Hallam, and to others working for

---

[226] Op. Cit. TUC, p.vii

[227] Op. Cit. Taylor, p.187. Other contemporary accounts state Jackson was granted £600.

Broadhead, were hidden from the union's accounts; they would incriminate Broadhead had they not been. The amounts paid were considerable; £20 in 1864 equates to around £11,620 at today's value.[228] On being questioned by the Commissioners, who were also keen to find out how this money was hidden from the union's members, Broadhead explained an elaborate scheme by which he falsely recorded the earnings of members in the books, recording less than the actual amount but taking the correct percentage in subscriptions and putting the difference to one side for the purpose of paying his ratteners and trade guerrillas. Although there were some alterations in the books they were not detected by the union's auditors. Broadhead explained:

'You must understand it was not scratched out in such large numbers that it would strike the eye-it would only be done at certain places and at certain times. I made the selections of them in such a way that they (auditors) *should not see them.'*[229]

However, had the union's books been given proper scrutiny it would have incriminated Broadhead as an embezzler and the instigator of the bombings and shootings. Broadhead was aware of this and took the precaution of destroying the books from around the times that these crimes were committed. In mitigation he explained that his actions were solely for the benefit of the trade.

---

[228] For historic monetary values see the following Internet web page:
http://freepages.history.rootsweb.ancestry.com/~calderdaleco mpanion/qq_105.html
[229] Op. Cit. TUC, 12,439

Sketch of Sheffield grinders, 1864
(Illustrated London News)

The Blowing Up of Joseph Helliwell

'He came home with his hair singed off, and his face and bosom burnt; and blind too he was!'[230]

1859

Joseph Wilson had manufactured saws for 22-23 years by the time that he gave evidence to the Commission of Inquiry and he had premises in Milton Street, Sheffield but in 1859 he also rented a hull at the Tower Wheel. There he employed three men who had been apprenticed to James Linley; Henry Garfit, Denis Clark and George Shaw.[231] Of the three Garfit and Clark worked for him on a regular basis but Shaw only occasionally. He also employed Matthew Woollen who had been apprentice to Thomas Fearnehough, who would fall victim to the outrages in 1866 (see below). Sometime in 1859 all four of them joined the Saw Grinders' Union and left Wilson, who was well-known for his objections to trade unions and their methods. The men's departure left Wilson without men for a fortnight and he then took on a man named

---

[230] Rebecca Helliwell's description of her husband after being blown up. Op. Cit. TUC, 6,862
[231] In the 1851 census 32 year-old Joseph Wilson is recorded as employing 4 men, 2 women and 6 boys.

Joseph Helliwell who was a labourer but could turn his hand to grinding. He was also the brother of John Helliwell who was at that time being stalked by Samuel Crookes and his air gun (see below). The fact that Joseph Helliwell was not an apprentice trained saw grinder made his employment by Wilson even more obnoxious to the union and they both became targets for retribution. Helliwell approached Broadhead offering £5 to join the union but the committee denied him membership. He went to him again and offered £8 but was refused again. He saw Broadhead for a third time and offered £10 but as he wasn't apprenticed to the trade he was ineligible for membership under the union's rules and he was told that the committee wouldn't accept him at any price.

Although the four grinders had left Wilson's employ, they would often hang around his hull at the Tower Wheel. Denis *'Tucker'* Clark did a few jobs for William Broadhead at the Tower Wheel holing and hanging stones at 1s a piece, but at other times he was there to make mischief; taking Helliwell's tools and goading him as he worked. He would shout insults at Helliwell, who he called *'Topsey'*, making the point that the union would *'do him'* if he carried on working for Wilson. George Shaw would also call by and on one occasion threatened that Helliwell would *'get his head knocked off'* if he continued working for Wilson. On another occasion Henry Garfit called on him to complain that he was getting more work than him and they finished up fighting with Garfit getting the better of Helliwell. Over a number of weeks he was also in receipt of three threatening letters and he must have been aware that it would be just a matter of time before something untoward would occur. One of the anonymous letters stated that *'if he did not give up working*

for "Bulldog" Wilson he might expect what would follow'.[232]
There were also occasions away from work that threats were made. Helliwell was in the Corner Pin on the Wicker with his wife Rebecca one night when Clark, who was also in the pub with George Shaw and Henry Garfit, threatened that he would *'get him'*.

Denis Clark clearly had a close relationship with Broadhead and was somewhat favoured with regards to his membership of the Saw Grinders' Union. Clark paid £5 to join but he wasn't in full-time work and he was allowed to pay the fee in instalments out of his *'scale'*[233] money. Apart from the odd jobs he did for Broadhead and a few days here and there working for his father, who was a mason, at 3s or 4s a day, he was out of work and drew scale from the union for 8 years. Commissioner George Chance calculated that Clark was in receipt of around £200 from the union during this time for doing nothing in return. It transpired that Clark was doing other jobs for Broadhead that wouldn't be recorded in the books, including *'doing'* Joseph Helliwell.

After joining the union and leaving Wilson, George *'Putty'* Shaw, who was 20 years old and could not read or write, went to work for a man named Marshall at Cornhill, Sheffield. He got the nickname *'Putty'* after his father who was a plasterer. A fortnight after joining Mr Marshall, Clark approached Shaw and asked if he would join him in doing a job for *'Old Smite 'em'* and blow up *'Old Topsey'*. On

---

[232] Op. Cit. TUC, 6,848

[233] Scale: money paid to union members whilst they were out of work or kept off work by the union so as to control the labour market. *The Times* speculated that on average a third of the members of the Saw Grinders' Union were on scale money at any time to keep them out of the market, 29 June 1867

Wednesday 15 October 1859 he went with Clark to see Broadhead at the Greyhound, 185 Gibraltar Street, where he was the landlord. Here Clark went upstairs and came back down with three cans of gunpowder and told Shaw they would get £3 once the job was done. Shaw took the powder home where he lived with his widowed mother and his sister and put it under the mattress of his bed. Two days later, on the Friday, Shaw and Clark took the powder to the Tower Wheel and Shaw put half a can of powder in Helliwell's trough; the wheel was down at the time. Mixed with the grinding dust it would not be detected without close inspection but once sparks from the stone hit the trough it would blow up in the grinder's face. After laying their deadly trap they took the other two and a half cans to Hyde Park where they sold it to a man called Simmonite who was known to be a regular pigeon shooter. With the proceeds from the sale they went on a drinking spree at the Green Man at West Bar, where they also had a pig-hock for their lunch. They then went on to the Corner Pin in the Wicker where they stayed until they got rather drunk before going home to sleep it off.

On the morning of Saturday 18 October Joseph Helliwell turned up for work, got his tools together and readied the stone. Before he began grinding Rebecca Helliwell turned up with his breakfast and asked if she was to bring him some dinner later; they lived nearby in the Wicker and Joseph would probably go home for dinner most days but with his hull being down the previous day it was likely he would want to work through to make up the lost time. Rebecca returned home but within 10 minutes of getting there Joseph staggered through the door, his hair singed off, his face black and his chest burnt. No sooner had he bent over the stone to

146

grind his first saw blade the powder exploded in his face. *'They have done me at last'* he cried as he fumbled around for something solid to steady his shaking body; the flash from the powder had also blinded him.

Joseph Helliwell spent the next four weeks recovering from his ordeal; it took a fortnight before his sight returned. He went back to work but it was a while before he got back to full strength and able to earn what he usually did. However, had Shaw and Clark deposited the full three cans of powder that William Broadhead had given them into his trough he would have almost certainly been killed. Rebecca Helliwell approached Broadhead's wife, Mary Jane, who she had known since childhood, to ask if she could persuade the union to help them out seeing that Joseph's incapacity was due to the union's doing but nothing came of it. Meanwhile Shaw and Clark shared the £3 that they got from William Broadhead for doing the job and probably went on another drinking spree.

Sheffield saw manufacturing[234]

Initially, Denis Clark denied any involvement in the blowing up of Joseph Helliwell when questioned by the Commissioners but he eventually came clean after Shaw had admitted his part in the outrage and the realisation that he would no doubt be jailed for perjury had he not. In an attempt

---

[234] From the front page of *The Working Man – A Weekly Record of Social and Industrial Progress, Saturday 3 February 1866*

to gain some sympathy he also informed the court that he had lost his 23 year-old wife, Frances, and one of his daughters, Ann, as a result of the Sheffield Flood of 1864; Ann was just 12 days old. They weren't included in the official list of the dead released by John Jackson at the time but they died of the effects of being caught up in the filthy water as it flooded their home in Orchard Street. They were buried together at Burngreave Cemetery on 20 March 1864.[235] Clark submitted a claim for £500 against the Sheffield Waterworks Company for the loss of his wife, and a further claim for lost property from his Orchard Street home valued at £43 6s. He made no claim for the loss of his baby daughter, save for the expenses for her funeral which were included in the lost property claim.[236] It was ironic that Clark faced the judgement of William Overend in deciding his claims in 1864 and now here he was giving evidence in front of him again in 1867. Having been awarded just £27 for the loss of his wife, and only £17 for the lost contents of his house, one can understand his initial reluctance to co-operate with Commissioner Overend. In court he also divulged that he had lost another baby daughter, again named Ann, in 1861; she was only 1 year old. We know little about her death other than that she was scalded; presumably a tragic accident.[237]

It is worth considering the motive of Shaw and Clark in undertaking this outrage. In evidence at the Inquiry we hear

[235] Lightowler, Karen, *Sheffield Flood The Aftermath,* www.lulu.com, 2011, pp.90-96
Also: Op. Cit. Drewry, p.156 and p.158
[236] Sheffield Hallam University, *Sheffield Flood Claims Archive,* www2.shu.ac.uk/sfca, loss of life claim No. 71 and loss of personal property claim No. 3102
[237] Op. Cit. TUC, 8,194

how William Broadhead and others defended their actions in that they were acting on behalf of their members; defending them against the greedy masters who would exploit them in the extreme had they not waged this war against them and those who sided with them; there was nothing personal against the targets and no other gain was desired, it was purely for the cause. Yet here we have two union members purporting to be acting on behalf of that cause who, when given the means to undertake their work decide upon selling most of it to finance a drinking spree. Whilst willing to undertake criminal acts that could not only result in them going to jail but could possibly lead to them facing the hangman's noose, their motives appear to be more to do with personal gain than support of the trade union movement. In essence, Shaw and Clark were mere criminals.

Joseph Wilson and the Saw Grinders' Union

1859

Throughout the period from his men leaving him and up to the blowing up of Joseph Helliwell, Joseph Wilson had himself been receiving threatening letters; about twelve altogether. He had kept the first and the last of these letters and presented them to the Commissioners. The first was quite a long one:

'Dear Sir. Seeing you are plunging about and endeavouring to extricate yourself from the meshes which you have been placed in, and as all your efforts will be futile, let me advise you to give up your opposition, for to this it must come at last, and depend upon it, it will be the worst. You erroneously conceive the society to be your enemy. They only wish to place you on the same conditions as other houses, and this they have both means to do and will accomplish. So let me advise you to make peace, and take men according to rule, which I am sure once being done you will be much more comfortable and satisfied with than being as you are, for instead of being compelled to employ the most disreputable of characters (which is no benefit to you in the end) you will have the opportunity of employing some steady, industrious, honest men, such as when you was want to

employ when you employed Union men, and which you know you was much more comfortable with. I am aware that in these times of competition discounts and under prices are very tempting to an employer when he can squeeze them out of a workman's necessities, under the cry and guise of each man being free to make his own bargains, and said necessities are not unfrequently brought about by the men's unsteady, intemperate and general bad character. Having broken faith with all whom he has had dealings with, his necessities make him a fitting instrument for such an object. But a man of this kind I should think your past experience has taught you is dear at any price, as if he breaks faith with others he will break faith with you. I am quite aware you will answer by saying, I do not object to pay the price, as I am willing to pay the price to any man who will leave the society and work for me; but you know it was price that caused your disagreement with the society in the first place, and hence your opposition to the society. But men know full well if you were to pay it now, and they had not the protection of the Union, you would reduce them the very first chance you had. Consequently I believe it useless to expect to get any one in any other way than that according to the rules of the Union. I believe the Union has no ill-feeling towards you, and I have no doubt (as I have before stated) will be quite willing and glad to treat you on the same terms as other employers. So let me advise you to do with a good grace what you may depend upon you cannot avoid. Believe me, dear sir, no enemy of yours but your best adviser.'

This was written by an educated hand and it perspicaciously explained the situation that existed between Wilson and the union. It also made very clear the argument of the need for trade unions to protect the employee in the laissez-faire labour market of the 19th century. It was polite and to the point. But the tone of the last letter was in total contrast and most sinister:

'Dear Sir. I take this opportunity of just reminding you that you are trying on a dangerous game. You are taking the place of another, - the person whose name I need not mention – [this is a reference to James Linley who had recently been shot at his brother-in-law's house in the Wicker] *by running about to decoy boys to grind for you. It will save your life if you do not succeed, as it would cause you to come the next game, and in that case it is fifty to one upon your days being numbered. You may treat this lightly, and toss it into the fire, if you will, but so sure as you are a doomed man; and bear in mind I have hitherto always done what I have promised in this way to the fullest measure.'* [signed] *'Tantia Topee'*

There is no mistaking the deadly intent declared in this message. The reference to Wilson employing boys to grind for him was yet another misdemeanour and breach of union rules added to his employing a non-union and non-apprentice trained grinder. Both letters were written by William Broadhead who admitted to the Commissioners that *'Tantia Topee'* was a pseudonym that he used.[238] Wilson was sure that it was his employment of Joseph Helliwell that made him a potential target for *'outrage'* and after the blowing up of Helliwell at his hull he realised that he must

---

[238] Op. Cit. TUC, 13,335

be on his guard and take every precaution; not just at the Tower Wheel but also at home at 145 Fitzwilliam Street where his wife Sarah and three children would also be in danger.[239]

A Sheffield Grinder's 'Hull'[240]

Wilson was aware that the most familiar mode of attack was to drop a canister of gunpowder down the chimney or cellar grate of the intended victim's house. He considered that the cellar grates were the *'Achilles heel'* at home and he

---

[239] The 1851 census tells us that Joseph, then 32 years old, was living with his wife, 31 year-old Sarah; daughter Sarah J, aged 4; son Joseph, aged 1; and his mother Mary Wilson, aged 69. By 1859 another child had arrived and, as there is no mention of Mary in Joseph's evidence, it is likely that she would have passed away by this time.
[240] Op. Cit, Taylor, p.250

took precaution by setting up an elaborate alarm system on the grate to the cellar under the room where he and his wife slept should such an attack occur. He got together a load of old pots and cans and set them up under the cellar grate so that they would all tumble down should the grate be lifted. The clatter that this would make would raise the alarm. It worked. At about six o'clock in the morning of 24 November Wilson was awoken by the sound of the crashing pots and cans; the grate had been lifted. He dashed to the window and saw a figure running away and around the corner of the street. He could not see enough in the dark to be able to recognise his attacker but he knew that it would be someone from the union. He was a young man, about 5' 7", wearing either a dark frock coat or tail coat and a cap. Wilson got dressed and went down into the cellar and secured the grate. The noise from his impromptu alarm had taken his attacker by surprise, causing him to take to his heels before he was caught in the act, taking his bomb with him. Wilson had had a lucky escape but things weren't to work out so well next time.

The following week the house shook as there was a mighty explosion at its very foundations. The bomber had returned but this time lifted the second grate to the cellar under the living room, which Wilson had not alarmed. His three children slept in the room above the living room and the blast blew them all out of bed. Wilson quickly dressed and instructed his wife to get the children into the office, which adjoined the house, then went downstairs and tried to get into the living room but the door wouldn't budge. He then went out into the street where neighbours were already gathering to investigate the blast. He could see a glow through the smoke billowing out of the grate and fearing the house would catch fire he dropped down the grate and into the cellar where he found a piece of burning cloth that the powder was likely to have been wrapped in. He quickly put this out and took a look around. The cellar was in a mess, everywhere was blackened with dust and there was a distinct smell of burnt powder. As the smoke dispersed he spotted what was left of a tin can that he estimated would hold about 3 pints. The cloth had been tied around the can with clothes line; here were the remnants of the bomb that had been dropped down the cellar grate. Above the devastated cellar the living room floorboards had been lifted four to five inches. All the furniture in the living room was damaged and the blast had lifted the floorboards of the children's bedroom above by a good five inches and there were cracks in the walls. Mercifully no-one was hurt except the young boy who had got some powder in his eye, which was sore for a little while. After making sure that there were no other burning materials in the house and everyone was safe Wilson went to inform the Chief Constable.

John Jackson was still in bed but Wilson waited on him getting up and they both returned to the house where Jackson inspected the damage and viewed what remained of the bomb. Police enquiries determined that the can had been made by brazier Charles Smith of 3 Arundel Street, who confirmed that it was his work. The clothes line, it was found, had been made by rope and twine manufacturer Curtis Brady of 27 Baker's Hill. This information did not, however, establish who had bought and used them to make the bomb. Wilson was convinced it was *'Putty'* Shaw and *'Tucker'* Clark and after relating everything to the police about the threatening letters, the verbal threats and the blowing up of Joseph Helliwell, they were inclined to agree that they were the likely culprits but all this was circumstantial and what they needed was some proof. Curtis Brady had told officers that whoever used the rope would have some left over. If they could find this and perhaps some gunpowder or anything else connected to the bomb it would be evidence enough. To this end police inspector Sills went with Wilson to track down George Shaw but he wasn't at home. Shaw's mother told them that he hadn't been in all night. A search of the house found that there was nothing here to incriminate Shaw. They then went to find Denis Clark who was at this time living with his brother-in-law in the Park area. Again they found no incriminating evidence and there was little else that the police had to go on to find the culprits. It was only at the Commissioners Inquiry that the identity of the true perpetrator of this outrage came to light: Samuel Crookes.[241]

---

[241] Op. Cit. TUC, 13,552

Sheffield from The Victoria Hotel, postcard painting by 'Jotter' with the distinct towers of the Castle Mills and Blonk Bridge

The Fork Grinders' Union and the Ten Masters Ruling

'A fork grinder is an old cock at 30.'[242]

1859

The fork grinders had the most dangerous job to health of all the grinding branches. It was also one of the least paid, especially at times when there was no union. The grinding of forks was a dry grinding process and where there was no fan in the hull to take away the dust, which was generally the case, the fork grinders spent all of their working days drawing this dust into their lungs with disastrous consequences, and it didn't take many years to take effect. In a study undertaken in 1843 Dr. G Calvert Holland found that only 30 of 97 men employed grinding forks attained the age of 30 years and that two thirds of the men died before their 30th birthday.[243] A further study undertaken by Dr. J C Hall found in 1857 that the average age of the 160 men then

---

[242] Quote from a fork grinder interviewed by Dr. J C Hall during his study: *On The Prevention and treatment of the Sheffield Grinders' Disease,* Longman, Brown, Green, Longman & Roberts, 1857, p.23
[243] Holland, George Calvert M.D., *Vital Statistics of Sheffield,* London, 1843, p.193 Op. Cit. Johnson

working in the fork grinding trade was 29.[244] In his report that he read to the Social Science Congress in 1865 Dr Hall told his audience:

'There is no more melancholy object than a fork grinder, looking prematurely old and dying from dust inhaled in his trade; no object more deserving of our pity, as we see him often crawling to his hull to labour, when altogether unfitted by the grinders' disease for his calling: "his poverty and not his will consents."'[245]

If any job in mid-Victorian Sheffield exemplified the need for trade unions it was fork grinding.

In February 1859 the Fork Grinders' Union took a decision to limit the number of master fork makers in Sheffield that their members could work for. This was in response to a number of table knife grinders taking in fork work and upsetting the market, causing a reduction in prices of up to 50%. Ten master fork makers were selected by the committee and it decreed that their members could only work for one of these ten masters, who in turn were only allowed to employ union men. In addition to this, the ten masters were not to grind themselves but to simply manage their businesses; the work could only be done by members of the Fork Grinders' Union. There were around 120 fork grinders in the town in 1859 and they were earning about £2

---

[244] Op. Cit. Hall, p.19

[245] Dr. J C Hall, *The Trades of Sheffield as Influencing Life and Health – More Particularly File Cutters and Grinders,* Longman, Green and Co., London, read before the National Association for the Promotion of Social Science, 5 October 1865, p.15

per week and £2-10s to £2-12s per week for a man and boy.[246] Master fork makers were earning around £3 per week. This was when there was a union. When there was no union, fork grinders had to grind four to five gross of forks to earn the wages that they got for two to three gross when there was a union.[247] The decision raised no objections amongst the ten approved masters as it would increase demand for their work; it was well-known that masters earned more when there was a union.[248] However, resistance from the masters who were not sanctioned by the union and confrontation with grinders who were not members of the union was inevitable.

William Mason was a fork grinder working for Thomas Jackson at the Union Buildings, Nursery Street; Jackson was one of the ten masters sanctioned by the union. Mason hadn't been there long before work dried up and he moved his tools to Marsden's.[249] That very night Mason was attacked by 5 of a group of about 30 men in Corporation Street, knocking him to the floor and kicking him. He knew one of the men, John Smith, who was a fork grinder and a member of the union. Mason reported the assault to the Chief Constable and the 5 attackers were brought before the magistrates. Two of them were fined but the other three were acquitted for lack of evidence.

Following this attack Mason went to work for Samuel Burrows at the Furnace Hill Wheel. Samuel Burrows was not

---

[246] Ibid, 21,671

[247] Ibid, 21,693

[248] Ibid, 21,675

[249] Ibid, 21,411. This could be either John or William Marsden who both made forks at Grimesthorpe. We can assume whichever it was wasn't one of the 10 union approved masters.

one of the ten masters approved by the union. Mason had been working for Burrows about three weeks when on the morning of Tuesday 17 February he was blown up by powder that had been laid in his trough, which was ignited by the sparks off his grinding wheel when he began work. He suffered burns to his face, neck and arms. Had it not been for his wearing spectacles he would have also most likely been blinded. Once more John Jackson was informed but this time all investigations failed to find the perpetrators of this grievous attack. However, Mason was sure that he had been targeted for moving to a master who was not approved by the Fork Grinders' Union.

On the same morning, in a trough at John Askham's works in Broad Lane, fork grinder Thomas Roebuck saw a distinctive glitter amongst the grinding dust under the horsing that he was about to mount to begin his day's work. A beam of the morning sun shining through one of the windows caught the gunpowder that had been laid there, just as it had been at the Furnace Hill Wheel. Had he not noticed the powder he too would have been blown up when he started grinding.

Thomas Roebuck had been a master fork maker working out of the Oliver Wheel at Ecclesfield Common in 1854.[250] He had worked for John Askham in 1857 and then for 12 months, when the trade was bad and prices were low, he had been a policeman.[251] Roebuck must have been a well-respected man and good at his work as when the trade had improved John Askham sent for him to go back working for him at Broad Lane. Thomas Roebuck had been a member of the union at times, having first joined in 1857, but at this

---

[250] Kelly's Directory 1854
[251] Op. Cit. TUC, 21,465

moment he was not a member and John Askham was not one of the ten master fork makers approved by the union. Before returning to Askham's he was approached by another fork grinder called George Cooper and was warned that by working for John Askham he would be *'outside of the union rules'*.[252] Cooper was one of a group of grinders that Roebuck met who told him of the *'ten masters'* ruling, warning him that if he worked for Askham he would *'get done'*. They swore at him and called him names and one of them by the name of William Norton had even called on him at home to give him some verbal abuse, calling him a *'knobstick'*[253]. Despite this harassment Roebuck went back to work for John Askham in February 1859.

Thomas Roebuck estimated that around 2lb of gunpowder had been laid across the bottom of his trough. He collected some of the powder and took it to John Askham and the two of them went to see John Jackson. Showing him the gunpowder he told the Chief Constable what he had found and that he would have been within 2ft of the explosion had it gone off: *'It would have blown my head off'*. He also told him who he suspected of having laid the gunpowder; a man called Samuel Johnson, one of the five men who worked in the garret above the chamber where he worked. Johnson was the only other fork grinder at the wheel and he was a union man; he too had called him a *'knobstick'*. Roebuck had locked the door to his chamber on leaving work the previous evening, sometime between 6:00pm – 7:00pm, dropping the key off with the gate keeper, a man named Sharpe who was related to John Askham's first wife. When he arrived that morning at around 7:45am, Johnson was the

---

[252] Ibid, 21,484

[253] Knobstick: a blackleg or strike breaker.

only other man at the wheel. The door to Roebuck's workshop was locked as he had left it and there was no other way into the room; he was sure that no-one had been in the room overnight. After opening up Roebuck went back downstairs and across the yard to the privy and was away for about 3-4 minutes. It is during this time that he thought Johnson had come down from the garret, entered his room and laid the powder. The Chief Constable sent one of his detectives to search Johnson's house but nothing was found to connect him with the gunpowder and everything else was circumstantial.

Although no action was taken against Samuel Johnson in 1859, the Commissioners summoned him to appear at the Inquiry in 1867. William Overend explained to Johnson that they (the Commissioners) had the power to provide him with a certificate of indemnity for any wrongdoing that he may have been involved in with regards to trade union intimidation so long as he told them truthfully everything he knew. However, should he not tell the truth and he was later found to have been involved in criminal activity, he would face being prosecuted and punished accordingly. Johnson had heard the evidence given by Thomas Roebuck earlier in the day and Overend's line of questioning was to offer Johnson an opportunity to confess with impunity had he been responsible for laying the gunpowder in Roebuck's trough. However, Johnson's response was to deny any involvement and he contradicted many of the statements Roebuck had made. He also denounced the assumption that he actually had the opportunity to do it. He even went as far as to offer a name for the actual perpetrator.

Johnson recalled the morning of the incident and agreed that he was a member of the Fork Grinders' Union at the time and he knew that Roebuck wasn't. He denied calling Roebuck a *'knobstick'* but he did ask him whether he preferred being paid 2s or 2s-6d a gross for grinding forks. This was a sarcastic reference about John Askham telling Johnson that he would be paid the same price as Roebuck, who had agreed to work for the lower price. Whilst this may imply a motive for Johnson it didn't prove that he did it. Johnson claimed that he got to work that morning sometime between 8:00am and 9:00am and that Sharpe (the gateman) had let him in (Roebuck claimed that Johnson was already at the wheel when he arrived at around 7:45am). He also stated that he wasn't alone in his garret workshop as there was a lad known as *'Face'* already at work when he arrived. *'Face'* was a *'little lad'* aged 13 or 14 who worked for a bolster grinder called Samuel. He had lit a fire by the time Johnson had arrived. Johnson denied seeing Roebuck that morning and insisted that he could not see the yard from the garret when he was working so he wouldn't have known Roebuck had gone to the privy (Roebuck had said that the yard was visible from the garret and that Johnson could have seen him on his way to the privy). When asked by William Overend if he placed the powder in Roebuck's trough Johnson emphatically said *'no'*. He then asked him if he knew who had done it and at this Johnson hesitated and then said *'That is another question'*.[254] On being pressed further he told Overend that he could tell them who did it and continued:

'The man that told me who did it is dead and gone: but the man who did it is in the 82nd Regiment – Thomas Yates,

---

[254] Op. Cit. TUC, 22,344

fork grinder……George Cowper, who is dead and gone, told me.[255]'

Nothing in Johnson's statements can be corroborated. Neither the gate keeper nor the little lad was brought in for questioning, and the man that Johnson said told him who did it was dead. The man accused of doing the deed, Thomas Yates, who Johnson knew to be a union man, was with his regiment in the East Indies. Despite the plausibility of this story being highly questionable, particularly on how this man Yates, who didn't work at the wheel, was able to get in unseen by the gate man (Sharpe had told John Askham that Johnson was the only grinder who had gone through the gate that morning), Johnson stuck by it and the whole question remained the word of one man against the other. On summing up his questioning of Johnson, William Overend told him *'You have had your chance, if things turn out against you, you must not blame us for it'.*[256]

In addition to the attacks on Mason and Roebuck, three other fork grinders were blown up at their wheels that morning: Samuel Gunson; James Gamble and Charles Royston. They all worked at different places in Sheffield and they were all non-union men working for masters who were not sanctioned by the Fork Grinders' Union. In the case of James Gambles, a fork grinder named Sykes, who was one of the men who had harassed Thomas Roebuck, was fined for threatening to blow him up but there was no evidence to prove that he actually did. Sykes was subsequently jailed for 12 months for failing to pay the fine. However, after 6 months someone paid the fine for him, probably someone

---

[255] Ibid, 22,347-22,349
[256] Ibid, 22,458

from the union, and he then went to America, again probably at the union's expense. James Gambles had died prior to the Commissioners' Inquiry and the case was not investigated. Samuel Gunson had also gone to America prior to the Inquiry and there was no investigation into the case of Charles Royston. The Commissioners were informed that no further attacks against fork grinders had been reported since February 1859.

The *'ten masters'* ruling lasted for two years and at some point thereafter the Fork Grinders' Union was dissolved and then reformed in 1864. The secretary of the reformed union, George Bulloss, was summoned to give evidence at the Inquiry but he offered no information on the acts perpetrated in February 1859. He did however assure the Commissioners that rattening was not recognised by the reformed union. He had no books that covered 1859 and it was thought that they had been destroyed so as to hide their contents. Although Bulloss's evidence was sparse we do learn that by 1867 there were 134 members of the Fork Grinders' Union, including a good number of masters, and that there were about 40 non-union men in the town. Contributions were now 2s per man and 1s for a boy. The earnings of a fork grinder were 4s-6d for an 8 hour day although they were presently working a 7 hour day as demand for forks was down (less than 4s per day). A man and boy could earn around 7s-6d per 8 hour day. The fork grinders' earnings were considerably less than they were in 1859.

In their final analysis of the gunpowder attacks on these five defiant fork grinders the Commissioners reported that in their view they were encouraged and promoted by the Fork Grinders' Union.

General view of Sheffield from the east, print reproduced in *The Graphic*, 28 November 1874

The Acorn Street Outrage

1861

At the impressive Green Lane Works between the banks of the River Don and Green Lane at the end of Dun Street, was the manufactory of Henry Elliot Hoole[257], an alderman and Justice of the Peace who was one of a long line of industrialists to become mayor of the town (1859), that included Henry Vickers (1860); John Brown (1861-62); and Thomas Jessop (1863-64). Hoole employed in the region of 80 to 100 workers. Most, if not all of them, were members of their respective trade's union. In the summer of 1861 Henry Hoole instructed his manager in the stove grate department, 37 year-old John Sibrey, who had only taken up his position at Hoole's in April that year, to lay off one of the fender grinders who was *very unsteady and neglected his work a deal*[258] and to find a replacement. The grinder he found to replace the sacked worker was Charles Taylor, a non-union man from Masbrough who was out of work due

---

[257] Henry Elliot Hoole was one of the first Sheffield councillors elected following the town's incorporation in 1843. He was elected for the St. Philip's Ward. In May 1851 Hoole attended on Queen Victoria when she visited the Sheffield stand at the Great Exhibition.
[258] Op. Cit. TUC 19,775

to a long running strike there. On Taylor taking up a trough at Hoole's the rest of the grinders walked out on strike. The uncompromising Henry Hoole's response to this was to instruct Sibrey to find more men to take their place. Sibrey knew where a number of idle fender grinders were to be found and invited six more non-union men from Masbrough to join their former co-worker at the Green Lane Works: Henry Ripley; William Hulse; George Wastnidge; Richard and Joe White; and a man named Cooper. Although this could be considered a provocative move there was no immediate reaction from the Fender Grinders' Union but it wasn't long before Hoole received threatening letters; letters that threaten both him and Sibrey.

In the weeks and months that followed the walk-out at Hoole's, deputations from the union were made but no resolution to the dispute was found. Interestingly, although the dispute was with the Fender Grinders' Union, two of the union representatives to apply pressure on Hoole was William Broadhead (Saw Grinders' Union) and Charles Bagshaw (Fork Grinders' Union). It is likely that Broadhead's involvement led to the ante being raised by the unions in an attempt to break the impasse. The stakes increased when John Sibrey was attacked on Tuesday 5 November 1861 whilst on his way home from work. Being early evening it was dark and it was also a typically foggy night as he headed for the Midland Railway Station for his train to Rotherham, where he lived.[259] He was walking past

---

[259] Ibid, 19,832. This information comes from John Sibrey's own evidence at the Inquiry. However, in another statement by Samuel Cutler, one of the fender grinders involved in the conspiracy against Hoole's non-union members, it is suggested that Sibrey lived on Spital Hill Road (20,332). In

the Union Workhouse when he was approached by two men. One hit Sibrey in the mouth, probably with a knuckleduster, splitting his lip against his teeth. He staggered but maintained his feet as the attackers ran off into the night. According to evidence given at the Inquiry one of the attackers was stove grate grinder Bill Bayles who had since died before the Commission sat. The identity of his accomplice wasn't revealed. The wound needed the attention of a doctor but before continuing his way anywhere he went to the Police Station to report the incident to the Chief Constable, John Jackson. However, Jackson wasn't available and according to Sibrey there was no-one else on hand to help.It is ironic that Sibrey had handed Henry Hoole his notice before this attack took place. The threatening letters and what he had learned about the unions' violent tendencies in the short time that he had worked in the town were enough to persuade him that Sheffield wasn't a safe place to work. John Sibrey ended his employment at Hoole's on the following Saturday, four days after the attack, intimidated out of his job.

Hoole's non-union men were invited on a number of occasions to enjoy a pint or two of ale in a local pub at the expense of the Fender Grinders' Union who also offered them sums of money to induce them to leave the Green Lane Works but they resisted these sweeteners. It soon dawned on the union men that this approach wasn't going to work and they turned to other means of persuasion.

---

the 1861 census he is recorded as living at 6 Mosbro' Houses, Greasbro', with his 44 year-old wife, Elizabeth, and five children.

Of the seven non-union men who came from Masbrough, three were attacked around the same time as Sibrey; William Hulse, Richard White and Joe White were badly beaten in Water Lane in the Port Mahon district, one of the Whites being left for dead. Two others, Wastnidge and Cooper, were attacked as they walked up Dun Street by first one man and then a number of others who came out of a nearby public house, probably the Cup.[260] As they were clearly outnumbered they made a hasty retreat and took refuge at Wastnidge's house in nearby Acorn Street.

19th Century illustration of the entrance to the Green Lane works and a photograph of the same building being renovated in 2016

However, this was only the start of George Wastnidge's troubles. What followed became known as the 'Acorn Street

---

[260] This is the only public house on Dun Street recorded in Kelly's Directory 1854, although there is also a couple of beer retailers listed.

Outrage' and one of the most appalling and horrific acts of intimidation that came before the Commission.

On the night of 23 November 1861, George Wastnidge, also known as 'Redman' due to the distinct colour of his hair, his wife Harriett and their young son were asleep in the garret bedchamber of 24 Acorn Street. The terraced house was of three stories, each consisting of a single room. At street level were the living quarters that included a small kitchen area. Above this on the second floor was a bed chamber with the Wastnidge's chamber above that on the third floor. This layout is familiar to me having lived in such a house in Bradfield Road, Owlerton, as a small boy in the 1950s and early 1960s.[261] In the second floor chamber slept Mrs Bridget O'Rourke (also known as Bedelia O'Rourke), an elderly widow who lodged with the Wastnidges. At 1:00am in the morning all where awoken by the noise of smashing glass followed by the sound of someone running away from the house. Harriett was the first out of bed and she went to the window and saw figures in the shadows, perhaps three or four, disappearing down the street towards Green Lane. She then ventured downstairs and into Mrs O'Rourke's bed chamber. On entering she found the old lady standing in a corner by her bed holding a small parcel that was fizzing and sparking. The window of the chamber was the one they had all heard smash and the parcel that the old lady was holding was the missile that had been thrown through it. Harriett shouted to her to throw it back out of the window but the frightened old widow was frozen to the spot and in a daze. Harriett snatched the missile from her hands to throw it out but as she did so the parcel exploded with a mighty flash throwing the two women apart. The force of the

---

[261] Op. Cit. Drewry, p.82

blast damaged the floor and ceiling, splitting a wooden beam that supported the garret chamber floor. Both women were seriously injured and the room was set alight. George Wastnidge had followed his wife down the stairs but arrived just after the explosion. Instinctively Harriett turned away and ran for the door making her way back upstairs to the garret chamber, her night dress still burning. George ran after her and on reaching her, ripped the burning night dress off her body exposing the severe nature of her burns. Her face was blackened and bloody, and she was partially blinded by the flash of the explosion. Naked and in a state of trauma and panic, she headed for the window and jumped out, falling to the street three stories below, where by now a number of the neighbours had gathered following the commotion. One brought a ladder and put it up to the house but it only reached the second floor window. The garret was now full of acrid smoke and the only way out for George and his son was to follow his wife out of the window. Coughing and choking on the smoke he managed to lift his young son through the garret casement and was able to drop him safely into the arms of a neighbour before managing to locate the ladder and climbing down himself.

Corner of Green Lane and Acorn Street[262]

By this time his wife had been taken into a neighbour's house and George ventured back into the burning house in search of Bridget O'Rourke, who he found had made her way into the cellar in a state of confusion. Her naked body was severely scorched and blistered, her night dress having burnt away around her. She was in great pain and in a terrible condition. Although George hadn't yet realised it, he too had suffered burns from the flames that had burnt through the garret chamber floor. His legs were badly burned as he struggled to get his young son out of the window. As the situation calmed and the adrenalin abated George began to feel the pain that alerted him to the extent of his own injuries.

By the time all were out of the house two or three policemen had arrived and before long a cab was acquired

[262] Sheffield Local Studies Library; Picture Sheffield u00847

and the four victims were taken to the General Infirmary. The neighbours set to and put the fire out in the house, which emitted the distinct smell of burnt gunpowder. The policemen retrieved what was left of the canister that had been wrapped in the parcel, and the remains of a fuse. The inside of the house was badly damaged and the window of the second floor bedchamber had been blown out. The walls in the room were scorched and blood spattered. There was little doubt that the house had been bombed and all who knew Wastnidge would conclude that this despicable act had *'trade outrage'* written all over it.

The parcel exploded with a mighty flash throwing the
two women apart.

Having been aware of the attacks on Sibrey and the other rebel grinders the police were also of the opinion that this incident was related to the dispute between Hoole's men and the Fender Grinders' Union. John Jackson, was not too long in picking up a suspect for the Acorn Street Outrage; a fender grinder named Joseph Thompson.

By the time Thompson had been arrested Bridget O'Rourke had died from the extensive burns that she suffered. She never regained consciousness and died in the infirmary a fortnight after the incident. Harriet Wastnidge had too suffered extensive burns and press reports suggested that these would also prove fatal; the house surgeon at the infirmary, Henry John Knight, had stated that she would probably not survive long. This prompted the magistrate, Vincent Corbett, John Jackson and Thompson's legal representative, solicitor Charles Broadbent, to urgently undertake interviewing Harriet Wastnidge at the infirmary before she died. However she did survive but suffered blindness for a while and was permanently disabled by her injuries. She lived long enough to relate the extent of her injuries to the Commissioners in 1867:

Commissioner Thomas Barstow: *'Were you very much burnt?'*

Harriett Wastnidge: *'Yes'*

Thomas Barstow: *Were you blinded at the time?*

Harriett Wastnidge: *'Yes'*

Thomas Barstow: *'Do you feel any injury from that now?'*

Harriett Wastnidge: *'Yes, I do'*

Thomas Barstow: *'What is that?'*

Harriett Wastnidge: *'My right knee fails me very badly, and I have no use in my right hand'*

Thomas Barstow: *'Is that from a burn?'*

Harriett Wastnidge: *'Yes'*

Thomas Barstow: *'And is the knee also from a burn?'*

Harriett Wastnidge: *'Yes'*

Thomas Barstow: *'How long were you blind?'*

Harriett Wastnidge: *'I daresay about a fortnight'*

Thomas Barstow: *'You have the marks of the powder in one of your eyes now, I believe?'*

Harriett Wastnidge: *'Yes'*

Thomas Barstow: *'Were you blackened all over with the powder?'*

Harriett Wastnidge: *'Yes'*

Thomas Barstow: *'Do any of those marks continue about you now?'*

Harriett Wastnidge: *Oh, yes, fearful'*[263]

Portrait of John Jackson, Chief Constable.
(*Courtesy of National Emergency Services Museum*)

---

[263] Op. Cit. TUC, 20,057-20,066

Joseph Thompson had been brought to the attention of Jackson as a known active member of the Fender Grinders' Union and likely to have been involved in the attacks on Hoole's men. John Jackson and a number of his detectives tracked Joseph Thompson down and apprehended him at home in bed. A number of implicating items were found in the house, including a tin of gunpowder that had been plugged and seemingly readied for another bombing. Also found were a pistol with a box of caps, and a thick stick weighted at one end so as to be used as a club. Following Jackson's investigation Joseph Thompson was sent to York Assizes to be tried for the murder of Bridget O'Rourke on 19 December.

Thompson maintained his innocence and the Fender Grinders' Union came to his aid by providing counsel for his defence, although it was Charles Bagshaw of the Fork Grinders' Union who retained Charles Broadbent to act for him. Did Bagshaw know the identity of the real culprit? Broadbent's fees and the court costs would amount to around £100 and this was paid not solely from the union's funds but also by voluntary subscription of £1 each from many of the union's members. Bagshaw and Broadbent concluded that the key to Thompson's defence was to provide an alibi and that witnesses should be called to this end.[264] This approach was evidently successful as Thompson was acquitted on 18 March 1862. The real culprit of this dastardly deed did not come to light until a confession was made under the protection of indemnity from prosecution engendered by the Royal Commission.

---

[264] Ibid, 21,264

Snig Hill around 1860[265]

There were a number of Fender Grinders' Union members involved in the intimidation of Henry Hoole's renegade grinders from Masbrough; some were members of the union's committee. The acting secretary of the union at the time, James Robertson, who would later become the full-

[265] Sheffield Local Studies Library; Picture Sheffield s19545

time secretary, provided the money for *'cajoling'* or *'persuading'* the men to leave Hoole's works but he kept a clear distance from the execution of any criminal activities. The payments were hidden through falsifying the union books. Stove grate grinders Bill Bayles and Samuel Cutler were the predominant players in *'watching'* the men and although Bayles wasn't alive to defend himself at the Commission, it was alleged that he was one of the men who attacked Sibrey and was also involved in the beatings that took place at Water Lane. For some reason George 'Redman' Wastnidge was particularly obnoxious to Bayles and Cutler and they singled him out. They approached a 37 year-old file grinder named Robert Renshaw who lived at Court 9 Princess Street, Brightside with his wife Eliza and their three children. Renshaw was known to them as a man likely to undertake such work for a price. At Joe Green's beer shop in Hawley Croft they first offered him 10s to give Wastnidge *'a knock on the head'.*[266] This proposition was hardly worth Renshaw's while and he declined but he did say that *'it would be* [a] *deal better to do him at home than to do him in the street'.*[267] This was agreed upon and Cutler gave Renshaw 10s to buy 3lb of gunpowder and they agreed a sum of £6 for doing the job. He took him to Acorn Street a week or so before the attack and pointed out Wastnidge's house.

Robert Renshaw was of the same ilk as Samuel Crookes; he wasn't interested in why these things were happening, he was doing it solely for the money. He bought the powder from either Shepherds & Irving at 25 Paradise Street or Twibell's at 50 Snig Hill (he couldn't remember which when

---

[266] Op. Cit. TUC, 20,090
[267] Ibid, 20,094

giving his evidence at the Inquiry but he did remember that it was the best 'Diamond' powder) and the fuse from Milners ironmongers at 33 Fargate. He took them home and filled a can with the powder and inserted the fuse. After sealing the can he wrapped it in brown paper and put it in his coat pocket. He carried the lethal weapon around in his pocket for a number of days before he came upon an ideal opportunity to complete the job.

Renshaw had been to the theatre[268] during the evening of 23 November and wasn't far from Acorn Street. Being after midnight there was no-one about and Renshaw had a good look around to ensure there were no curtains twitching or any local watchman doing his rounds. All was clear and he stepped into the gateway of the Watts & Stones Cannon Brewery, took the package out of his coat pocket and lit the fuse. He stepped into the street and hurled the spluttering parcel at the second floor window. As it smashed through the glass he ran off down the street towards Ebenezer Chapel where he hid in the chapel yard. After the explosion, Renshaw remained in his hidey-hole until the crowd gathered below the smoke billowing windows of No. 24. He then slipped out and joined the confusion, witnessing Harriett Wastnidge falling from the garret window and her fall being broken by someone in the crowd. He saw the frantic escape of 'Redman' and his son then had the audacity to help rescue Bridget O'Rourke from the cellar. According to his evidence the sight of the poor woman gave Renshaw

---

[268] Ibid, 20,104 The theatre in question could have been the Theatre Royal in Tudor Street or the Adelphi Theatre in Furnival Road. Conversely it could have been the Theatre Tavern public house in Arundel Street.

some grief and perhaps for a moment he felt some remorse for what he had done. However, he failed to show any.

During Renshaw's time in the witness box the Commissioners kept going over his insistence that he acted alone in the Acorn Street Outrage. They had taken evidence from Harriett Wastnidge and she insisted that there was more than one person running down the street when she first looked out of the garret window on hearing the crashing of the window below, perhaps even four or five persons. Renshaw maintained throughout that he acted alone and he had no reason to implicate anyone else. He alone had committed murder and he had got away with it, although he conceded that his life in Sheffield from this day forth may well not be worth living:

'What good will a [indemnity] *certificate do me when I get it? In the street they all stare at me; they say here is the b-------- wretch that has killed a woman.....I would rather put my head in any place than Sheffield.'*[269]

One curious aspect of the Acorn Street Outrage is Henry Hoole's slant on things. It is clear from reading between the lines of various witness statements that following the start of the trouble he would rather have had his original workers back and avoid all the hassle. In fact during his talks with Broadhead and Bagshaw it was Hoole who suggested that the union offer the Masbrough men money to leave.[270] Why did he suggest this when all he had to do was to lay them off and invite his old men back? It was simply to save face; he would rather not be seen to have made a mistake, even after

---

[269] Ibid, 20,292 and 20,294
[270] Ibid, 21,198 – 21,202

seeing his manager take a beating. Neither did he want to be seen to back down and accede to the unions.

Another point to consider is Hoole's lack of support for George Wastnidge following the outrage. Here was a man blown up with his wife and son in his own home; injured to the point of being unable to work for weeks and then only partially able due to his injuries; the contents of his home destroyed; a wife almost killed and left traumatised and permanently disabled; and all of this because he continued to work for Hoole at the Green Lane Works. Hoole offered him no compensation for his ordeal and the plight that he was now left in. On the morning after the attack Hoole called at the house and gave Wastnidge a sovereign (£1), then sent for it back in the afternoon. Wastnidge had to go to Hoole for help but he only lent him money, which he had to repay out of his wages at 5s per week.[271] Fifty-two year-old Henry Elliott Hoole, who lived at Crookesmoor House[272], Western Bank, with his 42 year-old wife Eliza Harriett and 10 year-old son Henry Laurance, and waited on by three servants, must have been one of Sheffield's wealthiest men; this was a period when the industrial capitalist was in the ascendancy, taking over from the landed gentry at the top of the socio-economic ladder. It is not surprising that Wastnidge took offence at this snub and once he had paid Hoole back the couple of sovereigns that he borrowed to tide him over he

---

[271] Ibid, 20,013

[272] In 1854 Crookesmoor House was burgled by Charlie Peace, the notorious Sheffield Murderer. Peace was apprehended after sending his mistress, Emma James, to pawn a pair of Henry Hoole's boots stolen in the burglary. Peace was sentenced to 4 years penal servitude for this and three other burglaries. See Bentley, David, *The Sheffield Murders – 1865-1965,* ALD Design & Print, 2003, pp.42-43

left Green Lane Works for the last time without giving notice. It wasn't trades union intimidation that drove 'Redman' Wastnidge away; it was the selfish attitude of a heartless, greedy master who cared nothing for him or his family.

Of course this aspect of the Acorn Street Outrage wasn't reported in William Leng's broadsheet. Yet Charles Reade touched upon the Sheffield masters' attitude towards their workers when his leading character, a forgeman and tool maker from London newly working for a Sheffield company, is warned by his foreman of a number of threatening letters that his master had received from the union, who objected to an outsider undertaking their members' work, and that his very life was in danger. He naively thought that the master would protect him from the threats but he had kept these letters to himself leaving the man totally unaware of the peril he was in. Why hadn't the master warned him of the situation? The foreman continued:

'Oh, he is no worse than the rest, believe me. What does any master care for a man's life? Profit and loss go down in figures; but life – that's a cypher in all their ledgers.'[273]

Reade's story may have been fiction but it reflected reality; labour was a plentiful resource that was there to be exploited by the masters for the benefit of the masters.

The value put on life during these times is illustrated by the amounts claimed for the loss of the lives of the people who perished in the Great Sheffield Flood of 1864, and the amounts paid out for the successful claims. Claims ranged from £5 for the life of an infant, to £2,650 for the life of one

---

[273] Op. Cit. Reade, p.26

particular 36 year-old file hardener named William Bethell. Payouts for the loss of a life ranged from £3-1s to £1,000 but many of the claims were dismissed. There was just one payout of £1,000 and that was to William Bethell's widow, Elizabeth.[274] Most payouts were less than £100.[275] Children in particular were considered of little value and only those that worked were deemed worthy of any compensation, and solely in relation to the amount of wages that they earned and would no longer contribute to their family.

This vicious attack on a fellow worker and his family in his own home was an abominable act, even by the standards of the times. The perpetrators were family men themselves. Thirty-seven year-old Robert and 34 year-old Eliza Renshaw had three young children: Samuel aged 15; Eliza Ann, 3; and 1 year-old Celina. Thirty-eight year-old Samuel Cutler and his wife, also Eliza aged 35, had six children at the time of the Acorn Street Outrage: Samuel junior aged 15; Archer J, 13; Emily, 8; Sarah, 5: Adah, 3; and 1 year-old Ralph.[276] Whilst Cutler appears to have some commitment to the union and was in part motivated by this interest, he chose not to undertake the mission himself but rather give the money he had taken from Broadhead to someone else, thus distancing himself too from the outrage. Renshaw wasn't at all involved in the dispute at Hoole's and he acted solely for the money; £6 amounted to about 6 weeks wages. As events turned out, had Renshaw been caught and successfully prosecuted he would have certainly been hanged, leaving Eliza and the children to fend for themselves. A similar tragedy could have befallen Samuel Cutler's family had his involvement in the

---

[274] Op. Cit. Drewry, p.63

[275] Ibid, pp.157-158

[276] The Cutlers lived at 61 New George Street, Sheffield

outrage come to light without the protection of a Commission Certificate; if he wasn't hanged for his part in the deed he would have faced a long prison sentence. These were consequences that fanatics like William Broadhead considered a price worth paying.

Joshua Tyzack and the Scythe Grinders' Union

1857-1866

Established in 1824, William Tyzack & Sons of 203 Rockingham Street and Abbey Dale Works were listed in the 1854 Kelly's Directory as *'steel converters and refiners; manufacturers of saws, files, scythes, sickles and reaping hooks; doctors for calico printers, knives for chaff and other machines; garden tools; etc.'* The company employed about 250 men. William Tyzack had three sons: Ebenezer, William junior and Joshua. William junior lived at the Abbey Dale Works and Joshua, who was also a magistrate, lived with his father at Wood Lodge, Abbey Dale. William's eldest son, Ebenezer, lived at 63 Gell Street, Sheffield. The Tyzacks took the lease for the Abbey Dale Works in 1849[277] and the family worked the site until its closure in 1935.[278] Ironically, the works had become available at this time when Dysons, the previous tenants, fell into arrears with their rent following uninsured losses sustained after their grinding shop was blown up in 1842, allegedly by members of the grinders' union.[279] The Abbey Dale area had its share of

---

[277] Op. Cit. Crossley et al, p.98
[278] Op. Cit. Hey, p.125
[279] Op. Cit. Crossley et al, p.98

trade outrages, including the blowing up of the house of a scythe maker by the name of Fisher who had not paid his union subscriptions for a number of years. Although he had not received the customary threatening letter he had heard that he was a *'wanted man'*. In the early hours of 16 April 1854 Fisher and his wife were awoken by the sound of breaking glass. As he looked out of the window there was an explosion in the next room, which was normally occupied by his apprentice. Fortunately for the young lad he was staying at his family home that night. On entering the room Fisher found the window frame and curtains ablaze, which he quickly extinguished, and the remains of what was described as a breakfast tin that had been filled with gunpowder to which a fuse had been attached and lit. The missile had been thrown through the bed chamber window. Had the perpetrator targeted Fisher's bed chamber window he and his wife would have been seriously injured if not killed.[280]

Being manufacturers of various products the Tyzacks would have necessarily had dealings with 11 or 12 different trade unions and inevitably experienced trade problems with all of them, and there were numerous incidents of rattening. In 1857, the first year covered by the Inquiry, 2 or 3 grinders' bands disappeared from the Abbey Dale Works. The reason for this rattening must go down as the most insignificant of indiscretions against the rules of the Saw Grinders' Union. A man by the name of Hazlewood was given the task of undertaking some re-glazing work that was not a job he was supposed to do. The value of the work was just 3d. Had Hazlewood not done as his master asked the work would have to have been sent some 3 or 4 miles away to be done at a far greater cost. None of the Tyzacks could have imagined

---

[280] Op. Cit. Drinkall, *Book of Days,* p.109

that this would attract the attention of William Broadhead and even if it did, such a trivial transgression would surely not be considered worthy of reprisal. They were wrong. Joshua Tyzack tackled Broadhead on one of his visits to Abbey Dale and asked *'what was the reason that you sent for our bands for such a paltry affair as that?'* It transpired that when Broadhead had been informed about Hazlewood's misdemeanour the extent of the work undertaken was exaggerated and he admitted that had the true value of the work been known to him, he would not have sanctioned the rattening:

'Well, my information was wrong, there was a great exaggeration of the amount of work that had been done; if I had known there had been such a small quantity they (the bands) *probably would not have gone.'*[281]

In 1858 three pairs of bellows were destroyed at the Abbey Dale forge due to their scythe finishers being in arrears with their *'natty'*. This was also the year that William Tyzack senior died, leaving the business to his three sons.

In January 1859 Tyzacks' scythe grinders were called out by their union without notice. Joshua Tyzack tried to track his men down but was told that they were sent abroad and that *'they were sailing on the high seas.'*[282] I doubt that they were literally out of the country but this was a way of telling Tyzack that his scythe grinders were no longer available to him and could not be contacted. Being unable to communicate with the scythe grinders Joshua Tyzack wrote to Joseph Machin, secretary of the Scythe Grinders' Union,

---

[281] Op. Cit. TUC, 18,325
[282] Ibid, 18,337

asking him why his men had been withdrawn. In response Machin summoned Joshua Tyzack to a meeting at the Wagon & Horses public house at Mill Houses on 18 January. Both Joshua and William junior attended at the given time expecting to meet with Machin and perhaps one or two of his men but when they arrived they found themselves confronted by about 30 men, most were unknown to them; they had been summoned to a meeting of an amalgamation of trade unions representing the scythe manufacturing trades. After a brief exchange of greetings, introductions and such pleasantries that the situation would allow, Machin presented the Tyzack brothers with a list of seven demands of the company in respect of their workers employed in the manufacture of scythes:

1.   *The company was to discontinue giving machine knives to grind to any other except the scythe grinders.*
2.   *The company was to immediately and without notice discharge Eccles* (presumably a worker obnoxious to the trade) *and others who were working at Ward's wheel at Dronfield* (this was the works that was blown up by Thomas Needham in 1856).
3.   *That the company ceased taking on apprentices.*
4.   *That the company changes its mode of management in the manufacture of scythes* (there were no details on what changes were demanded).
5.   *The company would take all the men back to their original situations without taking any law proceedings against them for breaking their engagements by the union*

having withdrawn them and sent 10 or 12 of them out of the country for several weeks.

6.   The company should allow the union men from other rival manufacturers to come in to inspect the works and mode of working when they thought fit.

7.   The company should pay the expenses of those men while they were away from their work in their homes.[283]

It was made clear that Tyzacks' men would not return to work until these terms and conditions were met. Joshua indicated that the company would need time to consider these demands and called for an adjournment. Before bringing the proceedings to a close, Machin quizzed the brothers about work being contracted out whilst their men were out. Tyzacks had received a large export order and some of the work had been placed with a neighbouring general manufacturing company owned by Mr Horne (possibly William Ibbotson Horne & Co. steel manufacturers of Bridge Street in Sheffield and at Wisewood). Immediately following this disclosure a whispered discussion took place amongst the union men and three or four of them left the room. It was no coincidence that the following morning Joshua Tyzack learned that Horne's premises had been broken into overnight and a quantity of tools had been destroyed.[284]

In the following weeks some compromises were reached between Tyzacks and the unions and the men returned to work after four or five weeks. In the meantime Tyzacks made a payment of between £5 and £6 to Mr Horne to cover his losses as it was obvious to everyone that the rattening

---

[283] Ibid, 18,342
[284] Ibid, 18,357

was due to the dispute between Tyzacks and the unions, although once more nothing was proven.

In July 1859 13 grinders' bands went missing at the Abbey Dale Works following the company's engagement of a man contrary to the Scythe Grinders' Union rules. The manufacture of scythes at this time was aligned to the agricultural season and they could only be made during a certain period of the year. This was due to the increase in demand for scythes as harvest time approached. The rule agreed with the trades unions was that no men could be hired before the start of the *'season'*, which was 6 July. In contravention of this ruling a man named Kay was set on before this date, which resulted in the bands being taken. The action stopped production of scythes at a crucial moment as it was time for the hay harvest. The company was prevented from supplying its products at the height of their demand. Although just 10 days production was lost it cost the company dearly. The man Kay was fined £10 by the union and the bands were found in a nearby corn field following a note informing of their whereabouts being pinned to one of the grinders' door. The note was signed by *'Tidd Pratt'*.

Although the blowing up of Tyzacks' scythe making workshop at Dronfield in 1856 preceded the ten year period that came under the scrutiny of the Royal Commission, the incident came back to haunt Joshua Tyzack at his own instigation in 1862 and what occurred then was certainly within the Commissioners' remit.

Although he was accompanied by Samuel Crookes and Michael Thompson on the night, Thomas Needham was the sole person convicted for the blowing up of Ward's wheel at Dronfield in 1856 and he was sentenced to four years penal servitude. Whilst in custody at Derby gaol, Joshua Tyzack visited Needham to quiz him about the role of Michael Thompson, who was secretary of the Scythe Grinders' Union at the time; he was sure in his own mind that Thompson and the union were behind the attack and that Needham was protecting them. During this interview Needham admitted that Thompson had instigated the attack and that he had paid him £3 up front and another £7 once the job was done. However, Joshua Tyzack could not persuade him to give evidence that would incriminate Thompson or the union. Tyzack's intention to bring Thompson to justice was stymied but Thompson was made aware of his visit to see Needham in prison (Needham had written to him from his prison cell) and he was no doubt relieved when no action was taken following the visit. He would have assumed that Needham would keep his counsel and remain loyal to the union, which was financially supporting his wife, Mary Ann, whilst he was in prison. However, Joshua Tyzack had not given up on his quest for justice and when Needham was released in 1860 he set about trying to track him down so as to get him to give evidence against Thompson. He made extensive enquiries as to Needham's whereabouts; he even hired a young file cutter named George Watson to help him track Needham down but to no avail, although he was in Sheffield at that time. Thomas Needham later went to America, sometime between 1863 and 1864; probably at the expense of the Scythe Grinders' Union and out of harm's way.

Although Joshua Tyzack never spoke to Needham again it was well known about town that he was trying to track him down now that he was out of prison and that he was looking to bring him before a court in an effort to prosecute Michael Thompson. One night during the first week of November 1862, at about 8.30pm, Joshua Tyzack was driving his gig

194

along Abbey Dale Road, about three quarters of a mile out of Sheffield just beyond Broadfield Bar, on his way home when two shots rang out from a revolver. He turned towards where he thought the shots came from as a third shot rang out and he saw the flash of the gun from behind a wall or fence near Gatefield House belonging to Thomas Bagshaw Cockayne about 12-15 yards away. He felt this third shot glance by his head just above his ear, parting his hair as it went through the brim of his hat *'leaving a hole the size of a half-crown'*.[285] At this Tyzack dropped down into his gig and the horse instinctively stopped. He now considered he was a *'sitting duck'* and that he should get away as fast as he could. He sat up and gave the horse a good crack of the whip and two more shots rang out as the gig sped off. He arrived home safe but somewhat shaken by the experience. In spite of this he didn't tell his wife of his ordeal that night, nor did he report it to the police. On being quizzed by the Commissioners about this he explained that he had only recently married and that he didn't want to worry his wife, who was a stranger to the area. He eventually told her of the shooting about a month later.[286]

The person who shot at Joshua Tyzack that night was never identified but he was sure that the reason for the shooting was his endeavours to track down Thomas Needham and that the Scythe Grinders' Union was behind what was undoubtedly an attempt on his life. The shooting occurred within a week of him making enquiries about Needham and he could think of no other reason for such an

---

[285] Ibid, 18,249 Half-crown: a silver coin worth 2s 6d that was a little over an inch in diameter.
[286] Ibid, 18,431

attack. However, despite the efforts of the Commissioners to prove this theory they concluded that:

'We are unable to satisfy ourselves from the evidence before us that this was an outrage promoted or encouraged by any trade union.' [287]

To say that the evidence given at the Inquiry was inconclusive is an understatement; in fact it was somewhat bizarre.

It is no surprise to find that Michael Thompson denied all knowledge of the shooting but Joseph Machin, his successor as secretary of the Scythe Grinders' Union, instigated the appearance at the Inquiry of a potential witness to the events on the night of the shooting; a young woman named Harriett Ann Morton. Machin had heard second hand that this woman had related an interesting story of what had happened as she walked home along Abbey Dale Road at the same time as Joshua Tyzack drove home on the night of the shooting. He tracked her down at the Angel Hotel in Angel Street where she worked as a *'sempstress'* [sic]. He asked her if what he had heard was true, which she confirmed, and then persuaded her to attend the Inquiry to tell her story to the Commissioners. She took the stand on 28 June 1867, the twentieth day of the Inquiry.

---

[287] Ibid, p.xv

Advertisement from White's 1871 directory.

Harriett Ann Morton told the court that she was walking alone along Abbey Dale Road one January night (the attack happened in November) about nine years previous (second inaccuracy as this would be 1856) when she heard a gig approaching her from behind. She flagged the driver down to ask him for a lift and recognised him as Joshua Tyzack (she insisted that she knew him by sight and by the sound of his voice[288]). Tyzack declined her request saying that the gig was fully loaded and that he didn't pick people up at that time of night. He drove off and after about 100 yards she heard five shots in quick succession and saw the flash of each one. She continued to walk on and was soon caught up by a man called Ebenezer Hall of the firm of Martin Hall & Co.

---

[288] Ibid, 18,916-18,927

of Broad Street, Sheffield. She told her new companion what had just happened and he opined that it may well have been Mr Tyzack who had fired the revolver as *'there was some disturbance with his workmen; they had turned out the week before.'*[289] He even suggested that he might have been shooting at her, mistaking her for one of the men in disguise.[290] They continued walking together along Abbey Dale Road as far as Ebenezer Hall was going, which wasn't far from where Harriett lived. Harriett arrived home safe but *'terrified'* by the experience. She insisted that she had told a number of people about the event including Thomas Bamford of Dore who was also in court that day having been summoned to give evidence on the Elisha Parker affair. After a session of cross examination by William Overend and George Chance, Harriett withdrew from the stand and the Commissioners recalled Joshua Tyzack and put her account to him; he insisted *'there wasn't a single word of truth about it'.*[291] Ebenezer Hall was sworn in and Harriett Ann Morton's story was put to him; he was adamant that no such thing ever occurred.[292] Thomas Bamford was sworn in and examined; although he recognised Harriett Ann Morton he denied ever having a conversation with her on the subject and that he wasn't aware of the shooting at all until that very morning.

---

[289] Ibid, 18,944
[290] Ibid, 18,966
[291] Ibid, 19,036
[292] Ibid, 19,064

William Tyzack & Sons' Abbey Dale grinders' workshop, now part of the Abbeydale Industrial Hamlet Museum[293]

The Commissioners then recalled Harriett Ann Morton and advised her of the serious nature of committing perjury and that given Joshua Tyzack, Ebenezer Hall and Thomas Bamford had all denied her story she was open to be indicted. William Overend then gave her a final chance to make a clean breast of things but even under threat of prosecution for perjury she stood by her story. Whether Harriett Ann Morton was totally mistaken or deliberately trying to mislead we may never know. There appears to be no motive for her attending court other than to oblige Machin, who appears to have gained nothing from it, or perhaps to have her 15 minutes of fame knowing that the proceedings were reported daily in the press. This whole aspect of the case was

[293] Sheffield Local Studies Library; Picture Sheffield u02412

strange; with so much contradictory evidence it is difficult to determine just who to believe. The Commissioners had the same difficulty and the case remained inconclusive.

What do we make of Joshua Tyzack's role in all this? Not only was he a high profile master at odds with the trade unions, he was also a magistrate. Surely if any master were to attempt to fight the unions using the law he was a man to do it. But he succumbed to trade union intimidation and didn't even inform the police of the attempt on his life. In response to William Overend asking if he had talked to the police about any of the attacks he replied *'I have never made a case known. I kept them as quiet as possible.'*[294] Yet he was quite open about his enquiries into Thomas Needham's whereabouts and almost broadcast his intentions so that Michael Thompson was sure to find out. Perhaps it was due to his experience as a magistrate that he knew the police were powerless in such cases as only 1 in 50 rattening attacks got as far as the magistrates' bench. Perhaps he deliberately tried to draw Thompson out into the open hoping that he would drop his guard. Following the shooting Joshua Tyzack took to carrying a loaded revolver and he travelled around in a phaeton[295] rather than an open gig. There were no further attempts on his life but it wasn't the end of rattening at William Tyzack & Sons.

A number of Tyzacks' workshops were broken into and tools taken in 1863 and in 1865. Two workshops were broken into and tools were thrown into a nearby dam and along the Midland Railway line, which was under

---

[294] Op. Cit. TUC, 18,422

[295] Phaeton: a light open four-wheeled carriage usually pulled by 2 horses.

construction at the time. This was also due to the men getting behind with their union subscriptions. It was alleged that the secretary of the Scythe Finishers' Union, George Austin, was behind these rattenings.

In February 1866 William Tyzack & Sons crossed swords with the Patent Scythe Makers' Union after their men employed in the production of these scythes withdrew from the union. The men were being paid more than the union rate and considered their membership wasn't worthwhile. Charles Bagshaw, secretary of the Patent Scythe Makers' Union and the Fork Grinders' Union thought otherwise and a large quantity of bands went missing. Joshua Tyzack also received the following unsigned, phonetic threatening letter dated 14 February:

'Sir, You say you will not pay the price asked for, but you will have to pay and glad you can. Mr. Charles Bagshaw says we can make you pay any price we have a mind to ask for. Mr. Bagshaw says you are robbing your men of their rites for not letting them 'ave there own apprentices; he says you are ruining the Trade for 'aving so many lads in your firm insted of your men having them, and men also working at the trade that don't work in harmony with us for they don't pay to the trade. But Mr. Bagshaw says we must stop it and very quick, he as sugested a plan which i think will suckceed very well, that is to fire your place at Abbydale insted of Blowing up the place with gunpowder so as it cannot be detected as a trade outrage. He says every man out to have two pounds ten shillings that as a union if not it is there own fault. He says yow out to give your men a price that will earn that amount and live in smaller mansions than you do, the Bargain is made to fire your place if you don't give the price

and get shut of the Boys and men that Bore and lap up; i tell you the money is paid and the job will be done by the same man that took your bands and threw them in the dam. Mr. Bagshaw says he got the fork grinders their price which they are now having and he says he can get us ours if we stick to him, and do as he tells us; we are sure to win the victory; i think Mr. Bagshaw is worthy of great prase for what he has done in Sheffield for the working men that belong to a union; I hope this will be sufficient warning to you to comply with the trade and save your place from being burnt down. [296]

A number of threatening letters were received by William Tyzack & Sons during disputes with several different unions during the 10 year period covered by the Inquiry. All had been handed to the incumbent Chief Constable; Thomas Raynor prior to 1859, and then John Jackson, who was now in possession of the above letter. How seriously these letters were investigated is open to question. One can imagine the difficulty of tracing authors of anonymous letters without the forensic technology that is available to the police force today. Even with the specific mention of Charles Bagshaw in this last letter and what he is supposed to have said, there is no evidence of him actually having committed an offence, and he obviously didn't write the letter himself. Throughout the whole period of the Sheffield Outrages I have found no instance of anyone being prosecuted for sending a *'Mary Ann'* letter.[297]

---

[296] Op. Cit. TUC, 18,396

[297] *'Mary Ann'* was one of a number of signatures to these threatening letters. Others include *'Man in the Moon'*; *'Nathan'*; *'Shy Maiden'*; *'Sweep'*; *'Tidd Pratt'*; and *'Tantia Topee'*.

These letters were part of the Sheffield trades' culture; custom and practice for the unions and, for the masters the accepted prelude to inevitable rattening or outrage. As threatening letters go they were not unique but their use in Sheffield did take a particular pattern that Charles Reade describes as *'the literature of outrage'*.[298] In the first instance the master would receive a letter informing him of his transgression. The letter had three features: it was courteous; of good grammar; and signed by the writer, usually the secretary of the union. At this stage there is no threat implied, just a polite message informing the master that the union was aware of what was going on. Should the master disregard this preamble it was quickly followed by a second letter. This too would be grammatically correct or with the odd minor error; although still polite it is with an insincere tone; the master is reminded of any of his previous misdemeanours and their consequences; and is either anonymous or signed by the *'man in the moon'* or other such pseudonym. Should this reminder be ignored, a further, penultimate communiqué would be received that was anything but polite if not totally disrespectful; attention to grammar is disregarded; it would more graphically describe the potential consequences of non-compliance; it too would be anonymous or signed with a mischievous pseudonym. Finally, should the master dare to ignore this warning, he would receive the ultimate threatening letter that would be written phonetically and in what Reade describes as the *'Dash Dialect'* – offensive language that could not be put into print at that time and the offending words replaced by a dash (such as in the above account from the minutes of the Commission where master brickmaker James Robinson's men are described as

---

[298] Op. Cit. Reade, p.81

'Robinson's b------ '); it would again be anonymous or signed by the same *'man in the moon'.* This vile piece of prose would be the last on the subject and the next thing the master would receive was news of a visit to his premises from a rattener or perpetrator of outrage. In Joshua Tyzack's case it was five bullets from a revolver.

Christopher Rotherham and the Sickle & Reaping Hook Grinders' Union

1859-1865

By the time Christopher Thomas Rotherham faced the Commissioners in 1867 he had been a sickle manufacturer for very nearly 60 years.[299] He lived and worked at Dronfield, about 5 miles from Sheffield town, where the manufacture of sickles was concentrated in the Eckington parish.[300] For the purpose of the Inquiry, this fell within the definition of being within the town's *'immediate neighbourhood'* and the Commissioners heard his evidence on the seventh day of the Inquiry on 25 June.

---

[299] The Rotherham family business goes back to at least 1787 when William and Thomas Rotherham were listed in the Directory of Sheffield as sickle manufacturers at Troway. Christopher Rotherham was 71 years-old at the time of the 1861 census when he was living at Unstone Lane, Eckington, with his daughter, 27 year-old Fanny Helliwell, recorded as a farmer's wife; his grand-daughter, 3 year-old Ann; his brother-in-law, Mark Staniforth, aged 55, also a sickle maker; and a 16 year-old servant girl called Mary Bennitt. Christopher Rotherham is also recorded as being a sickle manufacturer and farmer of 10 acres employing 1 man.
[300] Op. Cit. Hey, p.65

Christopher Rotherham told the Commissioners that he had *'been at war with the union for forty years.'*[301] The union in question was the Sickle and Reaping Hook Grinders' Union, which was based at Hackenthorpe where its committee met at the New Inn public house kept by George Staniforth. Rotherham's first encounter with the union, which fell outside of the 10 year timescale of the Commission, came about when the union asked him to give a job to a man who had been in prison and then had gone to America leaving his poor wife and children to fend for themselves. He had failed to make anything of himself in America and returned to England whereupon he asked Christopher Rotherham for work. Rotherham took an instant dislike to the man and when he learnt of his past he refused to take him on. He did not elaborate on what actions the union took against him at this rebuff as it fell outside of the Commission's remit. The story that the Commissioners were interested in began in late 1859 when Rotherham started getting threatening letters about his men not being members of the union. The letters implied that if he didn't force his men into joining the union he would be *'blown to pieces!'*[302] He ignored the letters and nothing untoward occurred until the following year when, after receiving yet another threatening letter, the boiler at his works was blown up. There was evidence to establish that this was no accident; the remains of a cask of gunpowder that had been put under the boiler were found by the police. Rotherham put up a reward of £100 to bring the culprits to justice and a man by the name of Coggin was arrested by the police but there wasn't enough

---

[301] Op. Cit. TUC, 15,974
[302] Ibid, 15,908

evidence to tie him to the incident and he was later discharged.

The threatening letters continued, all designed to terrorize Rotherham into forcing his men to join the union. Principal of these men were three of his nephews: John; George; and Christopher; all with the Rotherham surname. Numerous incidents of rattening occurred at the works following the blowing up of the boiler. On one occasion 9 pairs of bellows and 12 bands were cut. On another, anvils were thrown into the works' dams. Then a more sinister incident occurred when a canister of gunpowder was thrown through the window of a house where two of his nephews lived. [303] The house in question was at Troway and belonged to Christopher Rotherham. The nephews were upstairs in bed when the missile was thrown through the ground floor window at the back of the house. The blast lifted the floor above and blew out the windows. The walls of the house were damaged and the roof was blown to pieces. [304] The nephews escaped injury but were severely shaken by the attack. Once more this incident followed the receipt of a threatening letter demanding that Rotherham forced his men

---

[303] The nephews in question were sickle grinders George Rotherham, aged 26, and John Rotherham, aged 19, who lived with their mother, Jane, aged 56 and head of the family; their sister Ann, aged 23 and a dress maker; and Jane's 9 year-old grand-daughter, also called Jane. Their mother was recorded as being a farmer of 6 acres. The other nephew, Christopher Rotherham, aged 30, also lived at Troway with his wife, 29 year-old Mary; daughters Harriet, aged 10; Alice, 8; Elizabeth, 5; and sons George, aged 6; and 1 year-old John (1861 census).

[304] Op. Cit. TUC, 15,932

to pay to the union. There was little doubt in his mind that this was the work of the union.

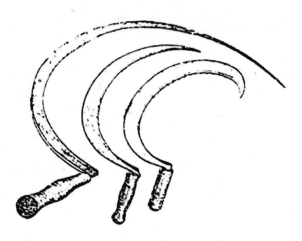

19th century sickles. Reaping hooks had a similar crescent shaped blade but were heavier and had a smooth blade rather than the serrated cutting edge of the sickle.

Christopher Rotherham finally succumbed to the union's attacks in 1865 when a 2 gallon bottle filled with gunpowder with a lengthy fuse attached was discovered in his warehouse one morning. The warehouse doors had been broken and the bottle had been left with the fuse lit sometime during the night. Fortunately, especially for his nephew and family who slept in adjoining rooms, the fuse had gone out before reaching the bottle. Had the fuse completed its deadly course the resulting explosion would have caused serious injuries to, if not killed, members of the unsuspecting family, which included a mother and four children.

Following Christopher Rotherham's submission to the Inquiry the secretary of the Sickle and Reaping Hook Grinders' Union, George Castles, was summonsed to attend the court and to produce the union's books. From his evidence we learn that the union, which in 1867 had around 60 members, was organised by district and each district had a representative on the committee. The nearest organised district to Dronfield was based at the Old Skelper Wheel at Eckington, about 2-3 miles away, and a grinder named Mark Fox collected the *'natty'* in that area. In a similar fashion to the saw trades, the sickle grinders were in an informal amalgamation with the scythe smiths and the patent scythe and hook makers. Castles had been a member of the union since completing his apprenticeship in 1848 but he claimed that he didn't even know of Christopher Rotherham and knew nothing of the gunpowder attacks or the rattenings.

On inspecting the union's minute book the Commissioners found that a number of pages had been torn out for a period up until October 1860, i.e. the time that Rotherham's boiler was blown up and his bellows and bands were cut. Castles claimed he didn't know who had removed the pages as it was prior to him becoming secretary in 1863. The union's cash book was new and only recorded transactions from 5 September 1866. Castles told the Commissioners that the old book had been burnt by one of the committee members at that time.[305] Although the burning of the book took place in his presence, Castles made no attempt to prevent it or to retrieve the book from the flames. The Commissioners were convinced that these actions were

---

[305] Ibid, 16,497. Castles claimed that the book was burnt by one of three committee men; Mark Fox, Elias Havenhand or Oliver Turner.

to cover up the union's culpability in the attacks on Christopher Rotherham. George Castles had to acknowledge that it did at least appear suspicious.[306] In their final Report the Commissioners concluded that *'these outrages were promoted and encouraged by the Sickle Grinders' Union.'*[307]

Christopher Thomas Rotherham's sickle manufacturing business folded in January 1874 and he was declared bankrupt.[308]

---

[306] Ibid, 16,506
[307] Ibid, p.xi
[308] *The London Gazette*, 3 February 1874

Nail Makers' Workshops Blown Up at Thorpe Hesley

1861

Although the village of Thorpe Hesley was beyond the Sheffield boundary, it did fall within the geographical area of *'its immediate Neighbourhood'* as specified by the Commissioners' Warrant issued on 3 May 1867, and as such a number of incidents that occurred in the village in December 1861 where brought to the attention of the Commissioners.

The incidents at Thorpe Hesley, a village renowned for its nail making, concerned two nail makers who worked for a Rotherham master nail maker called William Favell. Forty-nine year-old John Hattersley and 45 year-old Charles Butcher each had his own workshop about a quarter of a mile apart at each end of the village. A description of a 19th century nail maker's workshop is provided by Eric Hopkins:

'The best kind are little brick shops of about 15 feet long by 12 feet wide in which seven or eight individuals constantly work together, with no ventilation except the door and two slits or loopholes in the wall; but the great majority...are very much smaller, filthily dirty, and looking in one of them when the fire is lighted, it presents the appearance of a dilapidated coal-hole, or little black den...The effluvia of

these little work-dens, from the filthiness on the ground, from the half-ragged, half-washed persons at work, and from the hot smoke, ashes, water, and clouds of dust (besides the frequent smell of tobacco) are really dreadful'[309]

William Favell was having problems with the Nailmakers' Union, which was based at Belper in Derbyshire, due to him paying below the union rate. Union members were out on strike but a small number of non-union men continued to do work for Favell, including Hattersley and Butcher.

John Hattersley had been at odds with the Nailmakers' Union in 1859 when there was a previous strike at Favell's that he did not get involved with. He did, however, attend a

19th century nail forge.

meeting of the striking union men where he came under pressure to join them. He not only resisted the attempts to persuade him to join their ranks, he actually reported back to William Favell what had gone on at the meeting. The others got suspicious of him and refused his admittance at further

---

[309] Op. Cit. Hopkins, p.4

meetings. He continued to work at Nail Stove House at the Kimberworth end of Thorpe Hesley alongside his brother, Joseph Hattersley and another non-union man called George Walter. He had nothing further to do with the union but he soon found himself at the thick end of some mischief.

On a number of occasions John Hattersley was awoken in the night by stones smashing through the bedroom windows. Apart from the damage to the windows the stones could have easily injured him and his family: his 26 year-old wife Maryam; his 5 year-old daughter Sarah; and his two sons Richard and John aged 6 and 2 respectively.[310] On another occasion he was working early in the morning, at about 3.00am, when someone threw a piece of wood at him through an open window of the workshop, which was detached from the house. As it was dark he couldn't see who it was or how many were outside; he thought there could have been as many as four men. He closed the window and locked the door and carried on with his work. Whoever was outside went around the other side of the workshop and started throwing pieces of cinder at the door, one he estimated to have weighed about 7lb. Again he ignored them, and he certainly wasn't venturing outside under the circumstances. Within a minute or so the window was knocked out along with its shutter by a large piece of wood. After this it went quiet and whoever it was disappeared into the night. Hattersley had no quarrel with anyone and came to the conclusion that his tormentors were union men.

---

[310] It is alleged that nail makers had large families to provide labour for the workshop: Ibid, p.203. However, this doesn't appear to be the case here, although John Hattersley seems to have married late and to a much younger woman.

Around the same time of these attacks on John Hattersley, during the early weeks of December 1861, Charles Butcher also had a near miss at his workshop at the Wentworth end of the village. One morning one of his men arrived at the workshop and in preparing for the day's work found a tin can dangling down the chimney over the stove. On retrieving the can he found it full of gunpowder with a fuse attached. He went over to the house and informed Butcher of what he had found. There was over a pound of gunpowder in the tin and had it not been found before the stove was lit the inevitable explosion would have likely killed anyone in the workshop. Just like John Hattersley, Charles Butcher was of a mind that the attack was the work of the Nailmakers' Union. Within the next couple of weeks their suspicions would be confirmed as they would feel the hand of mischief once more. This time they would both have their workshops blown up.

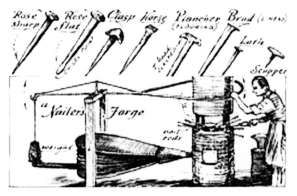

Some examples of 19th century hand-made nails and a nail maker at his forge.

Isaac Emanuel Watson was a nail maker living in Chesterfield. He was not a member of the union but was familiar with the organisation and he was engaged to undertake further attacks on the wayward Thorpe Hesley men in a curious fashion. He received an anonymous letter from Belper; not a threatening letter but one informing him *'that a job wanted doing and if we should do it we should be paid for it.'*[311] In place of a signature the letter ended *'Burn as soon as read.'* He didn't know the handwriting but being from Belper he understood that someone from the union had sent him the letter, which he did burn as directed. A second similar letter gave him some instructions on how to proceed with the job. He was to meet a certain train and to receive a parcel from a party who would be on it. Watson went to the station to meet the train detailed in the letter and on its arrival at the platform a *'gentleman'* put his head out of the window and said *'Will you get me a ticket for Whittington?'* Watson took the stranger's money to get the ticket for him but then turned back to him and said *'I beg your pardon sir but I am looking after a party.'* The gentleman replied *'Is your name Watson?'* He replied in the affirmative and the man then gave him a parcel, which contained between 6lb and 8lb of gunpowder.[312] No further discussion took place and it is not clear whether the unknown gentleman actually got his ticket to Whittington, or if indeed he really wanted one. It is likely that the request was used as a means of making the contact. It is interesting that Watson describes his co-conspirator as a *'gentleman'*. Whilst today we would use the term for any man who is polite and of good character, in mid-19th century Britain a gentleman was a man of property, wealth and high

---

[311] Op. Cit. TUC, 22,875
[312] Ibid, 22,882

social standing. Did such a man get involved in the criminal activities of the trades? Whilst there may be some supporters of trade unionism amongst the gentry, would any of them support criminal wrongdoings to achieve its objectives? Possibly so, or was this simply an elaborate disguise put on for the occasion?

It is not clear from the evidence that Watson gave at the Inquiry whether the job of blowing up Hattersley's and Butcher's workshops was expected to be done by Watson alone or with the assistance of others but he obtained the help of two fellow nail makers to join him in the undertaking: Joseph Tomlinson and Samuel Proctor. Having taken possession of the gunpowder, Watson purchased two cans from a street vendor near to Commercial Inn Yard in Chesterfield. This would have caused no suspicion as they were the sort of cans used for storing nails. Tomlinson put the powder in the cans and taking a good length of fuse the three of them set off for Thorpe Hesley on the night of 21 December 1861. They travelled by train from Chesterfield to Masbro' then walked the rest of the way to the village. They arrived at Thorpe Hesley sometime between 10 and 11 o'clock at night. Watson and Tomlinson were familiar with the geography of the village and knew where to find the two workshops; Watson had actually been brought up in the village. Their first target was Charles Butcher's shop, a single storey building with one chimney above the stove that rose to about three feet above the roof. The shop was in darkness and had been locked up for the night. A length of fuse about 5 or 6 yards long was attached to one of the cans of powder which was then tied to a length of string and lowered down the inside of the chimney stack to a depth of about six feet. The fuse was lit and they ran off towards the other end of the village to where John Hattersley lived. Here they suspended the second can of gunpowder down the chimney stack of Hattersley's workshop in the same manner as they had at Butcher's with the same devastating result; both workshops had the roof blown off and all of the windows blown out. However, the chimney stack at Hattersley's remained intact.

The three raiders made their way back to Chesterfield by a different route to the one that took them there so as to avoid their earlier target. It was likely that people would now be out and about following the first explosion and them being strangers the locals would soon put two and two together and guess that they had had something to do with it. On the following Monday Watson went to the railway station in Chesterfield to seek out someone from the Nailmakers' Union for his £3; the amount specified that he would get for doing the job in one of the anonymous letters. Union officials travelled from Belper to Rotherham every Monday to pay the strikers their 8s per week *'box'* money. Watson hoped to catch them on the train at Chesterfield but there was no-one on the train that he knew. He then took the train to Rotherham himself and went to the Cutler's Arms where the *'box'* money was paid to the men. Here he asked for the *'Belper men'* and was beckoned over by Charles Webster, one of the Nailmakers' Union committee members who was a district secretary (the Nailmakers' Union was divided into five districts, each with its own administration). Webster asked him if he was Watson. On Watson confirming who he was Webster gave him £2, not the £3 that he was expecting. Despite the letter stating he would be paid £3, the committee only sanctioned £2 for the job. In his submission to the Commissioners, Watson does not elaborate any further as to what occurred next in relation to the other sovereign owed him, other than he never received it, but he did confirm that he was accosted and prosecuted for his part in the Thorpe Hesley bombings, along with Joseph Tomlinson. However, in a bizarre judicial farce, Watson's brother, James, was indicted instead of Samuel Proctor.

Isaac Emanuel Watson, his brother James Watson and Joseph Tomlinson were all tried and found guilty of the Thorpe Hesley outrages at the York Spring Assizes in 1862 and sentenced to 14 years transportation. The fact that James Watson was innocent eventually determined that they would all be pardoned and released. Supported by the Nailmakers' Union, they lodged an intercession claiming that they had been wrongly convicted; the union paid all the appeal hearing expenses, which amounted to around £40 - £50. At the appeal hearing 15 witnesses attended and between them gave alibis for the three men at the time that the crimes were committed. Those who gave an alibi for James Watson were, of course, telling the truth as indeed he didn't take part in the crimes and was at Belper at the time. The others, who gave an alibi for either Isaac Watson or Joseph Tomlinson, did not commit perjury deliberately as there was some confusion about the date of the attacks; they were of the opinion that they took place on Christmas Eve and not 21 December.[313] Not surprisingly, neither Watson nor Tomlinson made them any the wiser. However, the truth of the matter unfolded at the Commissioners Inquiry, where indemnity was assured.

The identity of the culprits who planted the first, unsuccessful can of powder down Charles Butcher's chimney a couple of weeks previously was never disclosed but Isaac Emanuel Watson declared that it wasn't him.

---

[313] Ibid, 22,951

The only remaining nail forge in Britain at Hoylandswaine, near Barnsley *(Courtesy South Yorkshire Industrial Heritage Society)*

The Hoylandswaine nail forge furnace and bellows
(Courtesy South Yorkshire Industrial Heritage Society)

James Bacon Addis –
The London Interloper

1864

There is little doubt that James Bacon Addis (1829-1889) was the inspiration for Charles Reade's leading character in his story set at the height of the Sheffield Outrages: wood carving tool maker Henry Little. Like Addis, Little was a superior craftsman in the production of wood carving tools who came from London to take up work in Sheffield. Henry Little's experiences at the hands of the Sheffield trades unions is a tale of fiction but for James Bacon Addis it was a frightful reality.

James Bacon Addis had not only been involved in the production of carving tools since infancy, he was also an accomplished carver and as such understood the requirements of the tools of the wood carving art, far more so than the manufacturers who simply made them from patterns. His father, Joseph James Addis (1792-1858), and grandfather, Samuel Bayton Addis (1768-1832), had both spent a lifetime in the manufacture of edge tools and wood carving tools in their native Deptford in Kent. His grandfather was also an inventor of tools. The Addis family had been in business since 1717[314] and making wood carving

---

[314] Laroff, Gary P, *Addis History and Carving Tool Imprint Overview,* 2006

tools since the early 1790s.[315] James and his brother, Samuel Joseph Addis (1811-1871), learnt their trade as apprentices to their father. Both brothers exhibited at the Great Exhibition of 1851. The quality of James Addis's tools was unsurpassed in the country. He was the only wood carving tool maker to be awarded a Prize Medal at the Great Exhibition and he was awarded a further Prize Medal in 1862. Samuel was awarded a runners-up Honourable Mention at the Great Exhibition which prompted him to make an official complaint against James claiming that the tools he had been showing, for which he had been awarded the Prize Medal, were actually his. James denied that this was the case and as it was one brother's word against the other's the truth of the matter was never resolved. The incident caused a huge rift between the brothers and from that point on they went their separate ways setting up in business independent of each other: Samuel at Gravel Lane, Southwark; and James at Charlotte Street/Blackfriars Road and Lucas Street at Deptford.[316]

James Bacon Addis arrived in Sheffield in the autumn of 1864, after he had approached David Ward of Ward & Payne edge tool and sheep-shear manufacturers following his being declared bankrupt for a second time, the first in 1855; despite being a quality craftsman he doesn't appear to have been a good businessman. David Ward was impressed by Addis and being aware that there were few companies manufacturing wood carving tools in Sheffield he was keen to take him on but he was also well aware of the potential for trouble with the trades unions that such a move may provoke and advised

---

[315] Tweedale, Geoffrey, *Addis: A Famous Name in Carving Tools,* www.wkfinetools.com, 2015, p.1
[316] Ibid

Addis to seek membership of the Edge Tool Makers' Union before committing to employ him. He pointed him in the direction of James Reaney, secretary of the union and suggested offering him generous terms. Addis proposed paying a £15 entrance fee, to pay the appropriate weekly subscriptions and not to call upon the benefits of the union for a period of two years. Reaney's response was to advise Addis that there were enough men in Sheffield to do this work and that the committee would not take him at any price; no London interloper was welcome in the Sheffield trades. This put an end to Addis and Ward's immediate aspirations and James Addis returned to London. To all intents and purposes the potential threat of the Sheffield trades unions' possible reprisals had put an end to Addis promoting his skills in the town but other forces would intervene. London was the centre for trade, especially for international trade. There was great competition for wood carving tools from Russia and Germany in particular and the superior standard of James Bacon Addis's tools were recognised as perhaps the best in Britain. Consequently traders took a keen interest in his work and David Ward found that his company's big orders secured by their London connections were now at threat. One of the major London traders was prepared to give them considerable orders for wood carving tools but insisted on them being made by Addis. No orders would be forthcoming if the tools were to be made by Sheffield men. Unless David Ward could tempt Addis back to Sheffield Ward & Payne would lose out on these lucrative orders. Consequently Ward wrote to James Addis proposing to set him up in premises away from the eyes of the union men. Addis agreed and a small workshop was provided for him in Rockingham Street.

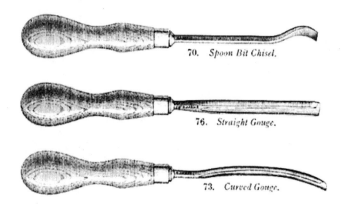

70. *Spoon Bit Chisel.*

76. *Straight Gouge.*

73. *Curved Gouge.*

Examples of James Bacon Addis's wood carving tools[317]

James Addis's work was indeed found to be superior to that of the Sheffield trades, so much so that the grinders found his forged tools much easier to grind than those of the Sheffield men, less effort was required and they could do more work in a day. This also meant that they could earn more money when grinding his work. Addis also earned much more than his union counterparts, sometimes as much as £10 per week. Out of this he paid for the keep of a lad who worked for him, including his clothes, and he gave him 1s 6d per week pocket money. Such was the Addis phenomenon that it would be impossible for it to remain a secret from the trades unions and before long the dissatisfaction of the Edge Tool Makers' Union was made clear to David Ward; and to James Addis.

---

[317] Ibid

Thirty three year-old James Bacon Addis had moved his wife, 34 year-old Jane, and two children, 11 year-old James Bacon Jnr. and 9 year-old Margaret, to be with him in Sheffield and they lived together at a house in Trippet Lane[318] around the corner from his workshop in Rockingham Street. At a nearby beerhouse called the Red Lion at 89 Trippet Lane, they befriended the keeper, one William Scamadine. About three months or so after they had moved to Sheffield William Scamadine was taken ill and Addis's wife and children accompanied him to London to visit a hospital there (we must assume that the hospital was known

1860s Ward & Payne advertisement

---

to Addis and it either specialised in the illness that afflicted William Scamadine or Addis had connections there). It was a rainy night at around 10:40pm that James Addis went across to the Red Lion to see if there was any news of their return. In the beerhouse were four men who also worked for Ward & Payne and one of them by the name of Jephson approached him and rebuked him for taking his work: *'Here is a bloody Irishman wants to insult me; come to take my part.'*[319] At this Addis ordered some beers and invited Jephson to have a drink with him and proposed *'let us be comfortable together.'* There was nothing *'comfortable'* forthcoming. Jephson retorted *'How many trades unions meetings have we had through you, you bloody cockney?'*[320] One of the others barred the door and then they all set about him knocking him to the floor where they kicked out at him. They left him with two cuts to his head some 2 or 3 inches long, and bruises to the length of his body. Following the attack Addis applied for a warrant against the men and they were arrested and brought before the magistrates where Addis curiously spoke up for Jephson, apparently due to him being a fellow member of a club that Addis had joined. The magistrate seems to have taken heed of Addis's representation as he fined Jephson £3 plus costs but the others he fined £5 each.

Despite Jephson's fine and Addis's attempts to square things with him, the assailant continued to threaten him and a further confrontation occurred in another public house. Addis was stood drinking at the bar when Jephson offered to fight him: *'Now, you bloody cockney, you have made me pay this fine. If you want to fight come and take it out of me. I am*

---

[319] Op. Cit. TUC, 4,646
[320] Ibid, 4,655

ready to fight you whenever you are ready. [321] Addis simply ignored him and moved away. On another occasion one of the other assailants offered to fight him for 3d. Again he ignored the man and walked away. There were no further physical attacks upon James Bacon Addis but Ward & Payne faced its own challenge from the trades unions.

James Reaney claimed that James Addis had come to Sheffield to learn how to forge and once this had been achieved he would take his newly acquired skills back to London and set up in competition with the Sheffield trades. In response David Ward insisted that Addis produced work far superior to that of the unions' men and his employment was essential to the company. Numerous meetings took place between the parties over a period of six months. It was clear that there needed to be a compromise to resolve the dispute and Ward proposed that the Edge Tool Makers' Union accept Addis into their fold. Following a further half-hour debate Reaney agreed to take the proposal to his committee for reconsideration. He would inform Ward of the decision in due course. The committee's decision was to deny Addis admittance to the union and to up the ante.

At this time Ward & Payne rented 16 troughs at Messrs. Marsden Brothers at their Bridge Street works. Security here was not as tight as it was at Ward's premises and one night the nuts off all of the troughs disappeared. David Ward did not connect the incident with the James Addis affair straight away but it became clear via information from his men that the rattening was the unions' response to his proposal. Ward sent for Reaney; the dispute had to be resolved.

A final summit took place at Ward's office which was attended by numerous union leaders: Samuel Stacey and

[321] Ibid, 4,664

James Higginbottom of the edge tool grinders; George Fox of the sheep shear forgers, who was also a foreman at Ward & Payne; Henry Mitchell of the edge tool forgers, also employed by Ward & Payne; and James Reaney, who led the negotiations for the trades unions. Reaney told Ward that the union was compelled to ratten to make the manufacturers comply with their demands. The nuts would only be returned when Addis ended his employment at Ward & Payne. Ward saw no way out of this dilemma. Sixteen of his grinders were stood and it was costing the company dearly. He had little alternative but to agree to let Addis go. Then came another bombshell; Reaney requested a payment of £30 to

The name of Ward & Payne amongst other Sheffield companies at the Great Exhibition, 1851.

cover the expense of the union's actions. Again, Ward reluctantly agreed and handed Reaney a cheque for £30. Astonishingly Reaney signed a receipt for the money, which was clearly recorded in the company's accounts as a payment to the union. This receipt could possibly incriminate Reaney at some future date. He must have subsequently realised this and wrote to the local papers to say that the £30 had been given to charities, although few people actually believed that it had. Having agreed to these demands Ward made a final throw of the dice. He informed the union men that although he would end Addis's employment with the company he simply could not do without him and it was his intention to set James Bacon Addis up as a small manufacturer on his own account; he would be his own master and contract with Ward & Payne to supply his wood carving tools. James Reaney and his cohort had no answer to this.

David Ward was true to his word and rented a small workshop for Addis to manufacture his wood carving tools and provided him with the steel. Addis would invoice the finished goods back to Ward & Payne on a weekly basis and Ward would charge Addis for the steel. There was no division of labour here as James Addis undertook the forging, the hardening and tempering, the grinding, and the finishing solely with the help of one lad. Although this was costlier than employing Addis, it was a successful arrangement and continued to be so at the time that James Bacon Addis and David Ward gave evidence to the Royal Commission in 1867.

In 1870 James Bacon Addis picked up another Prize Medal whilst working from the Arctic Works. In the 1871 census we find that James Bacon Addis continued his wood carving tool business living at Ct.16 Rockingham Street and that he now employed ten men. The family had also gained a grandson called George Koemp, who was 2 months old, and had a 15 year-old lodger by the name of Thomas Newton living with them. However, sources state that Addis was declared bankrupt for a third time in 1868.[322] The business relationship between Addis and Ward & Payne came to an end sometime before 1871 when he was then registered as a carving tool manufacturer at 127 Portobello.[323] In 1872 James Bacon Addis advertised his wood carving tools under the *'J. B. Addis & Sons'* brand, asserting that the only true Addis-made tools carried this stamp; they no longer bore the Ward & Payne mark. By 1879 James Bacon and Jane Addis had moved to 46 Newcastle Street and his son, James Bacon Jnr., lived nearby at the Arctic Works on Rockingham Street. James Bacon Addis gained a total of 10 Prize Medals for his wood carving tools, the last one being won in 1889, the year of his death at home in Newcastle Street on 31 December, aged 60. His two sons (a second son, George Kennedy Addis, was born in 1869) continued the family business and James Bacon Jnr. moved into the house next door to his widowed mother at number 44 Newcastle Street.

The company of J. B. Addis & Sons continued to trade well into the 20th century under the management of James Bacon's grandsons, Samuel Joseph Addis (1879-1952) and James Bacon Addis (1881-1944) and operated from Mowbray Street in the 1950s. J. B. Addis & Sons ceased trading in 1970.[324]

---

[322] McConnell, Don, of Eureka Springs, Arizona in reply to a question about Addis Tools on the internet.
[323] Op. Cit. Laroff and Op. Cit. Tweedale, p.2
[324] Op. Cit. Tweedale, p.8

James Bacon Addis's brother, Samuel James, died on 3 June 1871, aged 59, and Ward & Payne bought the rights to his mark of *'S. J. Addis of London'* and started marketing wood carving tools under this brand.[325] Ward & Payne continued to use the S. J. Addis brand on their carving tools, which were made at their Limbrick Works at Hillsborough, up until the 1960s. Ward & Payne also ceased trading around 1970.

David Ward was Master Cutler in 1877 and in 1879 he became mayor of Sheffield. He died in 1889, aged 55, leaving an estate worth over £58,000. In contrast, on his death later the same year, James Bacon Addis left personal property valued at just £350.[326]

---

[325] Op. Cit. Laroff
[326] Op. Cit. Tweedale, p.7

PRIZE MEDAL CARVING TOOLS.

Under the Distinguished Patronage of

H.R.H. THE PRINCE OF WALES, THE PRINCESS OF TECK, LORD LICHFIELD,

ETC., ETC

CARVING TOOLS.

J. B. ADDIS & SONS,

ARCTIC WORKS, SHEFFIELD.

(Brother to the late Mr. S. J. Addis, of 68 & 70, Worship Street, Finsbury, London.)

CARVING TOOL MANUFACTURERS.

BEWARE OF SPURIOUS IMITATIONS

We beg most respectfully to inform the Merchants and Manufacturers of Sheffield and the Neighbourhood that we are the only Manufacturers of the name of Addis in any part of the United Kingdom making Carving Tools, &c.

Messrs. J. B. Addis & Sons also beg to say that they have ceased to have any connection with the firm of Ward & Payne, Sheffield.

The only Prize Medals that are awarded in the United Kingdom have been to J. B. Addis & Sons. A Gold Medal was also subscribed for by the Merchants Manufacturers and Workmen of Sheffield for superior workmanship.

All Orders to be addressed to J. B. ADDIS & SONS, Carving Tool Manufacturers, Arctic Works, Sheffield, England.

N.B.—All Tools made by J. B. Addis & Sons are marked "J. B. Addis & Sons 9 Prize Medals, 1851 and 1862."
Protected by Act of Parliament

J. B. Addis & Sons advertisement published following the death of
Samuel Joseph Addis and his split from Ward & Payne, probably
1871-2.

Ward & Payne trade mark

John Hague and the Edge Tool Grinders' Union

1865

It is not clear whether John Hague was summoned to the Trades Unions Commission of Inquiry or whether he gate-crashed the proceedings in an attempt to achieve redress for his losses, allegedly at the hands of the Edge Tool Grinders' Union, following an incident sometime in 1865. He didn't report the incident to the police so neither they nor the magistrates would have brought it to the attention of the Commissioners. As cases that were investigated by the Commissioners went, John Hague's was not spectacular, it did little to either criticize or flatter trades unions, nor did it denounce or absolve any master. In fact it probably had the least impact upon the Commissioners' report of all the cases investigated and was most likely included in the final report simply because it was the only case of intimidation alleged against the Edge Tool Grinders' Union. However, on reading some of Hague's statements during his two spells in the witness box, which were recorded verbatim in the minutes of the Commission, the case gives a fascinating insight into the life of one particular Sheffield working man in these hard and pitiless times.

John Hague was a sheep shear and weavers' shear grinder brought up in the trade by his father but he was never apprenticed. His father died in 1830 when John was about 6 or 7 years old leaving his mother to struggle with six children (John had four brothers and a sister). Following his father's death he worked for his mother before taking up work on his own account. He probably had little education, although he did learn to read and write. I think it fair to assume that John's early family life was what sociologists today would call *'dysfunctional'* but such circumstances were not unusual at these times. That a young lad in these circumstances would stray off the straight and narrow is of no surprise but in 1841 17-year-old John Hague not only found himself before a Rotherham judge, but also at the wrong end of a sentence of 7 years transportation. The case is a peculiar one if we are to believe John Hague's story. During his second stint in the witness box, Commissioner Barstow was curious to know what Hague had done to deserve 7 years transportation:

Thomas Barstow: *'Why were you transported?'*

John Hague: *'For stealing a pair of trousers, me and another boy.'*

Thomas Barstow: *'How long ago was that?'*

John Hague: *'In 1841. I came back in 1848. I went to Van Diemen's Land.'* [327]

Thomas Barstow: *'Do you mean seriously to say that you and another boy were transported for stealing one pair of trousers?'*

John Hague: *'No; the other boy got one month, and I got seven years.'*

Thomas Barstow: *'Where were you tried?'*

John Hague: *'At Rotherham.'*

---

[327] Van Diemen's Land: now Tasmania.

Thomas Barstow: *'How old were you?'*

John Hague: *'I think I was about 17 or 18.'*

William Overend interjects: *'Was the boy much younger than you?'*

John Hague: *'I think he was.'*

William Overend: *'Then they thought that you had led him into mischief.'*

John Hague: *'Very likely; no doubt about that.'*

William Overend: *'Was it your first offence?'*

John Hague: *'Well, I think I had been a time or two.'*

William Overend: *'You had been a time or two and had got a little boy into trouble?'*

John Hague: *'Yes; I shall tell nothing but the truth I can tell you.'*[328]

Seven years transportation for stealing a pair of trousers may seem harsh but at this time justice was intensely bias in favour of property; the penalty for stealing a few pounds worth of goods could be 10 years transportation.[329] Two cases that were heard in Sheffield on 17 March 1841 distinctly illustrate this bias. The first was that of ratteners Thomas Booth and John Gregory who were convicted of destroying machinery at Spring Grove Wheel near Oughtibridge and sentenced to 7 years transportation. On the very same day William Hepworth and George Eastwood were convicted of the manslaughter of one Ann Schorach at Swinton and sentenced to 2 months imprisonment.[330] On 26 August 1841 Booth's and Gregory's sentence was

---

[328] Op. Cit. TUC, 10,063-10.074

[329] Op. Cit. Chesney, p.92

[330] Op. Cit. Leader, 1841, p.351

commuted to 1 year in gaol[331] but still the contrast with 2 months for manslaughter is stark. Terms of less than 14 years transportation were discontinued in 1853.[332]

Thomas Barstow returned to questioning Hague and asked if he had been in any trouble since his return to England in 1848.[333] Hague affirmed that he had and what followed was another intriguing exchange that at times appeared to amuse Hague but riled William Overend:

John Hague: *'I once had three months.'*
William Overend: *'When was that?'*
John Hague: *'I am sure I cannot recollect. It was a few years back. I cannot read very well myself.'*
William Overend: *'It is nothing to be proud of, you need not laugh!'*
John Hague: *'No, it is not.'*
William Overend: *'When was it?'*
John Hague: *'I cannot tell, three or four years ago.'*
Thomas Barstow: *'What was that for?'*
John Hague: *'It was for burning my own clothes.'*
Thomas Barstow: *'I am not aware that that is a crime at all?'*
John Hague: *'But it is a crime.'*
Thomas Barstow: *'Will you explain what you mean?'*

---

[331] Ibid, p.359
[332] Op. Cit. Chesney, p.29
[333] We have no way of knowing how John Hague managed to return to England as he would have had to pay for his fare, which was beyond the pockets of most convicts. Only a small number of transported convicts returned home.

John Hague: *'I will explain it. I will show you how I burnt my own clothes. My wife died and I got in company with another girl.'*

Thomas Barstow: *'Do not laugh about it, but speak the truth!'*

John Hague: *'Of course I bought those clothes and the girl wore them. I bought everything she had on her back from her foot to her head, and the girl left me then, and I thought I would be revenged upon her, and I thought I would buy two pennyworth of vitriol[334], and I thought I would sprinkle her with it just a bit.'*

William Overend: *'You are a greater scoundrel than I thought you were.'*

John Hague: *'Yes, no doubt.'*

By now the Commissioners had had enough and what little interest they had shown in the case of intimidation Hague alleged against the union had disappeared altogether and they dispensed with further questioning. The case was not broached when the secretaries of both the Edge Tool Makers Union, James Reaney, and the Edge Tool Grinders' Union, Samuel Stacey, were later sworn in and examined (the two unions were amalgamated with the Sheep Shearers' Union to form the Edge Tools and Sheep Shearers' Union).

To return to Hague's complaint against the Edge Tool Grinders' Union, he had told the Commissioners that when he started working for himself he faced insults from men in the union who called him a *'knobstick'*. He went to work for a Mr. Greaves at Ratcliff's Wheel on a six months contract. On nearing the end of the six months, Greaves was approached by James Reaney, secretary of the Edge Tool

---

[334] Vitriol: Sulphuric acid.

Makers' Union, and was persuaded not to renew Hague's contract (probably due to Hague not having been apprenticed and therefore not a union member). On arriving at work one Tuesday morning, about a week after Reaney's intervention, John Hague was met by the works' engine tenter who greeted him by saying *'Well, old ----, they have done thee at last.'*[335] Taking him to the boiler house, he showed him Hague's axle-trees[336] that had been shoved under the boiler and had been burnt. On-going up to the garret, where he had his hull, he found that it had been broken into and his bands and tools had been burnt, and his shank stone broken. His horsing had also been broken up and burnt. In total £15 worth of tools and equipment had been destroyed. Hague went to see Greaves but he simply didn't want to know; whatever Reaney had said or threatened had convinced him that Hague was bad news. He then went to see Samuel Stacey, secretary of the Edge Tool Grinders' Union, at the Yellow Lion public house at the bottom of Shambles, Market Place. He met Stacey and another union man called Turner and asked them if they could help him and he offered to pay £20 to join the union. Stacey said he knew nothing about the rattening but he said they would see what they could do to help him join the union. However, it would be up to the general meeting to admit him into the union.

Soon after, two or three men came to him at his home in Earl Street and told him to come to the Yellow Lion for the next committee meeting. Hague attended and was asked to sit downstairs until called for. He waited until the men began

---

[335] Op. Cit. TUC, 9,713. The omitted word was undoubtedly something offensive and considered unfit to print.
[336] Axle-tree: A fixed bar or beam of wood on which wheels and pulleys revolve.

coming downstairs and leaving; the meeting had obviously finished. The men laughed at him as they left; clearly the men who came to his house had been leading him on. In total Hague attended at the Yellow Lion five times and he was never called into the meeting. On the fifth and final time he went upstairs to confront Stacey but this time there was no offer of help and Stacey claimed to know nothing about the destruction of his tools or his joining the union.

Hague was desperate to join the union as he feared his tools would be burnt again in the night. By now he was working on his own account again with the help of an apprentice. He had taken to carrying his tools home at night so as to keep them safe and did so for a number of months. So desperate was he to be admitted into the union that he paid 5s for a newspaper advertisement pleading his case. He brought a copy of the advertisement to the Inquiry:

'To the gentlemen of the Edge-tool and Sheep-shear Grinding Trades,

My father ground weavers' shears. He died in the year 1830, leaving five boys and one girl. I worked at the same trade when a boy, but I had the misfortune in 1841 to be transported for seven years. I returned in 1848. I had no trade to fly to, but sheep shears and edge tools. I have continued at the same up to the present time. I am quite willing to join the trade and pay to it. I think you are not behaving right to me by you not allowing me a hearing. I have been five times to the committee by their order, and they have refused me a hearing. I have a wife and four children depending on me for support, and one of the four capable of work, but is going to school and does not work. I am willing *to work for my family while the Lord will allow me. I am also willing to join and pay to the trade.*

Yours respectfully, JOHN HAGUE. [337]

Clearly John Hague was desperate to join the union to protect his living and that of his apprentice. Hague and his lad earned between £3 and £4 per week and out of this he kept the lad and bought his clothes. He also paid him some pocket money on a weekly basis, the amount of which depended on what they earned that week; it could be 1s or 1s-6d, sometimes it would be nothing at all if they had had a bad week. When the fair came to town at Christmas and at Whitsuntide Hague would give the lad half-a-crown (2s-6d) or 3s as a treat. We also learn from this open plea to the unions that Hague was married and had four children so we can appreciate his desperation. Unfortunately there was no sympathy forthcoming from any of the unions and his plea was ignored. Union men continued to insult him in the street and he continued to carry his tools home every night to keep them safe.

There is one other intriguing aspect to John Hague's story. One day, about six months prior to his giving evidence at the Inquiry, John and his wife were walking through town when a man called Dronfield, who was a pocket blade grinder at Ratcliff's Wheel when Hague was there, came up to him and told him that he knew who it was that burnt his tools. He suggested that they have a chat over a pint of ale and the three of them went to a nearby public house. Having got their drinks Hague pressed the man to tell what he knew but he changed tack saying *'I am sure I will not say anything about it. If you and your wife will come up to my house on Sunday to have your tea I will tell you who burnt your tools.'*

---

[337] Op. Cit. TUC, 9,755

[338] Dronfield lived at Wadsley and although Hague said that they would go, his wife thought better of it and suspected that it was a ruse that would lead them to more trouble. Hague was getting over the tools incident and wanted no more bother so they didn't go.

[338] Ibid, 9,779

William Darwin and the Scissor Forgers' Society

1866

Few victims of the ratteners had the satisfaction of seeing their intimidators apprehended, prosecuted and punished. In this regard, in 1866, scissor manufacturer William Darwin was one of the few. William Darwin lived at Hadfield Street, Walkley,[339] and had a workshop on Snow Lane where he employed four members of the Scissor Forgers' Society, a trade union that had been founded as recent as March 1864. He also had a number of journeymen forgers working for him who worked their own tools at their own workshops; these were known as *'out-workers'*. Conversely, the men who worked at Darwin's workshop were known as *'in-workers'*. In the summer of 1866, by arrangement with Darwin, one of the in-workers named Hague moved out of Snow Lane to work his own tools so as to open up a place there for his brother, who was not a member of the union. This new man Hague refused to join the union, which caused

---

[339] Thirty-eight year-old William Darwin lived here with his 35 year-old wife Mary; daughters Ann E, aged 15; Mary E, aged 5; and 1 month-old son Thomas. Also in the household was William's grandfather, 68 year-old John, also a scissor grinder, and 65 year-old grandmother. Elizabeth (1861 census).

a little resentment amongst the other three scissor forgers. William Darwin took advantage of the situation and apportioned more work to Hague, who had agreed to work at below the union rate and had lowered his price by 10%. Darwin told the other three forgers that work was short but if they too would agree to reduce their price by 10% he would find more work for them. With great reluctance, and no doubt out of fear of losing their jobs, two of the men accepted Darwin's ruthless proposition. The other scissor forger, named John Clarke, refused to work for anything but the union price.[340] Darwin, having got three of his four forgers to reduce their price by 10%, put all the work their way and Clarke soon found himself without work and having to go *on the box*.

John Clarke went to see Joseph Thompson,[341] secretary of the Scissor Forgers' Society, who was also keeper of the Corner Pin public house on Allen Street, and told him of what had happened at Darwin's and asked him for permission to ratten Hague by cutting his bellows and removing all of his tools. Thompson objected to the bellows being cut but agreed that Clarke could remove Hague's smaller tools. Whilst recognising the impact that Darwin's action could have on the scissor trade, Thompson didn't want to start an all-out war. Tools could be returned when the dispute was resolved but according to his evidence at the

---

[340] An example of the union price given to the Commissioners was for five inch scissors at 1s-2d per dozen, Op. Cit TUC, 1,423

[341] Joseph Thompson, 34, and his wife, Ann, 36, lived at No. 2 Court 5 Radford Street, off Allen Street. They had a 9 year-old daughter called Hannah, and a 6 year-old son, called John. (1861 census, all ages as of 1866)

Inquiry he distinctly told Clarke not to cut the bellows.[342] He agreed to pay Clarke a sovereign for the job and, according to Clarke, he drew him a pattern for a key that would lift the locks at Snow Lane. Clarke went back to his own workshop and made the key that very night.[343] Thompson also asked Clarke to ratten Hague's brother, the one who was out-working for Darwin, and who had rented a scissor shop at James Dixon's works at Cornish Place.

James Dixon's works at Cornish Place[344]

On the night of 1 August 1866 John Clarke entered Darwin's workshop at Snow Lane using his newly fashioned key and a jemmy. Despite Thompson's instructions he cut Hague's bellows and destroyed some of his tools, then set off for Cornish Place to undertake the same job on his

---

[342] Op. Cit. TUC, 1,490
[343] Ibid, 7,691
[344] Op. Cit. Taylor, p.287

brother. However, before he got there he was apprehended by a watchman for being in possession of the jemmy and *'without shoes'*,[345] a ploy used by criminals at night so as to silence their footsteps. The following morning he was charged with the break-in at Snow Lane; the police were satisfied that the jemmy in Clarke's possession had been used to gain entry there. He was held in custody at the Town Hall for a week and following his appearance before the magistrates was transferred to Wakefield House of Correction to await trial at Leeds Assizes.

Whilst he was in custody at the Town Hall, Clarke was visited by his wife Ann, who had been informed of his arrest by her brother. She had been to plead with John Jackson and he had consented to her seeing him. She was in a state of distress at the thought of her husband going to prison and having no means of supporting herself. John Clarke told her not to worry and to go and see Joseph Thompson and to ask him if he would do anything for her while he was away. Ann went to find Thompson at the Star Inn at the bottom of Copper Street where the union paid out the scale money and held its meetings. It was obvious to Thompson that Ann Clarke was at her wits' end and liable to expose him and connect the Society with the rattening at Darwin's. She suggested that she could go to see William Darwin and offer to replace the things Clarke had destroyed so as to make amends; perhaps he would withdraw the charges. Thompson told her she must not do anything of the kind. He would see her husband right and do whatever he could for her but she was not to go near William Darwin. Thompson then took Ann Clarke to see solicitor John Chambers where Thompson paid him two guineas to represent John Clarke at the

---

[345] Op. Cit. TUC, 7,720

magistrates' court, from where he was sent for trial at Leeds. Chambers wanted another £20 to represent Clarke at Leeds, which Thompson thought was too much, especially as at this point the money was being paid out of his own pocket. He managed to find another solicitor at a lower fee. At the end of the whole process Clarke's legal fees amounted to £17. Thompson's biggest fear at this point was that Clarke may implicate him and the Society, and that he too could find himself behind bars.

John Clarke was convicted at Leeds and sentenced to 9 months imprisonment. True to his word Thompson took care of Ann Clarke and visited her at home on a weekly basis paying her 6s per week for the nine months that her husband was locked up. This money was also paid out of Thompson's own pocket and the other members of the union committee were totally unaware that he was providing for her. He had asked Ann Clarke to keep the arrangement to herself and not to inform anyone else; if it was known to the authorities it would implicate him and the union in the rattening. However, she couldn't hold her tongue for long and there soon arose rumours of the support that she was getting from the union with figures of from 4s to 10s per week being bounded around. Not surprisingly word got back to members of the union committee and in December Thompson was called to account by the newly appointed president, Thomas Gillott. Gillott, who had been president of the Scissor Forgers' Society on a previous occasion, had specifically taken up the position again to get to the truth of the matter (officers of the Scissor Forgers' Society were at this time appointed every three months). Gillott had received a report from his works manager at Messrs Nowill's of Scotland Street that Ann Clarke was receiving an allowance from the union but he knew that such an arrangement had not been sanctioned by the committee, nor had any such thing been discussed at its meetings. He had asked around other members of the union but couldn't find out if the report was true. At his first committee meeting on taking up the position of president Gillott asked Thompson how much the trade was allowing Clarke's wife. *'Nothing'* was his reply and he told the committee that if members would give him a week he would provide them with sufficient proof that the Society was not giving her maintenance.[346] Joseph Thompson still feared being brought before the courts as a co-conspirator in the Darwin rattening and following this meeting he drew up a document stating that no remuneration was being paid by the union to Ann Clarke and he got her to sign it with her mark; she couldn't read or write:

> *'In consequence of reports having been circulated to the effect that I, Ann, wife of John Clarke, am in receipt of a certain weekly maintenance from the Scissor Forgers' Society, I beg most emphatically to deny that I am receiving any such; and further state that all such reports are false.*
> *ANN CLARKE* **X** *Her mark'*[347]

Thompson told Ann Clarke that he was paying the 6s per week that she was getting and that the Society knew nothing about it. He read the document to her and explained that he needed her to sign that she was not receiving any maintenance from the trade. He told her it would be a deal better for him should she sign. She thought this was strange as she assumed that the Society had been behind her

---

[346] Ibid, 1,512
[347] Ibid, 1,514

husband's crime and that it was now supporting her; why would anybody else want to support her? Nevertheless she put her mark to the paper; after all the money had been given her by Thompson alone and she had not been in contact with anyone else from the Society; as long as she was getting her 6s per week it was of no concern to her who it was that was paying it.

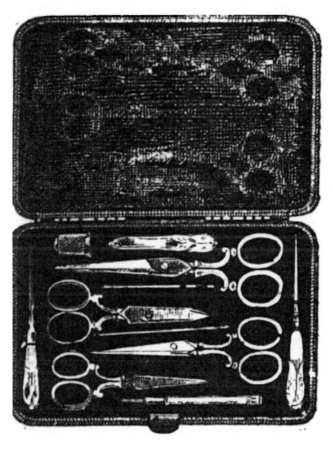

19th century Sheffield scissors and sewing kit.

Thompson took the document to the committee and suggested having copies printed off and circulated amongst the employers so as to quash the rumours. However, the committee saw no need for further action and was satisfied with having possession of the disclaimer and that the Society had not paid Ann Clarke any money. Thompson had managed to put the lid on things for now but there was still the problem of the money. Whilst he had paid Clarke's legal fees and his wife's maintenance out of his own pocket he took the opportunity of recouping some of the money from the Society by falsifying the books. He was in charge of collecting contributions and distributing the scale money on Saturday evenings at the Star Inn. He inserted men's names in the scale book that were not actually paid and pocketed sums of between 9s and £1. The treasurer suspected nothing. During the first three months of Clarke's imprisonment Thompson siphoned £10-6s-6d from the Society's funds to recover some of his costs; he stopped taking the money when the new committee was appointed and Gillott had started asking questions about Ann Clarke's maintenance.

The truth of the matter finally came to light at the Inquiry and following Thompson's confession on Tuesday 4 June 1867, Gillott called a meeting of the Scissor Forgers' Society's committee for the following night. As Thompson didn't turn up at the meeting the committee sent for him to account for his conduct regarding the money. When he eventually arrived Thompson proposed that a general meeting be called where he could explain his actions to the full membership of the Society. It was resolved that a general meeting of the Society would be held the following night, Thursday 6 June. There were upwards of 100 members that attended the general meeting which began at 8 o'clock in a room upstairs at the Star Inn. Downstairs awaiting the outcome, and probably at Thompson's instigation, was a reporter from the *Sheffield & Rotherham Independent*. On opening the meeting Gillott called upon Thompson to address the assembled members and to explain his conduct following his revelations at the Inquiry. Thompson rose to his feet and gave his account of what had taken place putting great emphasis on the fact that the Society's money had not been used for his personal gain but for the benefit of the trade; he could not accept that what he had done amounted to embezzlement. Nevertheless he felt that having acted without seeking the approval of the committee he had no alternative but to tender his resignation as secretary. Having listened to his statement, which gave no further information than what was already known from the press reports of his evidence given at the Inquiry, the members became agitated and there were calls to *'hang him'* and *'throw him out the window';* although some thought Thompson had acted in good faith it was clear from the uproar that most were angry at what he had done. Gillott managed to quieten the meeting down and proposed the election of a new secretary; John Earnshaw was duly elected. It appears that the proceedings took quite a while and a number of men, having lost interest, left the meeting following Earnshaw's election. It was approaching 11 o'clock when Thompson handed Gillott a written resolution that he had prepared for him to put to the meeting. Gillott read the resolution to those that remained:

'That this meeting is of the opinion that the monies taken by the secretary were not embezzled, inasmuch as they were taken and paid for services rendered to the trade.'[348]

---

[348] Ibid, 4,196

There followed what Thomas Gillott called *'a fearful state of excitement'* owing to the continued interruptions of one particular irate member named Charles Thomas who wouldn't let anyone else get a word in. Gillott had to repeatedly call him to order. As the chaos ensued more of the members drifted away and by the time a vote was taken there were no more than 25 members left in the room, and of those a number were at the door eager to leave shouting *'put it, put it!'* (to the vote). Gillott called the vote and 18 raised their hand in favour; the meeting broke up before a vote against could be called. A report of the chaotic meeting, including the full text of the resolution, was included in the following day's *Independent*.

Although it was William Darwin who had approached the Commissioners asking them to look into this particular incident he was not called to give evidence at the Inquiry. However, having heard of Darwin's submission, and having been summonsed to attend the court on other matters, Joseph Thompson had written to the secretary of the Commission:

'Mr. Barker,

Sir – I am willing to give information respecting the destruction of small tools on the premises of Mr. Darwin, scissors manufacturer, Snow lane, which took place ten months ago.

Yours Truly

Joseph Thompson, Secretary to the Scissor Forgers' Society' [349]

---

[349] Ibid, 1,733

Thompson was anxious to tell his story under the protection of immunity and he gave evidence on the second day of the Commission on Tuesday 4 June 1867, where he gave a full account of the incident at Darwin's as related above. At this point, no other member of the Scissor Forgers' Society was fully aware of what had occurred. John Clarke was summonsed to attend the Inquiry and gave evidence on 14 June; Ann Clarke and Thomas Gillott were called to give evidence the following day. The crux of Thompson's story was confirmed by John Clarke, the only difference in their accounts related to whether Thompson sanctioned the bellows being cut or that Clarke had done it against Thompson's wishes. I am inclined to believe Clarke. He went to Thompson to ask his permission to cut the bellows; had Thompson told him not to, would he blatantly ignore him and risk falling foul of the Society? If he was intent on cutting Hague's bellows he would have done so without bothering to ask anyone's permission to do it. Thompson was clearly concerned about his being implicated in the rattening and had he not been complicit with the bellows being cut he could have denounced Clarke to the committee and saved the personal expense of providing his legal fees and for the maintenance of his wife. Instead he went to great lengths to keep his involvement in the rattening from the other members of the union who, on the face of it, would have been hostile to such actions; they were aware that rattening went on in the scissor trade but it must not be seen to be encouraged by the Society.

On his release from prison John Clarke, not surprisingly, was unable to find work and, at least up to his attending the Commission, was in receipt of scale money from the Society of 11s per week; 8s for him and 3s for Ann. However, he never received the sovereign that Thompson promised him for the rattening at Darwin's. Although Joseph Thompson had resigned his position as secretary over the misappropriation of the Society's money, he was still to be found at the Star Inn on Saturday 22 June 1867 paying out the scale money, although the treasurer, William Habbigham, actually handled the money.[350] The Society had passed a resolution to the effect that Thompson had not embezzled the Society but had used the money for trade purposes.[351]

Darwin's was one of three incidents involving the Scissor Forgers' Society that were brought to the attention of the Commissioners. The other two were of a similar nature and involved the cutting of bellows belonging to workmen who had refused to join the union.

Joseph Thompson had just taken the role of secretary of the union in June 1864; three months after it was founded, and he began a recruitment campaign by writing to the masters whose men had not joined. One of the scissor manufacturers that he wrote to was George Gill who had a smithy in Lambert Place. Gill showed the letter to the six forgers that he employed; four joined and two didn't. One of the dissenters was Joseph Hague.[352] In early February 1865, Thompson, along with two other committee men, Richard Newbold and Robert Lingard, visited Lambert Place to try to persuade Hague to join the Society. Despite veiled threats Hague refused to contribute to the Society. On 22 February

---

[350] Ibid, 17,466

[351] Op. Cit. Pollard

[352] This is possibly the same Hague at the root of the trouble at Darwin's in 1866

a pair of bellows belonging to George Gill was cut; the repair cost him a guinea (£1-1s).

One day in early August 1865, Robert Winter, who worked for his father, Robert senior, a scissors manufacturer at Copper Street, met the Scissor Forgers' Society treasurer, at the time a man called Mills, in the street. Mills asked him if he was joining the union. Winter said that he would not, at which Mills replied that he had better or *'Nathan'*[353] would come![354] Winter told Mills that he didn't care whether he came or not, he wasn't joining the union. On Thursday 10 August Winter found his little dog dead in the house and that tools belonging to two of the other forgers who had joined the Society but had ceased paying their contributions in January, Henry Pressley and James Hallas, had gone missing and their bellows had been cut. He suspected that the dog had been poisoned; it was one of two dogs at Copper Street, the other was a larger dog that was chained up in the yard to guard the premises. The dog that was found dead had been free to roam the house and the yard. Robert Winter took the dead dog to a chemist to see if he could determine whether it had been poisoned or not. He was told that the contents of the dog's stomach would have to be removed and sent to London to be analysed and that this would cost two guineas. Winter thought this was too much of an expense but the rattening was reported to John Jackson. It was clear that the non-union men working at Winter's smithy had been targeted and suspicion fell on one of the union members who worked there; one William Fernley.

---

[353] Nathan: one of the signatures to threatening letters, on this occasion used to suggest Winter would be rattened should he not join the Society

[354] Op. Cit. TUC, 17,267

The police were unable to determine Fernley's guilt but he admitted the crime to the Commissioners; he had cut Pressley's and Hallas's bellows before leaving the smithy the previous night, hence there was no sign of a break-in, and he had taken the tools and had thrown them into Green Lane Dyke. There was no reference made to the dead dog in the Commissioners' questioning but it is unlikely that Fernley had poisoned it. Killing the dog would not have prevented Robert Winter working and the only plausible motive for doing such a thing was pure spite. Fernley was known to the dogs and they would not deter his wrongdoing; Robert Winter had told the court that Fernley would often bring the little dog bits of bread.[355] Whilst admitting the crime Fernley insisted that he did it off his own bat and that there had been no official sanction of the Society for him to do it, nor had it been instigated by Joseph Thompson. Nevertheless, the Commissioners came to a different conclusion and they were satisfied that the Society was behind the rattening at Robert Winter's, as they were those at William Darwin's and George Gill's:

'We report that all these outrages were encouraged and promoted by the Scissor Forgers' Union.'[356]

It is interesting to note that at the conclusion of the Inquiry on 8 July 1867, William Fernley was granted a certificate of indemnity but Hubert Henri Sugg's application on behalf of Joseph Thompson was refused by the Commissioners as in their view he had not made a full

---

[355] Ibid, 17,321
[356] Ibid, p.xiii

disclosure or a true statement.[357] Thompson, who was in court, asked to speak to William Overend but the Chairman cut him short saying *'We have considered his case, and we do not believe what he has said.'*

Whilst these incidents were definitely committed by members of the Scissor Forgers' Society, and certainly in respect of the rattening at Darwin's, with the complicity of an officer of the Society, I am not convinced that the Society as a body officially sanctioned them.

---

[357] Ibid, p.449

Edwin Sykes and the Scissor Grinders' Union

1865-1866

Scissor grinders' worked on both dry and wet stones and the most harmful process that they undertook was when shaping the rounded form to a scissor blade, a process known as *'humping'*. In 1857 there were 300 men and 200 boys employed in scissor grinding in Sheffield. According to Dr. Hall's research *'hundreds of these men perish before reaching the age of forty. The average age of the men now at work is thirty-two.'*[358]

Edwin Sykes had been a scissor manufacturer for about 40 years and lived at 33 Wentworth Street, St Philip's.[359] He also had a workshop at Burnt Tree Lane and appears to have occasionally rented a hull at Gibson's Wheel on Watery Lane. Sykes was a master scissor grinder and had been a member of the Scissor Grinders' Union. He was familiar with the ways of the trades unions and the practice of rattening; in an act of revenge he had taken the bands of men

---

[358] Op. Cit. Dr. Hall, *Sheffield Grinders' Disease,* p.21

[359] Edwin Sykes would have been 59 years old in 1865. His wife, Alice, would also have been 59. In 1861 the couple had a 14 year-old apprentice scissor grinder called Martin Quinland living with them (1861 census).

who he suspected of taking his bands at the Union Wheel in 1838. This however was outside of the scope of the Commissioners but other instances of intimidation at the hands of members of the Scissor Grinders' Union were investigated at the Inquiry.

In December 1865 Edwin Sykes employed a young lad named Leadbetter on a temporary basis after the lad's father had asked him if he could find him a couple of weeks work whilst his master was away as he couldn't afford to keep the lad. The lad came to the attention of Robert Holmshaw,[360] president and treasurer of the Scissor Grinders' Union, whilst collecting subscriptions at the works on 11 December. A couple of days later Holmshaw returned and pulled young Leadbetter off his horsing telling him he must go home and threatened to fetch a policeman to him; we must assume that Sykes employing the lad, albeit for just a couple of weeks, was in contravention of the union's rules - from the evidence given by Joe Gale,[361] secretary of the Scissor Grinders' Union, the employment of apprentices had to be sanctioned by the committee.[362] Sykes witnessed this and immediately confronted Holmshaw and threatened to take a strap to

---

[360] Robert Holmshaw would have been 46 years old in 1865. He too lived on Wentworth Street at No. 104. His wife, Eliza, would have been 34 and the couple had a 19 year-old son called Robert and a 7 year-old daughter called Fanny (1861 census).

[361] Joe Gale would have been 27 years old in 1865. He was married to 24 year-old Sarah M and they had a 5 year old daughter called Eliza. In 1861 they lived at 44 Clarence Street, off Broomhall Street, Gillcar with 57 year-old bricklayer, mason and builder George Gale (probably Joe's father); his wife Ann, aged 52; and 21 year-old son Ben, who was also a bricklayer, mason and builder (1861 census).

[362] Op. Cit. TUC, 2,991

him.[363] A disgruntled Holmshaw took his leave and Sykes stopped paying to the union. He must have considered Holmshaw's action a bit extreme and totally uncalled-for. It was about six months after this episode that Sykes next saw Holmshaw when their paths crossed in Pelham Street and the following exchange took place:

> **Holmshaw:** *'You do not pay to the trade now.'*
> **Sykes:** *'No, I never shall do.'*
> **Holmshaw:** *'I will serve you out!'*
> **Sykes:** *'If you would go out in the street I would dare take it out in your bones.'*[364]

There was obviously no love lost between Sykes and Holmshaw, especially after their confrontation over young Leadbetter. The pair kept their distance from each other and nothing further untoward occurred until later in the year.

In August 1866 Sykes took on a young man named Pryor, who was the son of a scissor grinder who had recently died. Pryor was about 18 or 19 years old and not of an age to join the union and he had not been apprenticed to anyone in the scissor trade. Following the death of his father his mother approached Holmshaw and asked if the union would admit him to the trade. The committee considered the distraught mother's request at one of their regular meetings at the Punch Ball public house in Bridge Street but decided that allowing Pryor in was contrary to the rules and they refused. Despite this, Sykes decided to offer Pryor work. It isn't clear whether he did so out of pity for the lad or to take advantage of him; it may well be a case of both. Whatever his motives

---

[363] Ibid, 18,087
[364] Ibid, 18.092

his employing young Pryor led to another confrontation with the union. On 10 December 1866 a set of Sykes's bands went missing from his hull at Gibson's Wheel. He got word from his men that the rattening was due to his employing Pryor. Sykes reported the missing bands to John Jackson telling him that he was sure it was a *'trade affair'*. Nothing came of the Chief Constable's investigation and Sykes had to purchase new bands. On 26 December the Wheel was broken into again and £24-£25 worth of tools were damaged and 17 glaziers[365] were stolen. The glaziers were later found in a well on Easter Monday.[366]

Sykes employed three grinders at the wheel but he didn't know whether they were members of the union or not; he didn't care to find out. Had any of the three been members they would have come under suspicion for the rattenings but there was no suggestion that any of them had been involved. In evidence given by Joe Gale at the Inquiry it transpired that the only member of the union known to have taken any bands was a man named Joseph Parrott, who was now conveniently dead. Gale insisted that although it was known that rattenings had occurred within the scissor trade, the union never promoted or encouraged them, and he had no knowledge of who was responsible for them; he didn't want to know. Parrott was the only exception as he confessed to a number of rattenings before dying. Gale and Holmshaw gave evidence early in the Commissioners Inquiry, both taking the stand on the third day, Wednesday 5 June 1867, and at this time the Commissioners were keen to learn more about the

---

[365] Glazier wheels were made of wood covered in leather and dressed with glue and emery. They ranged in size from 4 inches to 4 feet in diameter, depending on the product.
[366] Op. Cit. TUC, 18,112

killings and gunpowder attacks. William Overend asked Gale if any person associated with the scissor trade had been blown up. Gales reply was *'They have not the pluck to blow them up in our trade.'*[367]

From the evidence given at the Inquiry we learn that the Scissor Grinders' Union had been dissolved at least twice before reforming again in March 1862. On its reformation members paid 4d per week and apprentices paid 2d. Masters were allowed in and received the same benefits as the men; there were 12 masters on the books in 1867. The *'natty'* increased to 8d per week in March 1864 when the scissor grinders achieved a 10% increase in prices.[368] In 1865, following an initiative by Joe Gale, the Union also became a sick and funeral club and the *'natty'* further increased to 1s 6d per week. Gale argued that this initiative reduced the number of rattening instances as it enhanced the incentive for members to pay their subscriptions. Membership in 1867 stood at 230 and there were about 30 non-union scissor grinders known to Robert Holmshaw.[369] George Shackley,[370] a scissor grinder at the Soho Wheel at Coulston Crofts, must have been one of the 30 as his bands were cut to pieces just days before the Commissioners began their Inquiry.[371]

---

[367] Ibid, 2,970

[368] Ibid, 2,631

[369] Ibid, 2,442

[370] In 1861 George Shackley was recorded as being a 30 year old scissor grinder living at 53 Oborne Street, Bridge Houses. His wife Mary was 28 and he had four daughters: Lucy, aged 7; Sarah, aged 5; Eliza, aged 3; and 2 months old Elizabeth. Lodging with them was William and Eva Crookes (1861 census).

[371] Op. Cit. TUC, 2,968

A selection of bands from a 19th century advertisement.

George Platts and the Scissor Grinders' Union

1863

George Platts,[372] who had been in business manufacturing scissors since 1857, lived at Talbot Place in the Park area. He was an early victim of rattening soon after the Scissor Grinders' Union was reformed in 1862. During 1862 Platts was approached several times at the Old Park grinding wheel on Sheaf Street, where he rented a hull, and was asked to join by a union collector called Knott but he had consistently refused. However, by the end of the year Platts had a change of mind and he began paying 8d per week to the union; 4d for himself and 2d each for two apprentices. He also employed two journeymen but they would be responsible for their own contributions assuming they were members. It wasn't long after joining the union that he began to lapse into arrears with his 'natty' and trouble began in late May 1863. Early one Tuesday morning he was alerted at home by one of his apprentices that the hull had been broken into. He had

---

[372] George Platts would have been 40 years old in 1863 living with his 33 year-old wife Harriet; 12 year-old son Arthur; and 10 year-old daughter, Emily. In 1861 they had two apprentice scissor grinders living with them called James Southwich, aged 22; and 19 year-old Charles Pigott (1861 census).

left the place secure the previous night but when he arrived he found that a partition board between his hull and another had been broken through and that 6 bands had been taken with a value of between 50s and £3. He could think of no possible reason for this other than it being a *'trade affair'*. That evening he went to the Punch Ball to confront the union committee. Amongst those present were Robert Holmshaw and Joe Gale. He asked why his bands had been taken and he was told that they knew nothing about his bands but they were aware that he was £1-13s in arrears. Whilst he might have been a little behind he was certain that it was not as much as that and he objected. Platts was asked to leave the room while the committee discussed the matter. When called back in Holmshaw told him that he must pay the full amount; £1 contributions and 15s for *'expenses'* (it transpired some time later that the collector had pocketed some of Platts' contributions). Once more Platts protested about the amount and as he only had 15s on him offered to pay that but they refused and things got a bit heated. One of the committee men called William Saddler, who was a bit worse for drink, used *'vile epithets'* and grabbed Platts' neck-tie.[373] Platts said he would pay £1 as that was probably the amount he owed in back contributions but as he only had 15s on him he said that he would pay this down and the other 5s later. This was not acceptable to the committee, they were adamant that he paid the full £1-15s. Platts saw that he was getting nowhere and left the Punch Ball to go to the Town Hall where he reported the matter to John Jackson.

We learn nothing about the Chief Constable's intervention from the minutes of the Inquiry but two days later, on the Thursday, Holmshaw and Gale were waiting for

---

[373] Op. Cit. TUC, 2,654

Platts in Sheaf Street opposite the Queen's Hotel. The following conversation between the parties is recorded in the minutes:

Holmshaw: *'Now then, let us make an end and this here little brother.'*

Platts: *'Why did not you make an end of it on Tuesday night when I offered you very fairly to pay a pound, which I know is as much as I owe?'*

Holmshaw: *'Well pay a pound now and there will be no more about it.'*

Platts: *'How about those bands, there are five of us idle. When can I have them?'*

Holmshaw: *'All right, you will have them tomorrow.'*[374]

Platts paid Holmshaw £1 and the following morning he went early to his workshop, arriving at about 6:15 am where he was met by the engine tenter who told him that the bands had come back and that they were under the gateway. Platts went to have a look and found that there were 10 bands where the man had told him. There were not only his 6 bands but also 4 others belonging to Henry Lee,[375] who also rented a hull at the Old Park grinding wheel and who had been rattened at the same time (this incident was not investigated by the Commissioners). George Platts made sure that he paid his contributions regularly in future and he had no further problems.

---

[374] Ibid, 2,676-2,678

[375] Henry Lee is recorded as being a 37 year-old scissor grinder living at 29 Old Street, off Broad Street, St John's (now the Park Hill area). He lived with his wife Mary, aged 36; and his son William, aged 17 and also a scissor grinder (1861 census).

The New Hereford Street Outrage

'In all great bodies there are black sheep, and in Sheffield
there are many mechanics, unionists and non-unionists,
who are highly paid, uneducated, vicious and reckless.'[376]

1862-1866

Derbyshire born Thomas Fearnehough had been a member
of the Saw Grinders' Union on and off since 1859. He had
also at times been a member of the Jobbing Grinders' Union.
He was 50 years old when he gave evidence to the
Commission in 1867. There had been occasions when he was
at odds with the unions by getting into arrears with his
contributions; working his own tools; and on more than one
occasion by being absent from work for days, sometimes
weeks on end due to his drinking. Although he was a good
saw grinder, the time he spent in the beer house often made
him unreliable. In 1862 he sold his house in Birkendale[377]
for £200 as he feared it would be blown up after receiving an

---

[376] Quote from Thomas Hughes (author of *Tom Brown's
School Days)* in a letter to *The Spectator* dated 24 October
1866 and printed in the 27 October edition, p.15, following the
New Hereford Street Outrage.
[377] Fearnehough's address at the time of the 1861 census was 2
Malinda Terrace, Upperthorpe.

anonymous threatening letter.[378] He had been asked to do some grinding for Ibbotson's[379] but he turned it down as the letter threatened that he would be blown up if he worked for them. His selling the house may have been out of a genuine fear for his and his family's safety, or perhaps there was another hitherto unknown motive for such a drastic move. It was probably at this point that he moved his family to a house in New Hereford Street.

In May 1863 he left the union once more to go to work for Hague, Clegg & Barton[380], saw and file manufacturers of Arundel Street, taking one of his sons to help him. The company's John Hague had sent to William Broadhead for the list of available saw grinders; it was a union ruling that only men on their list were eligible for employment. Although Fearnehough was *'on the box'* at the time his name didn't appear on the list. Hague was told that the list he had received wasn't the list of all available men so he sent back to Broadhead asking for the full list. However, Thomas Fearnehough's name was still absent. Hague went to see Broadhead and told him that he wanted to engage Fearnehough but he wasn't on the list despite him being *'on the box.'* Broadhead told him that Fearnehough had been employed by the company before and as such he could not re-engage him; this too was a ruling of the union. Hague insisted that the company had not engaged him before but Broadhead was of the opinion that it had and still refused

---

[378] Op. Cit. TUC, 10,400
[379] This could either be Richard Ibbotson of Shoreham Street or Thomas Ibbotson & Co. of Paternoster Row; both were saw manufacturers.
[380] The partnership of John Hague, Charles Clegg and John James Barton was dissolved on 31 December 1875.

Fearnehough's eligibility. Of course Broadhead couldn't prevent Hague engaging Fearnehough but he made it clear that if he did Fearnehough would lose his membership and all entitlement to benefit, which he was currently getting at 7s 6d per week (5s for him and 2s 6d for his son). Hague told Broadhead that he would offer him the job and take the consequences. Thomas Fearnehough accepted the offer and he too would have to take the consequences.

Being well aware of possible reprisals and of how vulnerable the company's workshops were, Hague rented troughs at Rayner's Wheel in Park Mills, which was more secure, and moved Fearnehough and his son there. There was no further communication between the parties until November 1864 when Broadhead approached Fearnehough and persuaded him to re-join the Saw Grinders' Union. Not long after he re-joined the union, the company's saw handle makers found themselves at odds with their union over non-payment of their contributions. There was an informal amalgamation of the saw trades unions at this time and William Broadhead offered Fearnehough 5s to 'do a job' for him; to ratten the handle makers at the Arundel Street workshop where Fearnehough now worked. He wanted him to remove their bands and leave a note, which he had already written and pressed into his hand. Fearnehough refused and went straight to John Hague and told him what Broadhead had asked of him. Knowing that someone else would take Broadhead's five shillings Hague asked him to remove the bands at the end of the working day and hide them in a safe place. Fearnehough complied and once more found himself 'obnoxious to the trade'.

In May 1865 the Arundel Street workshop was broken into, a glazier was cut and a band was taken despite precautions having been made as one of the other saw grinders, William Woodhead, had told Fearnehough that Arundel Street would be targeted because he was in arrears with his *'natty'*. Bands, nuts and all removable tools were locked away that night but one band had been overlooked. When John Hague arrived the following morning he found that a window, its shutter and its frame had been prized out. Hague and his business partner, Charles Clegg, went to see William Broadhead who confirmed that Fearnehough was 3 or 4 weeks in arrears but he denied all knowledge of the rattening. He agreed that it was undoubtedly a trade affair but it was nothing to do with him. Clegg then reported the incident to John Jackson who sent two inspectors (Wynn and Whitely) to investigate the rattening. The officers interviewed William Woodhead but he would not divulge the culprits, claiming he knew nothing about it. Charles Clegg was convinced that Woodhead was involved and dismissed him, barring him from the premises. The glazier was re-covered and put back into use but the band was never returned.

Following this incident Thomas Fearnehough lived in fear of further attacks, as did John Hague who eventually gave him notice in September 1865. In contravention of union rules, Fearnehough went to work his own tools at Butcher's Wheel at Kelham Island, where he felt much safer. He was replaced by a saw grinder called Charles Staniforth who would get indirectly embroiled in another plot at Hague, Clegg & Barton. During Staniforth's short time with the company (he left in June 1866 to work in Manchester) he allegedly overheard a conversation between George 'Putty' Shaw, who would occasionally call in at the yard and had sometimes helped Thomas Fearnehough, and James

Thomas, a smith and engineer who worked at Arundel Street. During their conversation Shaw inferred that there was someone wanting to *'blow up the place for £5'* but William Broadhead wouldn't sanction it.[381] This story is confused by the evidence given by Staniforth, Shaw and Thomas at the Inquiry. Staniforth said that he overheard a conversation between Shaw and Thomas; Thomas said he had heard Shaw and Staniforth discussing it; and Shaw denied saying anything at all except perhaps in jest. No-one mentioned the name of the person intent on blowing up Hague's but as nothing came of it we can assume that if there was such an objective Broadhead put a stop to it.

Meanwhile at Butcher's Wheel Thomas Fearnehough was still having trouble with the Saw Grinders' Union. On 24 November 1865 two of his bands went missing regardless of the high security of the place. He bought two new bands for £4 19s and took to leaving them in the timekeeper's house when he was away from the wheel. He knew that the union was behind the rattening as he had not paid any contributions since leaving Hague's and he was now working his own tools. The fact that the incident happened at Butcher's wheel suggested it was done by an insider; someone who had authorized access to the premises. Feeling vulnerable to attack once more he decided upon approaching Broadhead to see if he could re-join the union. It was at this time that Fearnehough was ill with a liver complaint; no doubt due to his excessive drinking. Being under-the-weather and obviously intimidated by *'Old Smite'em'* he made the approach through a third party; a saw grinder and butcher in Gibraltar Street called Benjamin Green. Green arranged a meeting with Broadhead who told Fearnehough

---

[381] Op. Cit. TUC, 5,045

he would have to pay £16 to make him straight.[382] Fearnehough hadn't this amount to hand and asked if he could knock £5 off for the missing bands, give him £3 now and pay the rest by instalments. Broadhead said that could not be done, he must pay £16 and he could have his bands back. They failed to agree and Fearnehough told Broadhead he would carry on as he was.

In February 1866 Fearnehough and his son, 21 year-old Tom, went to work for a company called Gray's in New George Street and then sometime during the summer months they moved back to Butcher's Wheel at Kelham Island where Thomas worked his own tools again. He had no further conversation with Broadhead and had suffered no further intimidation from the union men. Shortly after moving back to Butcher's Wheel he was contacted by Joseph Wragg, manager at Slack, Sellars & Grayson[383] who happened to be in dispute with the Saw Handle Makers' Union at the time. Wragg asked if he would do some grinding for them and he agreed. On completion of the work Wragg asked him to take in some more work and again Fearnehough agreed and continued to take in even more work until eventually, at Joseph Wragg's request, he dropped all of his other work to grind solely for Slack, Sellars & Grayson.

As mentioned above, the saw trades' unions had at this time formed an informal alliance and were working in support of each other when disputes arose. When any rattening was done in the saw trades it was usually against

---

[382] Ibid, 10,426

[383] Listed in Kelly's Directory for 1854 as manufacturers of improved saws, files, ledger blades, and all kinds of spiral cutters, steel converters and refiners

the grinders as once they were stopped, the whole saw making process came to a standstill. Joseph Barker[384],secretary of the Saw Handle Makers' Union, and Henry Skidmore[385], president of the Saw Makers' Society, had been made aware that Fearnehough was grinding for Slack, Sellars & Grayson and it was a matter of great concern. They were of the opinion that something had to be done to put a stop to it.

With this in mind they approached William Broadhead and asked that he did something to stop Fearnehough, and that they would share the expense between the three unions. Broadhead agreed and asked that they left it with him. Two or three weeks passed and nothing had been done so Joseph Barker went to see Broadhead again and he was told that *'the thing was in progress.'* Broadhead had delayed things as there was soon to be a Social Science Congress that he was to attend. The subject of the outrages in Sheffield was raised by the Christian Socialist writer Thomas Hughes,[386] who

---

[384] Joseph Barker had been a saw handle maker for all of his working life and was the son of a saw handle maker, John Barker. At the time of the 1861 census the 24-year-old Joseph lived at 17 Lansdowne Road with his wife Ellen, aged 21, and their 3 months-old daughter Mary E.

[385] At the time of the 1861 census 48-year-old Henry Skidmore was a widower (he had lost his wife, Margaret, sometime after the 1851 census when she was 38) living with his two sons, John, aged 19, and William H, aged 16, who were also saw makers, at 150 Fitzwilliam Street. Also living in was a 28-year-old servant named Mary Morton.

[386] Thomas Hughes (1822-1896): Author of *Tom Brown's School Days;* entered Lincoln's Inn 1845; barrister, Inner Temple, 1848; Queen's Counsel, 1869; principal of Working Men's College, 1872-1883; Liberal MP for Lambeth, 1865, for Frome, 1868-1874; county-court judge, 1882-1896. *The*

would sit on the parallel 1867 Royal Commission on Trade Unions in London, at the previous year's Congress held at the Alexandra Music Hall in Sheffield and Broadhead had replied in defence of the trades unions. What he had planned for Fearnehough would have made things difficult for him at this year's event if it were to occur beforehand. Just two days after the Social Science Congress came to a close, on the morning of Monday 8 October 1866, a can of gunpowder exploded in the cellar of Thomas Fearnehough's house in New Hereford Street.

Thomas Hughes

Concise Dictionary of National Biography, Volume II G-M, Oxford University Press, 1994, p.1510

Lord Brougham opens the Social Sciences Congress
at the Alexandra Music Hall, 1865[387]

Although Thomas Fearnehough, his wife, 49 year-old
Mary Ann, his two sons Arthur, aged 10, and Joseph, aged
7, and his 19 year-old daughter Emma, were in the house at
the time no-one was hurt but the house was badly damaged;
it cost Fearnehough £25 10s for the repairs.[388] He had been

---

[387] The Illustrated London News, 14 October 1865
[388] Op. Cit. TUC, 10,692

aware that his home was a possible target as it had been threatened before when he lived at Birkendale. The fact that Butcher's Wheel was almost impenetrable restricted the potential for him being rattened, which would turn any potential adversary's attention to either accosting him on his way to and from work, or to use the well-known extreme tactic of blowing up the house where the *'knobstick'* lived. He had taken the precaution of fastening down the cellar grate and boarding up the fanlight over the door but he had made himself public enemy number one with the saw trades unions and such precautions had not prevented previous outrages. Broadhead had hired his trusty henchman Samuel Crookes to *'do'* Thomas Fearnehough, who in turn got Joseph Copley[389] to help him, paying him just £1 out of the £22 that Broadhead paid him.[390] *The Times* informed its readers that *'Broadhead himself planned the whole matter, making a sketch of the house, with the entrances to it, and showing how the thing could be done.'*[391] Crookes didn't need to be told how it could be done, he was a past master of the game; this was purely an example of press melodramatic conjecture. At the Commissioners Inquiry Crookes initially denied having anything to do with the New Hereford Street outrage but following the incriminating evidence of others he finally admitted all of his crimes.

---

[389] Joseph Copley was 29 years-old in 1866 and was living with his 28-year-old wife, Hannah, and three daughters: Ann Elizabeth, aged 6; Eliza, aged 3; and 1-year-old Adelaide. At the time of the 1861 census Joseph, Hannah and Ann Elizabeth lived at 70 High Street. By 1871 the family had moved to 91 Lord Street with the addition of another baby girl, 1-year-old Alice.
[390] Op. Cit. TUC, 13,141
[391] *The Times,* 29 June 1867

Once news of the New Hereford Street outrage hit the papers and press billboards there was a public outcry. Rewards amounting to £2,000 were offered for information leading to the identification of the perpetrators, including £1,000 from manufacturers; £100 from the government; £100 from the Sheffield trades unions; £10 from the Saw Grinders' Union and a personal pledge of £5 by the hypocritical William Broadhead.[392] In a letter to William Leng's *Sheffield Daily Telegraph,* Broadhead wrote:

'The foul deed in Hereford Street adds to the fearful catalogue of such things which are disgracing the fair fame of this largely increasing and prosperous town. All will join me in condemning this foolishly insane and wicked practice, and, personally entertaining such a view, I am subscribing five pounds for the discovery of the offender.[393]

Two days later there appeared a letter in reply signed by *'Constant Reader'*:

'Let Mr Broadhead lose no time in producing all his books for two years previous to Linley's death, and up to the present time, before the magistrates and John Jackson, or stand condemned. No shuffling, no grumbling, no stating that the books are lost or destroyed. Also let him state to the magistrates who have constituted the committee in those years and the secret committees during that time.'[394]

---

[392] Op. Cit. Derry, p.152
[393] *The Sheffield Daily Telegraph,* 12 October 1866
[394] *The Sheffield Daily Telegraph,* 14 October 1866

Clearly *'Constant Reader'* was familiar with the trades unions' code of behaviour and alleged criminal practices, and appalled at Broadhead's sheer hypocrisy; was it the editor? Despite this public finger-pointing, Broadhead remained aloof and no-one came to claim the reward or give evidence against the unions. The incident was discussed at the October meeting of the Town Council where the mayor, John Webster, opened a list for subscriptions for relief of the victims, which within a week reached a munificent £1,500.

As this chorus of public disapproval was unfolding, Henry Skidmore and Joseph Barker were getting the jitters. They were convinced that the blowing up of Fearnehough's house was undertaken at Broadhead's instruction and that they would be incriminated as co-conspirators should he be exposed. The day after the outrage they went to see Broadhead at the Royal George. They met in an upstairs room where Broadhead sat behind his desk. *'Well this is a rum affair'* proclaimed Barker *'We never engaged for anything of this sort you know.'* Broadhead smiled and told them he wanted £7 10s from each of them for their share of the cost. Skidmore retorted *'This is a shocking affair. I did not think it would come to this or else we should never have had anything to do with it.'* *'Well, it is done'* replied Broadhead. Skidmore said he would have to consult with the union's secretary, Thomas Smith, about the money.

It is the amount of money that they agreed to pay that gives the game away regarding Barker and Skidmore's feigned ignorance. They told the Commissioners that their approach to Broadhead to do something about Fearnehough was for him to be rattened, not to be physically attacked in any way. But it wasn't lost on the Commissioners that the going rate for removing bands or nuts was 5s, not £22, and that surely Skidmore and Barker would expect something more for their respective union's £7 10s contributions. William Overend also challenged Skidmore on his failure to denounce Broadhead if he felt he had overstepped the mark and acted without his knowledge or his agreement. To this he said he didn't want to implicate innocent people, i.e. Joseph Barker and Thomas Smith. Smith, who had been secretary of the Saw Makers' Society just 7 months, had told Skidmore he would not provide the money and that he would have nothing to do with the affair. When he saw Joseph Barker a couple of days later Smith told him that the handle makers would have to find the full £15, which he did by deducting £7 10s from the money owed to the saw makers. Despite Smith's refusal to pay the money out of the Saw Makers' Society funds, he allowed it to be paid indirectly by deducting £7 10s from the Saw Handle Makers' debt to the Saw Makers' Society, which at the time was around £17-£18.[395] In doing so he implicated himself whether he knew about the blowing up of Fearnehough beforehand or not. Barker gave the full £15 to Skidmore who in turn handed it Broadhead. The Commissioners were of the opinion that Skidmore, Barker and Smith knew all too well what Broadhead would do but regretted their involvement following the public outcry, which they feared would engender their downfall and lead to them being jailed. That is also my opinion. Skidmore and Smith were suspended from office but they were allowed to continue their union membership. Smith, who was unable to find employment following the scandal, was allowed *'scale'* money for longer than the union's customary 12 weeks limit.[396]

---

[395] Op. Cit. TUC, 14,404
[396] Op. Cit. Pollard

Although the *'Hereford Street Outrage'* was not the first of its kind, or indeed the worst, it became a focus for the attention of the national press following William Leng's coverage in the pages of the *Sheffield Daily Telegraph*; what had been a local concern now became a matter of national indignation. It gave rise to an attack on trade unions by the leader writers as being violent and dangerous groups and that

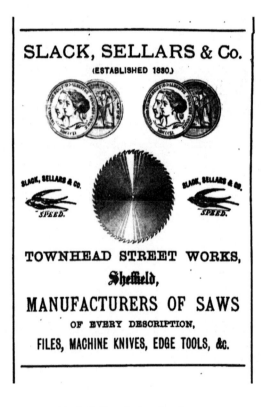

Slack, Sellars & Co advertisement.

they should be outlawed. In response, national union leaders condemned the Sheffield outrages and claimed that they were the work of local extremists and were unjustly associated with the wider trade union movement.

John Brown and the Ironworkers' Union

'We have abstained from employing unionists.'[397]

1867

One of the last cases looked into by the Commissioners was unusual in that it was the only case involving one of the large scale manufacturers: Messrs. John Brown and Co.,[398] who employed over 3,000 people at the Atlas Works on Saville Street East.[399] The incident in question was also one of the most recent occurrences, taking place in February and March 1867. In February the company had imposed a 10%

---

[397] Quote from Mr. William Bragge who was managing director of John Brown and Co. (Limited). Op. Cit TUC, 23,360

[398] Sir John Brown (1816-1896): one of Sheffield's leading dignitaries being twice elected town mayor in 1861 and 1862; pioneer of armour-plate manufacture; invented conical steel spring buffer for railway wagons, 1848; knighted 1867: *The Concise Dictionary of National Biography, Volume I A-F,* Oxford University Press, 1994, p.360 Sir John Brown was also Master Cutler in 1865 and 1866.

[399] In 1879 the Atlas Works of Messrs. John Brown and Co. were described as one of the largest iron and steel works in the world covering an area of 25 acres; Op. Cit. Taylor, p.232

reduction on the wages of their puddlers[400] in the ironworks; many of them were members of the Ironworkers' Union. In response the Ironworkers' Union called their members out and picketed the factory gates where a number of threatening incidents were reported. To avoid issues with the pickets the company employed policemen at the gates and brought in workers from outside of the town and billeted them within the factory, bringing in beds and a commissariat to keep them fed.[401] The new men would stay within the confines of the factory from Monday morning until Saturday night. This situation lasted for about three weeks at which point some of the men gave notice. However, most of the outsiders stayed with the company but the union men were not allowed back and John Brown and Co. adopted a non-union employment policy. Some of the regular men who were not members of the union and who had taken the 10% drop in wages gave notice of termination of their employment following pressure from their striking colleagues but once the state of siege was over most decided to stay with the company.

One of the puddlers brought in to replace the union men was Thomas Rock who came from Derby. One evening he ventured out of the factory to have supper at one of the local public houses with his foreman. On leaving the pub he was accosted by a number of the striking union men who told him that by working for John Brown he was working against his brother workers and what he was doing was morally wrong. Rock tried to evade them by going back into the pub but he

---

[400] Puddlers: workers who stirred molten iron with iron oxide in the furnace to produce wrought iron.

[401] In 1864 ironworks employers in Leeds and Bradford imported 40-50 puddlers from Belgium to break the unions. Op. Cit. Tholfsen, p.275

was jostled along to another public house that was used by the union where they told him that they would pay his fare back to Derby if he was to return home; they would pay the fares home for all the outsiders. That night Rock didn't go back to the factory but stayed at the public house at the expense of the union men. In the morning, after he had some breakfast, which they also paid for, some of the men walked him to the railway station and paid for his ticket back to Derby. In his evidence at the Inquiry Rock explained that he went back to Derby *'because I was afraid to stop there* [at John Brown and Co.] *'[402]*

Contemporary John Brown & Co. (Limited) advertisements[403]

---

[402] Op. Cit. TUC, 23,510-23,539
[403] Op. Cit. Taylor, pp. 424-425

Another outsider was John Skidmore who came from Garston near Liverpool. Skidmore was not billeted in the factory but stayed in lodgings at a house owned by a Mr. Jennings. Twice Skidmore was accosted on his way to work, once in Blonk Street by a union man called Dimond who rebuked him for working in the place of the strikers. Before long there was a crowd of about 20 strikers shouting at him and calling him a *'blackleg'*. Although he was seized by the collar he suffered no physical violence, only verbal abuse. On a second occasion, whilst walking down Bower Street, he passed three men who asked him for directions to a street he didn't know of. He continued on his way but the three men followed him and caught him up and asked him where he was going and if he was going to work. He told them that that was his business and carried on his way. By now Skidmore suspected that the men were striking puddlers from John Brown's and he increased his pace to get away from them. However, the men were determined and caught hold of him and threatened to *'knock his b----- head off'* if he didn't tell them where he was going to work. Skidmore protested that he wasn't puddling but working on the hammers. At this the men let him be.[404]

Edmund Higgatt had begun working for John Brown in 1862 and was a member of the Ironworkers' Union but he had left the company before the puddlers' strike. However, he returned whilst the union men were out having been sent for by the company despite previously being a member of the union.

---

[404] Ibid, 23,485-23,509

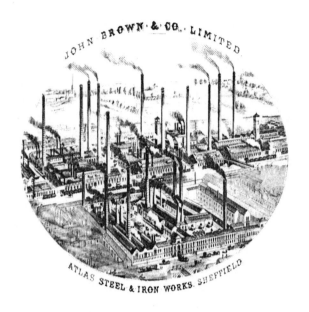

JOHN BROWN & CO., LIMITED

ATLAS STEEL & IRON WORKS, SHEFFIELD

One Saturday night Higgatt was having a drink in the Great Gun public house at 13-17 Wicker (known locally as the *'Big Gun'* and later renamed Big Gun[405]) when, from across the room he was pointed out by a union puddler called James Harris shouting *'There's that "Snip" that has taken Joe Smith's job'* ('Snip' was Higgatt's nickname and Joe Smith was another union puddler who was on strike). Harris and another union man called Joseph Trowman came over and Harris struck Higgatt in the face. Being outnumbered Higgatt didn't retaliate and further trouble was avoided that night but on the following Monday night Higgatt went for a drink at a

---

[405] Opened in 1796, it was still called the Great Gun in 1893; the latest reference I have found prior to it becoming the Big Gun

beerhouse known as Towers'[406] with James Dunhill, a fellow puddler at John Brown and Co., and found himself in Harris's and Trowman's company once more. Higgatt approached Harris this time asking him why he had hit him on Saturday night. Harris made it clear that it was due to him working at John Brown's doing the work of those who had been locked out following the strike, calling him and Dunhill *'blacklegs'*. There were five or six other men drinking with Harris and Trowman and it wasn't long before a fight broke out, although Higgatt described it as *only wrestling with each other'* and he didn't think many blows were exchanged. Dunhill claimed he was only hit the once. After the brief scuffle Higgatt and Dunhill ran out and retreated to the Great Gun where they hoped to have a quiet drink but after about five minutes Harris, Trowman and six or seven other men came through the door and set about them. This time there was a good scrap and being outnumbered Higgatt and Dunhill came out of it the worst having taken a good kicking. Higgatt was off work for two weeks partly due to his injuries, which consisted of bruised shins and ribs, but he admitted that he also had a cold at the time and that he *'played truant'* part of the fortnight. Dunhill had a pair of black eyes and cuts to his face. Following the attack Higgatt and Dunhill went to the magistrates and the attackers were prosecuted, each being bound over to keep the peace for six months.

The fight at the Great Gun that Monday night would have drawn little public attention as such encounters occurred on a regular basis in Sheffield's public houses; it was nothing out of the ordinary. The only noteworthy aspect of the fight was that it was between union and non-union

---

[406] Probably the beerhouse of James Towers at 123 Hanover Street.

men but even this wouldn't have been considered unusual. Such quarrels were a pretty regular occurrence, especially at times of union disputes such as that at John Brown's. There was nothing to suggest that the attack was organised by the Ironworkers' Union or by any of its leaders although clearly the attackers were union members. The Commissioners didn't bother to call in any of the union's leaders for examination and although they would have considered the attack a *'trade affair'* they concluded that *'We have not sufficient evidence before us to justify our reporting that these outrages were promoted or encouraged by the Ironworkers' Union.'*[407]

Sir John Brown

---

[407] Op. Cit. TUC, p.xv

Samuel Crookes & James Hallam:
Trade Mercenaries

'My character is gone, I am sorry to say – It is a bad one, and I am ashamed of it.[408]*'*

Samuel Crookes and James Hallam were not primarily concerned with the interests of the trades; they were clearly doing what they did for the money and were no more than the trades' mercenaries. Although both were apprentice trained neither of them had regular employment in the saw grinding trade. In giving evidence to the Commissioners Crookes told them *'when I got these jobs I did them; I did not ask any questions; I did not ask the reason.'*[409] By his own admission Crookes wasn't interested in undertaking the rattenings, they didn't pay as much as the bombings and the shootings, and these he undertook most liberally. Of course the risk in these undertakings was greater than the minor intimidations as any one of the bombings and shootings could have resulted in a murder charge and the possibility of facing the hangman's noose. Once he had got Linley's murder off his chest at the Inquiry, knowing he would not be

---

[408] Samuel Crookes' final statement to the Commissioners. Ibid, 13,758-13,759
[409] Ibid, 13,549

punished for his crimes, he admitted a catalogue of felonies undertaken for Broadhead and others, indicating a most lucrative business, far more profitable than saw grinding. According to William Broadhead, Crookes was paid a total of between £130 and £150 (around £75,500 - £87,000 at today's values) for the bombings and shootings that he instigated on behalf of the Saw Grinders' Union.[410]

Samuel Crookes was 36 years old at the time of the 1861 census and he was the head of a large family living at West Side, Crookes. His wife Sarah was 33 years old and the mother of seven children; five girls and two boys ranging in age from under 1 year to 14. At the same time, 23 year-old James Hallam was living with his parents, 49 year-old Samuel and 47 year-old Hannah, and eight siblings. Three of his brothers, 18 year-old Samuel junior; 16 year-old Robert; and 14 year-old Abraham, were also saw grinders by trade, as was his father.

There was nothing in Samuel Crookes' appearance to indicate his criminal tendencies. A contemporary description of him indicated that he had *'nothing of the ruffian or villain in his appearance...his countenance is rather refined...and his profile...would suggest that his character was that of a conscientious, intellectual, and rather thoughtful man...his aspect is grave and rather mild...and his manner earnest and straightforward.'* A workmate described him *'as quiet a fellow as you ever saw; to look at him you would not think that he could kill a fly...you'd almost take him to be a religious man.'*[411] The temptation for Crookes to earn the extra, easy money from these reprehensible activities, having such a large family to keep, was clearly too great for him.

---

[410] Ibid, 13,137
[411] *Sheffield Independent,* Op. Cit. Pollard

The fact that William Broadhead, chief amongst the Sheffield union leaders and who was educated and carried an air of authority, was employing him, would have also given the work some legitimacy in Crookes' mind. Hallam on the other hand, lived in a household of five wage earners and perhaps his needs were not so great; for him the incentive was easy money and simply having something to occupy him. I think Hallam had criminal inclinations irrespective of the circumstances; on one occasion he had even rattened his own father.[412] Had he not been familiar with Crookes he would have found mischief elsewhere with some other scoundrel. In essence James Hallam was a villain by today's standards but in 1860s Sheffield he wasn't out of place.

Samuel Crookes told the Commissioners that he, along with a scythe grinder and engine tenter named Thomas Needham,[413] dropped a canister of gunpowder down the chimney at the house of 65 year-old saw grinder Samuel Baxter at Normandale, near Loxley on 25 May 1859. Samuel Baxter was asleep alongside his 61 year-old wife Ann. Also in the house were their two sons, 28 year-old Charles and 21 year-old Joel, who were also saw grinders. Thomas

---

[412] Op. Cit. TUC, 12,193

[413] Samuel Crookes claimed that Thomas Needham accompanied him when he blew up Samuel Baxter's house (TUC, 13,540) but Needham would have been in prison in 1859. If Needham did accompany Crookes the attack must have occurred at a later date following his release from prison in 1860. Although Thomas Needham was the only person convicted of the Ward's wheel bombing he was accompanied by Samuel Crookes and Michael Thompson who was then secretary of the Scythe Grinders' Union and who paid Needham £10 for the job.

Needham had been convicted for a previous gunpowder attack at Tyzacks' scythe making workshop known as Ward's wheel at Dronfield in 1856. No-one was hurt in the blast at Loxley but there was much damage done to the house and furniture. Baxter was one of two non-union saw grinders working for Messrs. Firth & Sons, the other being John Helliwell, the brother of Joseph Helliwell who was blown up at the Tower Mill by Denis Clark and George Shaw around this time (see above), and who had previously worked at Newbould's and had left that company following a dispute over prices. He also left the union. Helliwell went to work at Firths, took on two apprentices and undercut the union prices causing much ill-feeling amongst union members; hence he became a target. Crookes went with the intention of shooting John Helliwell whilst he was at work at Firth's factory near the Wicker. He kept watch from the nearby Midland railway but he was unable to get a clear sighting of Helliwell. On this occasion he was accompanied by his old partner in crime James Hallam. As with James Linley, Crookes didn't want to kill John Helliwell, just wound him and he took the same air gun. Messrs. Firth & Sons was also the target of an unsuccessful attack on 5 June 1859. Again at Broadhead's behest Crookes attempted to blow up the chimney at their works but little damage was done.

It was whilst he was stalking John Helliwell that Crookes was approached by Broadhead and was told he had a more urgent job for him to do. Word had got around that Messrs Wheatman & Smith, saws, files and steel manufacturers at Kelham Island, had installed a machine for grinding long saws. Whilst this would make the process easier, more efficient and more profitable, Broadhead could only see it as a threat to his members' jobs and the union's control of the market on prices, although in time he did change his opinion on this.[414] He promised Crookes £15 for blowing up Wheatman & Smith's. Crookes considered the works' chimney to be the most suitable target, although Broadhead saw problems with this. Nevertheless he left Crookes to his own devices. Crookes naturally told Hallam about the job and they both went to see Broadhead at the Greyhound public house at 185 Gibraltar Street, Shales Moor, where he was then the inn keeper. Crookes went upstairs and came back down with £2 to buy the gunpowder for the job. They sourced the powder from two shops so as not to raise suspicion on what it was for. Hallam purchased a 2 gallon tin milk bottle for 4s-6d at Milner's on Fargate, a length of fuse from Twibell's on Snig Hill, and some sash line from a shop in Division Street; probably Oliver Turner, rope & twine maker. Crookes and Hallam first took their bomb to Kelham Island on Saturday 15 Jan 1860 but their undertaking was thwarted by the fact that men were still working and the chimney was hot; the powder would have exploded straight away had they attempted to put it in the stack. They secreted the bottle bomb in some waste material and left, returning the following night. On Sunday night yet again men were working and they were once more unable to proceed with their iniquitous task. They returned again on Monday and still men were about in the factory so they changed tack. They approached the factory from the river, crossing from the other bank in a small boat to where they knew there was a drain outlet. Having acquired a length of timber from a nearby wood yard they pushed the bottle as far up the drain as it would go having extended the fuse to a length of between five and six yards. They then blocked up

---

[414] Op. Cit. TUC, 12,132

the drain with stones from the river, lit the fuse and rowed back to the other bank. They then stood on Rutland Bridge to witness the fruits of their shady work; there was a mighty explosion. On being assured their attack had been a success they split up and headed home.

On Wednesday Hallam tracked down Broadhead to ensure that he was aware of their success at blowing up Wheatman & Smiths and to get his ill-gotten earnings. But Broadhead had hired Crookes and wasn't that keen on dealing with Hallam and he told him he wouldn't pay there and then but leant him 10s to tide him over. Hallam went to find Crookes in the Mowbray public house on Harvest Lane. Crookes was in company so they couldn't discuss the Wheatman & Smith bombing and they made arrangements to meet at the Blue Boar in West Bar on the following Saturday. Here Crookes gave Hallam £4, not the £7 10s he was expecting and Crookes told him that Broadhead had only given him half the money; he would get the rest next Saturday. They met up again a week later and Crookes gave him another sovereign and told him Broadhead still hadn't settled. When Hallam next saw Broadhead during the following week he asked him for the outstanding £2 10s but he insisted he had settled with Crookes the previous Saturday. I have been unable to find out if it was Broadhead or Crookes who was telling the truth about the money, or whether Hallam eventually got his outstanding £2 10s. Broadhead insisted in his evidence to the Inquiry that he paid the full £15 by instalments and that this included the £2 for the powder. The one good thing to come out of the Wheatman & Smith business was that John Helliwell was forgotten about and neither Crookes nor Hallam returned their attentions to him, but I doubt Helliwell was ever aware of this.

Whilst Hallam and Crookes undertook most of their unsavoury tasks for Broadhead and the Saw Grinders' Union, they would do jobs for anyone. They would also be approached by other trades unions to undertake physical attacks on members who had contravened trade rules. In 1861 John Broomhead, secretary of the Pen and Pocket Blade Grinders' Union, got word of Hallam's reputation as a hit man and offered him £7 to attack a surgical instrument maker called Samuel Sutcliffe who had broken a strike in the trade. Broomhead gave him instructions to *'make him so that he could not go to work for a week or two.'*[415] Hallam invited Crookes to join him in the job offering to share the £7. One of Hallam's tools of his trade was a home made life preserver[416] constructed of gutta-purcha.[417] He used this on Samuel Sutcliffe on the threshold of his home in Hoyle Street, coshing him several times about the head, as did Crookes who had his own life preserver. Sutcliffe was bedridden for a week as a result of the attack. The following day Hallam was approached by John Braithewaite of the Pen and Pocket Blade Grinders' Union in Eldon Street and was given a sovereign as part payment for the Sutcliffe job. Braithewaite told him that Broomhead would pay him the rest the following Saturday at the Washington Hotel in Fitzwilliam Street. When they met with Broomhead he gave

---

[415] Ibid, 11,007

[416] Life preserver: a short stick with heavily leaded end used as a cosh.

[417] Gutta-percha: rubber like condensed sap of trees found in Malaysia used as an electrical insulator. It was also used to make early golf and cricket balls.

Hallam £5 telling him that that was all the committee would allow. At this Hallam told him if that was the case he would have to pay the other £1 himself. They arranged to meet again on the following Tuesday at the Black Swan on Snig Hill. Broomhead took along another union man, probably for protection or as a witness to anything untoward that may take place; by this time Broomhead knew that Hallam was a nasty piece of work. Hallam beckoned them into an archway outside of the pub; Samuel Crookes was waiting nearby at the bottom of Snig Hill. Broomhead told Hallam that he hadn't got the money. At this Hallam turned on him angrily and took hold of him in a threatening manner. At this Broomhead must have thought that he was about to feel Hallam's life preserver himself but the situation was resolved when the other man went back into the Black Swan and returned with a sovereign to pay Hallam off. Hallam then went to join Crookes at the bottom of the hill to share the spoils.

Eighteen sixty-one was a busy year for Crookes and Hallam. On 1 December Crookes went solo with a canister of gunpowder on a warehouse in New George Street. The warehouse was the premises of Messrs Holdsworth and Ashburner, crinoline steel, saws and tools manufacturers. Harry Holdsworth had set up the partnership with a Mr Ashburner in September that year and did not acknowledge the trades unions *'in any shape or form'* but was not averse to his men being union members. The company had no particular policy and employed a mix of both union and non-union workers. However, it wasn't long before the Saw Grinders' Union took an interest in the set up and in October Harry Holdsworth received the first of a number of threatening letters from *'Tantia Topee'*. In the letter

Holdsworth was told to discharge one of his non-union saw grinders, one Jonathan Crapper. Holdsworth ignored the letter and its demand, then a second letter arrived two weeks later with the same ultimatum but this time vague threats were made against him with advice for him to look out when going home at night. He burnt this letter and continued to employ Crapper but, in his words, *'took proper precautions to defend himself'.*[418] Not long after this second letter some long saws that Holdsworth had sent for grinding at William Jackson & Co.'s Sheaf Island Works on Pond Hill disappeared. Jonathan Crapper confided in Holdsworth that he believed the saws had been taken due to a dispute he had with the Saw Grinders' Union; something other than him simply not being a member. The saws were returned to the Sheaf Island Works two days later. Whoever returned them did so undetected despite there being a watch put on the place. The following week Holdsworth received a further threatening letter with the same demand regarding Jonathan Crapper and a further threat of personal injury to Holdsworth. This letter was signed *'One whose hand never flinches'.*[419] This and a fourth letter of the same nature were handed to the Chief Constable, John Jackson.

On the morning of Monday 2 December 1861, Holdsworth arrived at the New George Street warehouse to find there had been an explosion that he estimated had caused damage to the value of £100 or more. His manager, William Roberts, reported that he had found the remains of a canister in the cellar below the warehouse.

---

[418] Op. Cit. TUC 9,159
[419] Ibid, 9,171

Grinding the blades of pocket knives.

Holdsworth knew that the culprit was not one of his men as the grate that had been lifted to drop the canister down into the cellar was one that had been soldered up and a second grate that was known to his men to be only chained would have been easier to lift. The culprit was Samuel Crookes who had been paid £15 by William Broadhead to do the job as *'some outlaws were working there'*.[420] This particular outrage was undertaken not just by the Saw Grinders' Union but was a joint affair by an amalgamation of the saw trades unions and the Jobbing Grinders' Union;

---

[420] Ibid, 13,671

the £15 cost was shared by the amalgamation, of which Broadhead was the treasurer.

After this incident some of Holdsworth's men suggested to him that it might be better to let Crapper go but Harry Holdsworth stood his ground. Others suggested that he advise Crapper to settle with the union but no, he wouldn't do that either. He told Jonathan Crapper *'I would stick to you as long as you stick to me'.*[421] As things turned out Crapper did settle his differences with the Saw Grinders' Union, the threatening letters ceased and there were no further incidents.

It is not clear just how much the explosion at New George Street impacted on the company's commercial viability but in March 1863 Harry Holdsworth was committed to prison for 12 months as a fraudulent bankrupt. At the time that he gave his evidence to the Royal Commission in 1867 he was working as the manager of the Hull branch of William Primrose lead and glass merchants of Corporation Street.

The relationship between Broadhead and his chief henchmen is interesting. As I have alluded to previously, Broadhead didn't like or trust Hallam but he was well aware that he was Crookes' right hand man. This didn't prevent him from putting his trust in Crookes despite the possibility of Hallam being able to incriminate them both. When being questioned by William Overend about the payments for the Wheatman & Smith job Broadhead stated that he *'had an objection to do with Hallam'* and *'I did not want to have anything to do with him.....I should have preferred paying it to Crookes because I should think the secret more likely to*

---

[421] Ibid, 9,192

be kept.[422] Being 13 years senior to Hallam, Crookes appears to have been the lead player in the deadly partnership and seemingly kept Hallam in check as a big brother would. Nevertheless, the possibility of Hallam breaking his confidence was a huge gamble for William Broadhead. Eventually Hallam did incriminate Crookes and Broadhead when called before the Commissioners in 1867, albeit after the ordeal of being jailed by William Overend for contempt of court when initially refusing to identify Crookes as his co-conspirator, and also with the full knowledge that if they all came clean they would not be prosecuted for their crimes.

Whilst Broadhead had more trust in Crookes, his number one henchman was not altogether straight with him. On the occasions that Crookes' enterprises did not totally fulfil the mischief intended, Broadhead would try to reduce the price that was agreed for the job. To counter this Crookes invented a fictitious accomplice called *'Nunk'* who he would still have to pay and any deviation in the price would mean that he would have to stand the difference as *'Nunk'* would have to be paid his agreed share. He could not risk upsetting *'Nunk'* as he may betray him. Broadhead was aware that should Crookes be compromised, then so would he and he couldn't risk that. Broadhead asked Crookes a number of times who this accomplice was but Crookes told him he only knew him as *'Nunk'*.[423]

It transpired that Crookes and Hallam were responsible for most of the serious outrages that made William Leng's headlines and brought the state of affairs to the attention of the government. But they weren't responsible for all of them.

[422] Ibid, 12,143-12,145
[423] Ibid, 13,569-13,591

At the conclusion of the Inquiry neither Crookes nor Hallam were in court to receive their certificates of indemnity. The procedure adopted was for a list of their offences to which they had confessed to be handed to each witness for them to consider and agree. Once they were satisfied that everything was in order, they would sign the papers and their certificate and any expenses would then be awarded. In their absence William Overend asked John Jackson if he would take Crookes' and Hallam's papers for them; the Chief Constable agreed. After due process both received their certificates but they were refused any expenses on the grounds that they *'did not come in the first instance and make a clear and full disclosure of all that they knew.'*[424]

File cutting.

---

[424] Ibid, p.449

William Broadhead – Villain or Working Class Hero?

'I am ruined, but I cannot complain, I must bear it.' [425]

William Broadhead was born in Whirlow[426] in September 1815 and became a saw grinder at a young age working in Sheffield and, according to one biography, the Loxley Valley,[427] although there may be some confusion here with regards to the mill on the River Loxley known as the Broadhead Wheel. This mill was tenanted by a man named William Broadhead but this was around 1741; obviously not our William Broadhead. Although no other Broadhead is associated with the mill it was known as the Broadhead Wheel up until 1868 when Edwin Denton bought the site, which had laid waste since the mill was swept away in the Great Inundation of 1864, and it was re-named 'Loxley Steel Works'.[428] He married 16 year-old Mary Jane Wilgos on 2

---

[425] William Broadhead after giving his evidence to the Commissioners, Ibid, 13,321

[426] In the 1851 census his place of birth is recorded as Ecclesall

[427] *The Concise Dictionary of National Biography, Volume I, A-F,* p.343

[428] Op. Cit. Crossley et al, p.39 For the story of Broadhead Wheel in the Great Inundation see Op. Cit. Drewry, pp.41-42

April 1836 and in 1841 was living in Garden Street with Mary Jane and their three children; Ann, aged 5; Martha, aged 2; and 1 month old Thomas Wilgos (we must assume that Mary Jane was pregnant with Ann when they married). Also in the household was 18 year-old servant girl Ann Horsefield and 16 year-old apprentice Henry Mann.[429]

William Broadhead

---

[429] 1841 census. It is unlikely that William Broadhead was also a licensee at Garden Street as the only public house I have found there is the Royal Exchange, number 64, and the earliest record I have found for it is 1856 when Edmund Darwent was the licensee. No house number is given on the 1841 census return and Broadhead is simply recorded as a saw grinder.

PLACE	HOUSES		NAMES of each Person who abode therein the preceding Night.	AGE and SEX		PROFESSION, TRADE, EMPLOYMENT, or of INDEPENDENT MEANS.	Where Born	
	Uninhabited or Building	Inhabited		Males	Females		Whether Born in same County	Whether Born in Scotland, Ireland, or Foreign Parts.
Gardens			William Broadhead	25		Saw G__ __r	y	
			Mary Jane do		20		y	
do			Ann __ do		5		y	
			Martha — do		2		y	
			Thomas do	1m			y	
do			Ann Horsfield		16	F V		
			Fanny Mann	16		F V	X	

Extract from 1841 census.

Broadhead acquired a good reputation amongst the Sheffield saw grinders and he became actively involved with the Saw Grinders' Union. He first acted as the organisation's secretary around 1842-43. In 1844 he was one of the signatories to an *'Address to the Public of Sheffield'* made by the grinding branches calling for legislation to address the unions' concerns about the working conditions of Sheffield grinders. Following a report by Dr. G C Holland entitled *'The Diseases of the Lungs from Mechanical Causes'*, which the unions had been involved in by helping to gather evidence, the Sheffield grinding trades made three demands upon the government: 1) *'A better ventilation in Grinding wheels through the medium of an apparatus, called a dust machine';* 2) *'That no boy or apprentice be put to work at the Grinding trades under 12 years of age';* 3) *'That all Grinding wheels should be cleaned annually, either by lime washing, or some other process.*[430] All three of these requirements and more were recommended by Dr. Holland but his report was not acted upon at this time and it was not until 1867 that these demands were partly met when the Factory and Workshops Acts prohibited children under 11 years of age working in grinding mills and the local Sanitary Inspector was given powers to enforce the installation of ventilation fans. It was not until 1908 that the grinding of metals was classed as a dangerous trade, and regulations on keeping grinding workshops clean were not introduced until October 1909.[431]

William Broadhead was elected secretary again in 1848 and was still in post at the time of the Royal Commission in 1867. Broadhead also became licensee of a public house and used some of the money he made from the business to support fellow saw grinders in times of need. He was landlord of a number of public houses over the years. In 1851 he and his family, which had now increased in number with the addition of daughters Caroline (8) and Catharine (6), and sons Joseph (4) and William (1), were living with his 24 year-old sister-in-law, Caroline Wilgos, licensee at the Burnt Tree Tavern at 83 Hoyle Street.[432] By 1852 William Broadhead had taken over the license there himself and he was also the keeper of the White Horse at 22 Copper Street.[433] He is recorded as having the Greyhound at 185 Gibraltar Street in 1856 whilst also still at the Burnt Tree

---

430 *Sheffield Independent,* 23 March 1844. One of the other signatories was John Drury, Secretary of the Razor Grinders' Union who was sentenced to 7 years transportation in 1848
431 Op. Cit. Johnson
432 Kelly's Directory 1854
433 White's Directory 1852

Tavern.[434] He was still at the Greyhound in 1862 but moved to the Royal George at 62 Carver Street in 1863 where he stayed until 1867. Throughout the years that he was secretary the Saw Grinders' Union committee would meet in a back room or an upstairs room away from the public bar in whichever pub Broadhead was keeping at the time. The Union's general meetings would also be held there.

The Greyhound, 185 Gibraltar Street prior to demolition. The greyhound relief above the entrance was saved and kept at the Kelham Island Industrial Museum but was subsequently stolen.

Broadhead's reputation as a local trade union leader grew as the saw grinders gained higher prices in the 1840s and became one of the best paid of the Sheffield trades; despite being a hard and physically demanding job, it was one of the more sought after occupations. Despite a slump in trade in 1857 Broadhead maintained high wages for the saw

---

[434] White's Directory 1856

grinders by strictly excluding newcomers and 'buying up' surplus labour by paying *'scale'* money to those *'on the box'* that almost matched what they would earn at the grindstone.[435] Between 1857 and 1867 there would be from between 50 and 80 of the 190 union members *'on the box'* at any one time, which cost the union about £40 per week. This of course had to be found from the subscriptions of the men in work and at times their *'natty'* reached as much as 4s-6d in the £ of their earnings.[436] However, during this period Sheffield saw makers' and saw handle makers' wages dropped by as much as 33% and 50%.[437] To many Sheffield saw grinders Broadhead was a hero.

William Broadhead and his family at the Burnt Tree, 83 Hoyle Street (1851 census)

His work with the Saw Grinders' Union brought William Broadhead into contact with other union leaders of various Sheffield trades and he became one of the founder members of the Sheffield Association of Organised Trades, the fore-

---

[435] Op. Cit. Pollard
[436] Ibid
[437] Ibid

runner of the Sheffield Trades Council, in 1858.[438] The Association was formed following a dispute in the printing trade when union members resisted a reduction in wages at the *Sheffield Times*. In October 1858, Samuel Harrison,[439] owner of the *Sheffield Times*, locked his workers out and recruited non-union men from London, implementing a strict non-union regime by way of *'the document';* a promise not to join a union enforced on his staff.[440] In response the print workers issued a pejorative statement entitled *'The Press Trampling on the Rights of Labour'.[441]* At this Harrison launched a <u>liable</u> action against George Bingham and William Dronfield, president and secretary respectively of the Sheffield Journeymen Printers' Association. In response to this legal threat a meeting of the Sheffield trades was called at the Town Hall on 10 November where a committee was appointed to carry out four resolutions agreed by the delegates present. The first three resolutions recognised the lock out at the *Sheffield Times* as an attack on all trade unions; condemned Samuel Harrison's liable action against

LIBEL!

---

[438] This was not the first time that Sheffield trade union leaders considered a local alliance. On 22 May 1843 it was reported that a meeting of trades' delegates passed resolutions in favour of a union of all the trades of the town: Op. Cit. Leader, 1843, p.385

[439] Samuel Harrison wrote the first book about the Sheffield Flood of 1864: *The Complete History of the Great Flood at Sheffield,* published by S Harrison, Sheffield Times Office, 1864

[440] This was not the first time that employers took the offensive by imposing *'the document'* on workers. The tactic was used by hard-line employers up and down the country following the Tolpuddle Martyrs case of 1836. Op. Cit. Hopkins, p.43

[441] www.sheffieldtuc.co.uk/history

the printers who issued the statement; and condemned the legal action against the Sheffield Journeymen Printers' Association. The fourth and most significant resolution, which was proposed by Mr. F. Wood of the white metal smiths and seconded by Mr. W. Hydes of the saw makers concluded:

'That this meeting cannot separate without the expression of a hope that the working classes will perceive in this case the necessity of banding themselves together, and maintaining a close connection on some permanent basis, with the view of securing for their labour that protection which will assure it against attacks of a similar character to that now complained of.'[442]

The appointment of a committee was the fifth and final resolution of the meeting and William Broadhead was one of those appointed. The dispute with Harrison was eventually resolved and he was persuaded to drop the ~~liable~~ action. However, it was a costly affair for the trade unions with legal and other fees amounting to around £1,000. It was clear to everyone that without coming together to fight Harrison the outcome would have been disastrous, not only for the printers' union but for the whole trade union movement. This ensured the success of the fourth resolution as formal rules were drawn up for the Association which were passed at another meeting of the Sheffield trades on 7 June 1859. The rules were confirmed at a further meeting on 22 June and an executive committee of the association, now called the Association of Organised Trades of Sheffield and Neighbourhood, was elected; Charles Bagshaw (Fork

---

[442] Ibid

Grinders Union) was elected president; William Dronfield, secretary; and William Broadhead, treasurer.[443]

The propensity for employer lock-outs increased into the 1860s, the most damaging in Sheffield being the 16 weeks lock-out of the file trades in 1866, and in July of that year the Sheffield Association called a conference of trade unions to try to establish a means of defending themselves against these tactics. This conference began the process of establishing a short-lived coalition of around 60 affiliated unions that between them claimed 60,000 members, calling itself the United Kingdom Alliance of Organised Trades.[444] The Alliance was inaugurated in December 1866 and being the main instigators of its creation the three executives of the Sheffield Association were elected to its respective executive positions: Charles Bagshaw was elected president; William Dronfield secretary; and William Broadhead treasurer.[445] Broadhead resigned his position on 20 June 1867 following his confessions at the Commissioners' Inquiry.[446] He also resigned as secretary of the Saw Grinders Union but the members voted their confidence in him and he was re-elected. However, he lost his license at the Royal

---

[443] Ibid

[444]Op. Cit. Fraser, p.41. This was not the first time that Sheffield trade unions considered a national alliance. It was reported in the *Sheffield Local Register*, p.441 on 10 May 1847 that *'Many of the trades of the town had meetings to hear explanations of the working and objects of the National Trades' Union, when several of them agreed to join.'*

[445] Op. Cit. www.sheffieldtuc.co.uk/history According to William Broadhead in his evidence at the Inquiry on 21 June 1867, George Austin, secretary of the Railway Spring Makers' Union was now president of the UK Alliance. Op. Cit. TUC, 12,939

[446] Op. Cit. TUC, 12,919

George, which was taken over by James Elshaw. By the end of 1867 the United Kingdom Alliance had collapsed after just two further meetings in 1867 (one in Manchester, the other in Preston) due to the unions' failure to regularly pay the necessary levies required to finance the organisation.[447] However, the initiative did not end there as in the following year (1868) a further national meeting of trade unions took place in Manchester which turned out to be the first Trades Union Congress (TUC).

Saw grinding[448]

When the Commissioners sat to take evidence in 1867 William Broadhead had been secretary of the Saw Grinders' Union for almost 20 years and although some people knew of his extreme methods, and many more suspected them, he

---

[447] Op. Cit' Pelling, p.59
[448] Op. Cit. Taylor, p.279

was still held in high esteem amongst his peers within the Sheffield trade union movement and nationally. It is also worth noting that despite huge sums being offered in rewards for bringing the perpetrators of outrage to justice, especially following the New Hereford Street outrage which caused such a great outcry, no-one was ever tempted to claim them by betraying Broadhead. Some would say this was out of a misguided sense of loyalty, others out of fear for their personal safety. Considering just how much a temptation such rewards would have been to people struggling to eke a living at this time I would argue the former was more likely the case. *The Times* commented on the general opinion of the negative response to the rewards:

'It was said…with all appearance of truth, that a million of money, if it were offered, would not produce the revelations desired…'[449]

However, following the revelations at the Inquiry Broadhead was cast as the villain of the piece and on at least one occasion when leaving the court he needed police protection from an angry crowd, although there would have been few, if any, saw grinders amongst it.

Charles Reade characterised William Broadhead in his novel with the iniquitous Mr. Grotait, who was also secretary of the Saw Grinders' Union with the nickname *'Old Smite 'em'*. There is no hiding Reade's bias in the saga, for him Broadhead/Grotait was pure villain but he was also capable of showing some compassion. In reality, according to one contemporary account, William Broadhead bore *'no resemblance to the common idea of an assassin or a*

---

[449] *The Times*, 29 June 1867

conspirator, but is a jolly, corpulent, good-looking man, apparently satisfied with life, and with whom the world has dealt kindly. [450] In another Broadhead is described as *'stout, ruddy, active, self-confident, and respectable-looking'* and in another *'a jolly, good-looking man, more like a well-to-do farmer than an artisan brought up to a dangerous and unwholesome trade.'* [451]

There is no doubt that, in his own words, Broadhead *'was ruined'* by the disclosures in court. But he still had a circle of supporters who stood by him despite the public vilification. Regardless of his wrongdoings, which included embezzlement of the union's funds to pay for the rattenings and outrages, there was a wide acceptance that everything he did, he did for the well-being of the Sheffield saw trades and for the benefit of the trade union movement, and that in doing what he did he put himself at great risk of prosecution which could have led him to the gallows; in the case of James Linley he was liable to have been tried as an accessory before the fact of murder. In this respect he had put his own life on the line for the cause.

Payments for the rattenings, shootings and gunpowder attacks were initially made by Broadhead using money siphoned off the contributions a little at a time; he had no authority to do this. Contributions to the Saw Grinders' Union at this time averaged around £40 per week. When a member paid him, say 10s, he would put 3s of it aside to cover these illegitimate expenses; there was no check on members' payments. In 1861 an investigating committee was set up within the union, separate to the regular committee, whose purpose was to investigate members who

[450] Op. Cit. Pollard, from *Beehive,* 22 June 1867
[451] Ibid, from *Sheffield Independent*

were in arrears with their contributions. This investigating committee consisted of four members: J. Coldwell; J. Turner; T. Parkin; and E. Machin. Broadhead would provide them with a list of members in arrears at the end of each month and they would decide on how best to deal with them. Broadhead would pay for any rattenings, which were usually undertaken by a union member who worked at the same wheel or workplace as the man in arrears. In June 1865 a new union ruling allowed the investigating committee to claim expenses from the union's funds. Although these expenses were to pay for illegal activities they were never divulged and no minute book was kept. Resolutions passed by the investigating committee were written on a sheet of paper and passed to Broadhead, who would then obtain the money from the treasurer to cover the costs of the committee's expenses. Payments were recorded in the union's accounts simply as 'expenses of the investigating committee'.[452] Broadhead destroyed the sheets and the books covering this period prior to the Commissioners Inquiry.

We have learnt that Broadhead didn't trust James Hallam, who was the first to incriminate him at the Inquiry, and had Hallam informed on Broadhead without the protection offered by the Act there would have been a more serious outcome for them both, and for Samuel Crookes. In fact from the evidence he gave at the Inquiry we learn that Hallam did make a statement to the Chief Constable, John Jackson, witnessed by solicitor William Fretson, confessing his involvement in a number of rattenings and outrages and he did indeed implicate Broadhead. He later retracted this statement out of fear for his personal safety but it isn't clear as to why he made it in the first place. At the Inquiry Hallam

---

[452] Op. Cit. TUC, 12,357

initially denied ever making the statement but we can be sure that he did as William Overend tricked him into saying something which confirmed that he was at Wheatman and Smith's on the night that gunpowder exploded in the drain under the works, just as he had told John Jackson and William Fretson, which he now claimed was a false statement:

Overend: *'Did you tell them* [Jackson and Fretson] *that it was about eleven o'clock at night, and that when you found there was no likelihood of the men going you resolved to fire it and take the consequences?'*

Hallam: *'Yes.'*

Overend: *'You told them that?'*

Hallam: *'Yes.'*

Overend: *'Did you tell them that it was a very cold, bitter night, and that you had to keep running up and down to keep your feet warm?'*

Hallam: *'Ah! It wur an all.'*

Overend: *'Then you were there were you? You said "Ah! It wur an all." You said that it was a very cold night, when you were there?'*

Hallam: *'I did not say I was there.'*

Overend: *'Well was it a cold night?'*

Hallam: *'That night it was done?'*

Overend: *'You did not mean to say that you intended to say that you were there.'*

Hallam: *'No, I was not there.'*[453]

Clearly Hallam was there, and despite continuing to deny it at this point, it was obvious to the Commissioners

---

[453] Ibid, 6,526-6,531

that he had also made the statement to John Jackson. This was confirmed later when Hallam returned to the witness box after his six days of solitary confinement in the Town Hall cell for contempt of court. What isn't clear is why the Chief Constable didn't act on this initial statement and question William Broadhead, who appears to have had a lucky escape at this time.

Broadhead never carried out violent attacks himself; he orchestrated others who were more accustomed to sorting things out with their fists or a life preserver; chiefly Samuel Crookes and James Hallam. He also hired the later to be convicted murderer Joseph Myers, a saw grinder and fellow member of the union, to run errands on occasions, paying him small sums of between two and four shillings, but not to undertake any criminal activities.[454] As for the shootings and bombings, such incidents had occurred in Sheffield long before Broadhead came on the scene. And even during his time in office not all of the outrages brought before the Commissioners were of Broadhead's instigation. Arguably the worst of all the outrages, at Acorn Street, was nothing to do with Broadhead at all yet no-one remembers Robert Renshaw. Although there was a great risk of killing someone with a can of gunpowder Broadhead never intended taking anyone's life, only to damage property. The shootings were also meant to disable and not to kill. He was indirectly responsible for the death of James Linley but he bitterly regretted it. The custom of threatening letters from *'Tantia Topee'* and other such pseudonyms were not sinister forewarnings of inevitable violence; they were designed as an attempt to resolve issues and to give time for reconciliation before resorting to violence. Those who

---

[454] Ibid, 13,211

received them knew exactly what to expect should they not take action to resolve their dispute with the trade.

The indemnity awarded by the Commissioners' certificate prevented Broadhead facing the full force of the law but he paid for his crimes in other ways. He found great difficulty in making his living in Sheffield after losing his licence at the Royal George. His status took a tumble and although he remained with the Saw Grinders' Union he had lost the power and influence that he once had within the trade and the wider trade union movement. Prior to all this he had also suffered the loss of his 26-year-old son Thomas Wilgos who had died on 25 April 1867 following an unspecified 'lingering illness'.[455]In 1869, with the help of his band of supporters in the saw trades and the Sheffield Emigration Committee, money was raised to pay for Broadhead's fare to America where he hoped to make a new life for himself working with his cousin at a Philadelphia saw mill.[456] However, what hopes he had failed to materialise as the job he was promised fell through just days before his arrival. Being unable to find work he returned to England in February the following year, walking straight into more controversy. His return to Sheffield was soon made known to the Emigration Committee and there were calls for the money given to him to be paid back.

---

[455] *Sheffield Independent, 26 April 1867*

[456] Having searched passenger lists to America for 1869 I have found just one William Broadhead, who is of the right age (54) but he is listed as a farmer. This may be an attempt to hide his true identity, being the now infamous secretary of the Sheffield Saw Grinders' Union. He travelled alone in steerage class on the Cunard Line's ship 'Etna' arriving in America on 18 December.

114 New Meadow Street with the Meadow Street Hotel on the
opposite corner of Sudbury Street (Drawing by author)

Within a week of his return Broadhead was called before
the committee, ironically at his former public house, the
Royal George, on 15 February to explain the reasons for his
return. The chair of the committee, Rev. John Francis Witty,
was of the opinion that he ought to have found other work in
America. Broadhead assured him that he had tried but to no
avail (it is possible that his involvement in the Sheffield
Outrages were now known to Philadelphia employers). The
committee was split on whether Broadhead should be made
to repay the money. After what must have been a heated
discussion it was finally agreed that Broadhead could keep
the money but two members of the committee were so

incensed by the decision that they resigned there and then. Another member, one Mr. Wright, made it known what he thought of the decision by declaring that the committee would no longer be welcome to hold its meetings in his house.[457]

Broadhead's now well publicised return to Sheffield (the outcome of the Emigration Committee's meeting was reported in the local press) didn't help his job prospects back in Sheffield either but he was able to set up a small grocery and provisions business at 114 New Meadow Street, on the corner of Sudbury Street across from the Meadow Street Hotel. From the 1871 census we find that William Broadhead junior, now 22 years old, had followed his father into the saw grinding trade and William Broadhead senior had become a grandfather. Daughter Catharine, now 25 years old, had married Joseph Baker, a 24 year-old fork and rivet maker and lived with the Broadhead family with their 8 month-old son John W Baker. We must assume that William Broadhead spent the rest of his days at New Meadow Street as his wife was still running the shop in 1879.[458] By 1881 the shop was Benjamin Taylor's furniture store.[459] William Broadhead died on 15 March 1879 aged 63 and was buried at Ecclesall. Two days later the *Sheffield Independent* printed an obituary on William Broadhead which indicated that public animosity towards him had waned since the exposure of his crimes, or perhaps the press now had a little more understanding of the reasoning behind them:

---

[457] Op. Cit. Drinkall, *Book of Days,* p.48
[458] White's Directory 1879
[459] Kelly's Directory 1881

'His crimes were due, not to malicious disposition, but to a grievously mistaken view of the interests of his trade and the duty he owed it.'[460]

I concur with this view and I believe William Broadhead was a casualty of his passion for trade unionism and what he perceived his duty towards those who he represented in the continuing conflict between capital and labour. We cannot condone his actions but he made no personal gain from his criminal activities and held no personal grudge against, nor had a quarrel with any of his victims; they were purely and simply *'obnoxious to the trade'*. It is clear that his motivation, albeit misguided, was to protect the saw trade and to progress the trade union cause. We must also consider his methods in the context of the times; Victorian Britain was a comparatively violent society and there were others who followed the same path to achieve the same objectives for their own trades. Broadhead took the opportunity offered by the very public questioning of the Commissioners to justify himself to a degree, and to argue the case for the legal recognition of trade unions and for the protection of their funds in law:

'I took this view, that there being no law for the trades I conceived the notion that I had a right to take those courses [outrages] *in the absence of a law, and that the end would justify the means.'*[461]

'I believe this, that if the law would give them [trade unions] *some power, if there was a law created to give them some power to recover contributions without having*

---

[460] Op. Cit. Pollard, *Sheffield Independent,* 17 March 1879
[461] Op. Cit. TUC, 12,970

recourse to such measures [rattenings and outrages] *there would be no more heard of them.* '[462]

'*I now wish to say for the benefit of my fellow working men and the country at large that if a legislative measure was adopted to meet these things it would destroy these acts that have taken place and which have placed me in this painful position.* '[463]

'*I wish to God for it* [intimidation] *to be abandoned and the protection of the law given in its stead.* '[464]

To round off his interrogation William Overend's last question to William Broadhead was to ask him about the threatening letters and if he wrote them. Broadhead confessed that he had written most of them but not all; he had written those signed 'Tantia Topee'.[465]

Nationally the trade unions were keen to distance themselves from Broadhead's crimes and a meeting of trade unionists was held at Exeter Hall in London, famous for its religious and philanthropic gatherings,[466] to express their horror and indignation at his unlawful activities.[467] Speaker after speaker expressed their detestation of Broadhead's regime of violent intimidation. However, one attendee of the meeting, Professor Edward Spencer Beesly, used the event as an opportunity to condemn the actions of the Jamaican

---

[462] Ibid, 13,241

[463] Ibid, 13,243

[464] Ibid, 12,203

[465] Ibid, 13,335

[466] Op. Cit. Chesney, p.15

[467] Harrison, Royden, *Professor Beesly and the Working Class Movement,* in Op. Cit. Briggs and Saville, p.225-226

Governor, Edward John Eyre,[468] by comparing the indignation of the middle-classes at Broadhead's outrages in the interests of the workers with those perpetrated by Eyre in the interests of property and wealth; there were no meetings called to denounce Governor Eyre.

Despite his methods being meant to benefit the trade unions Broadhead's notoriety prompted a euphemism for a course of action that would hold back or regress the trade unions which was used by George Howell, a member of the Trades Union Congress Parliamentary Committee, when he condemned Joseph Chamberlain's quadrilateral of 'Free Church; Free Land; Free Schools; Free Labour' as 'Broadheadism'.[469]

---

[468] John Edward Eyre (1815-1901) appointed Governor of Jamaica in 1864. He forcibly suppressed a native rebellion at Morant Bay in 1865, proclaiming martial law. Eyre confirmed the sentence of death on George William Gordon, a black member of the Jamaican legislature, and over 600 other natives: *The Concise Dictionary of National Biography, Volume I A-F,* Oxford University Press, 1994 p.956
[469] Op. Cit. Briggs and Saville, p.237

Sheffield Outrages: The Legacy

'I believe (and I think my colleagues agree with me) that great good will be found to arise from this inquiry, and that, however painful the inquiry may have been, the result of this investigation will be great benefit to this town and to the country generally.'[470]

All of the cases examined by the Commissioners had been reported to the police and the town magistrates immediately or soon after they had occurred and of the estimated 60 trade unions in Sheffield, just 12 were found to have been implicated in them. Therefore, some 48 trade unions had no charges made against them whatsoever. Of course this doesn't mean there was no complicity to rattenings or acts of violence amongst their members. In fact we can safely assume that over the half century or longer that rattenings had been customary within the Sheffield trades, not just the 10 years under the Commissioners' scrutiny, there would have been many such cases involving other unions that were simply not reported or recorded. Many that were reported were beyond the detection capabilities of the police. There were of course a number of incidents that were reported and

---

[470] William Overend in his closing statement on the final day of the Commissioners' Inquiry, Monday 8 July 1867

dealt with, the perpetrators being prosecuted and punished. Nevertheless, the official account of the Sheffield Outrages, as reported by the Royal Commission, indicated that just 20% of the trade unions were involved and that the other 80%, a good majority, were not involved in any of the violent attacks or high profile rattenings. If we look at the numbers in more detail, of the 14 trade unions that were implicated in the outrages, 9 were grinding unions but only a small number of union members were actually involved in the instigation or perpetration of the shootings or gunpowder attacks. *The Times,* on reviewing the Inquiry, whilst condemning the trade unions for the outrages, accepted that the actual perpetrators were a small minority:

'We have brought this review of the evidence to a point at which it becomes perfectly clear that the Sheffield 'trade outrages' are beyond any question the work of Trades' Unions – that is to say, they were perpetrated by union men, at the instance of a union officer, for union purposes, at the expense of union funds. We fear, too, that the officers of some of these unions must be charged with a species of connivance, for it is hardly creditable that they could have been blind, except of wilful purpose, to the abstraction of their money. But we can still remark with sincere satisfaction that the great body of unionists remain free from complicity in these crimes.' [471]

There were two deaths as a result of 'trade' violence and one other murder in Sheffield between 1854 and 1864; that being the murder of Alice Myers by her husband Joseph (see above). Neither of the 'trade' deaths was intended but when

---

[471] *The Times,* 29 June 1867

you shoot a gun at someone or drop bombs down cellar grates, or through people's windows, someone is inevitably going to be seriously hurt or killed. The deaths of James Linley and Bridget O'Rourke were what the Americans today would insensitively call 'collateral damage'. A look at the crime statistics for this period informs us that three murders in ten years was no more than the average number of murders in Sheffield at this time.[472] This also applies to the level of violent attacks, which was no more than the norm; there were far more violent attacks due to drink than there were due to 'trade affairs'. The Commissioners, in their questioning, nearly always asked the victims in the witness box whether they had any enemies or had had a quarrel with anyone prior to them being attacked so as to satisfy themselves that it was a trade union or members of a trade union that were behind each incident. In the wider picture 'trade affairs' would have been at the root of a very small proportion of the total number of violent incidents in Sheffield at a time when an exchange of words soon turned into an exchange of blows. Yet, when such incidents occurred the press was keen to emphasise that the unions were behind them. In essence the Sheffield press, led by William Leng, blew the issue up out of proportion so as to vilify and denounce the trade unions at the behest of the industrial masters; it was not simply sensational journalism but also capitalist propaganda in the ongoing conflict

---

[472] There were 5 people executed for murder in Sheffield between 1835 and 1853, Op. Cit. Bentley, *Sheffield Hanged,* p.79; 4 between 1875 and 1885; and 3 between 1887 and 1893. Op. Cit. Bentley, *Sheffield Murderers,* p.31

between industrial capital and labour.[473] Although the Outrages were a local issue they had wider implications. Leng knew that as Sheffield had historically taken a leading part in the development of trade unions the image of trade union violence in the town that he portrayed in the pages of the *Sheffield Daily Telegraph* would reflect upon and affect the image of the trade union movement nationally. William Leng was not alone amongst the anti-trade union press in Sheffield. Robert Leader, the editor of the *Sheffield Independent*, *Sheffield Local Register* and *Reminiscences of Old Sheffield,* was just as outspoken and even attacked Dr. G. Calvert Holland for his support of trade unions following his study into the health of Sheffield grinders in 1841.[474] In the Preface of his report Dr. Holland comments:

'We were fully prepared to meet with opposition, but scarcely from the press, of a character as dastardly as it is vindictive – as persecuting as it is unprincipled – and especially from the liberal *press, that boasts of the advantage of free inquiry – of unshackled discussion.'[475]*

He concludes the Preface by including a copy of one of the four articles printed by Leader in the 18 December issue of the *Sheffield Independent* to illustrate Leader's personal attacks upon him.

---

[473] Leng would later be rewarded with a knighthood (1887) and Sheffield's dignitaries presented him with his portraite by H.F. Crighton and 600 guineas (£630) from subscriptions.
[474] Holland, George Calvert M.D., *The Mortality, Sufferings and Diseases of Grinders Part II – Pen-Blade Grinders,* Ridge and Jackson, 1842, pp.iv-v
[475] Ibid

However, if the industrialists and leading civic dignitaries (who were very often one and the same) thought that the Inquiry would put an end to the trade unions' power to intervene in trade and the labour market, especially after the exposure of William Broadhead's crimes and the confessions of other union members to two murders, they were very much mistaken. In fact the Inquiry helped to bring about changes in the law that would strengthen the trade unions; changes that would prove to be crucial in the development of the trade union movement as a whole.

Of course the trade unions too had welcomed the Inquiries, especially the London version, which was used by them to good effect in convincing the Commissioners that the trade unions' legal position put them at a disadvantage and that it was that situation which engendered activities outside of the law as the only alternative, including the violent incidents that had occurred at Sheffield. In Sheffield, William Overend was also persuaded by Broadhead's assertion that if the unions had recourse to law to recover contributions, illegal means would probably never have been used:

'I daresay there is something in that, and it is for that reason I want it clearly shown to the legislature that they may have the means of legislating properly upon the subject if it ought to be legislated upon?'[476]

---

[476] Op. Cit. TUC, 13,242

In summing up at the end of the Sheffield Commissioners' Report, William Overend made the point that during the ten years that was covered by the Inquiry there had not occurred *'any act of intimidation, outrage, or wrong promoted, encouraged, or connived at by any association of employers.'*[477] However, he failed to include any comments on individual employers' actions that had provoked disputes with the trade unions, such as the 10% reduction in saw grinders' wages at Samuel Newbould's in

Robert Applegarth

1855; the 50% reduction in fork grinders' earnings in 1859 after table knife grinders took in fork grinding; William Darwin's 10% reduction of scissor grinders' wages in 1866; and the more recent bullying of the puddlers at John Brown

---

[477] Ibid, p.xvi

& Co. with another 10% reduction in wages imposed on them in February 1867. He also stated that matters connected to the rules of trade unions such as their setting of prices/wages; the number of apprentices allowed into the trades and their qualifications to join the respective trades; restrictions on outsiders; and general policies adopted by individual trade unions, would be purposely excluded from their Report and left for the consideration of the London Commissioners.

The Sheffield Report's final paragraph commented on the Commissioners' powers to grant certificates of indemnity to witnesses:

'We are convinced that the most material disclosures made to us were so made in reliance on our promise of indemnity made in conformity with the Act of Parliament. Had no such indemnity been offered, we are satisfied, that we should never have obtained any clear and conclusive evidence touching the most important subjects of our inquiry, and that the system of crime which has now been disclosed, as well as the perpetrators, would have remained undiscovered; we have therefore granted certificates to all witnesses whom we believe to have made a full and true disclosure of all offences in which they have been implicated.'[478]

The Report was signed by the three Commissioners on 2 August 1867.

The setting up of the London Royal Commission, although parallel to the Sheffield Commission, assumed a different approach in the selection of its members, who had

---

[478] Ibid

a more sympathetic attitude towards trade unions. This was partly due to the proactive approach of the national union leaders, later described by the social reformers and historians Sidney and Beatrice Webb as the *'Junta',*[479] who had demanded that at least two trade unionists sat on the bench. This of course was rejected by the government but they did accede to the unions nominating one of the Commissioners. The Junta's nominee was the Positivist[480] author and barrister Frederic Harrison.[481] The appointment of Liberal MP, barrister and Christian Socialist writer Thomas Hughes added a second trade union sympathiser to the London court. The chairman of the London Commission was Sir William Erle.[482]

---

[479] The five union leaders, who formed the Conference of Amalgamated Trades, were Robert Applegarth and William Allan of the Amalgamated Society of Engineers; Edwin Coulson, of the Operative Bricklayers' Society; George Odger, a shoemaker and secretary of the London Trades Council; and Daniel Guile of the Friendly Society of Iron Founders. Op. Cit. Pelling, p.48. Sidney and Beatrice Webb wrote *The History of Trade Unionism,* 1894.

[480] Positivism: Philosophical system of Auguste Comte, recognising only positive facts and observable phenomena, and rejecting metaphysics and theism. See Robertson, David, *Dictionary of Politics,* Penguin Books, 1993, p.392

[481] Frederic Harrison (1831-1923), called to the bar (Lincoln's Inn) 1858; president of English Positivist Committee, 1880-1905; secretary, Royal Commission for Digesting the Law, 1869-1870. *The Concise Dictionary of National Biography, Volume II G-M,* Oxford University Press, 1994, p.1334

[482] Sir William Erle (1793-1880), judge; MP for city of Oxford 1837; lord chief-justice of common pleas 1859-1866. *The Concise Dictionary of National Biography, Volume I A-F,* Oxford University Press, 1994, p.937

Two of the national union leaders, Robert Applegarth and William Allan of the Amalgamated Society of Engineers, proved to be impressive and most influential witnesses. Unlike at Sheffield, where the union leaders were at first in denial and then uncovered as being parties to criminal activities before going on the defence, the national leaders were able to present trade unions as predominantly friendly societies, arguing that far from being instigators of industrial conflict they were essentially a restraint on strikes.[483] They were more able than William Broadhead in presenting the argument for the legal protection of trade union funds. Applegarth, who along with William Dronfield had been consulted by the government on the format of the Inquiries and who had advocated the controversial indemnity element,[484] asserted that trade unions were a force for order and stability in industrial relations, not the violently disruptive organisations portrayed by the Sheffield industrialists and the Sheffield press. The Minority Report delivered to the government by Frederic Harrison strongly supported Applegarth's argument.

The government's response to Harrison's Report was almost immediate in bringing forward a number of interim measures to improve the trade unions' legal status. Their first move was to amend the Master and Servant Act. The original Act determined that an employee's breach of contract was a criminal act and could lead to a gaol sentence, whereas employers were only liable to civil action.[485] This meant that

---

[483] Op. Cit. Fraser, p.46

[484] Op. Cit. Derry, p.152

[485] Between 1858 and 1875 there was an average of 10,000 prosecutions and 6,000 convictions of workmen in England

employers could threaten strikers and their union leaders with legal action for breach of contract that could lead to their imprisonment. The amendment of 1867 limited criminal action to 'aggravated cases'.[486] In the following year a Bill introduced by Russell Gurney, MP for Southampton, provided for any organisation to take legal action in cases of larceny or embezzlement. Although not specifically mentioned in the Act, it included trade unions.[487] The Trades Unions' Funds Protection Act 1869 allowed a trade union, even in restraint of trade, to take legal action. The most significant piece of legislation that came out of the Minority Report was the Trade Union Act 1871, which permanently protected the funds of registered trade unions and removed any liability for being in restraint of trade.[488] In 1875 the Master and Servant Act was repealed and replaced with the Employers and Workmen Act which made both equal before the law.[489]

The changes in the law during the years following the two Royal Commissions, as well as the improvements in communication brought about by the expanding railways, technical advances in telegraphy, the spread of literacy and the availability of cheaper newspapers, engendered an increase in the number of trade union members and enhanced the development of trade unionism. The very first Trade Union Congress met in 1868 when there were 118,367 TUC affiliated trade union members. Ten years later there were

---

and Wales per year under the Master and Servant Act. Op. Cit. Best, p.297

[486] Op. Cit. Pelling, p.53

[487] Op. Cit. Fraser, p.46

[488] Ibid

[489] Op. Cit. Best, p.298 and Op. Cit. Fraser, p.69

114 affiliated unions with 623,957 affiliated members. By 1898 the numbers had grown to 188 affiliated unions and 1,093,191 affiliated union members.[490] Adding the trade unions not affiliated to the TUC, there were a total of 1,326 trade unions registered in Great Britain and Northern Ireland in 1898 with a total membership of 1,752,000.[491] By 1900 trade union membership had grown to 2 million; 12% of Britain's labour force.[492] This period also saw the emergence of large national trade unions amongst the skilled workforce. By 1880 the Amalgamated Society of Engineers had a membership of 44,000; the Amalgamated Carpenters' Society had 18,000 members; the Operative Stonemasons' Society, 13,000; and the Society of Boilermakers had 18,000 members.[493]

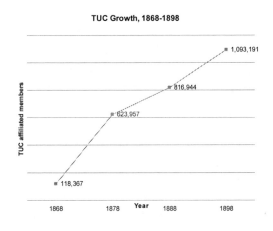

TUC Growth, 1868-1898

[490] Coates, Ken and Topham, Tony, *Trade Unions in Britain,* Fontana Press, 1988, p.131
[491] Op. Cit. Pelling, p.302
[492] Op. Cit. Thompson, p.241
[493] Op. Cit. Fraser, p.52

There is little doubt that the Sheffield Outrages were a catalyst for change in British industrial relations to the benefit of trade unions and that trade unions have since played a significant role in shaping Britain; a role that they continue to perform despite the decline in trade union membership in recent years and successive political attacks upon them, chiefly from Tory governments.[494] One wonders what direction the conflict between capital and labour might have taken had there not been those Royal Commissions in 1867; what would the alternative social and economic history of Britain have looked like and what sort of society would we be living in today had there been no Sheffield Outrages?

To echo the sentiments of my first book, on the Great Sheffield Flood of 1864, I believe that the Sheffield Outrages have also been somewhat airbrushed out of the city's history. Ask people in the streets of Sheffield today what they know about the Sheffield Outrages and too many will look at you with a blank face and shrug their shoulders. Only those with a keen interest in local history will be able to tell you anything about them. Few local historians have taken more than a cursory interest in the subject and there is scarce coverage on the shelves of local book stores. The civic dignitaries of the 1860s naturally took a keen interest in the subject matter but I remember nothing of a civic commemoration of any kind in the 1960s; my apologies to anyone whose event I may have missed but at that time I too was one of those who knew nothing about the Sheffield

---

[494] As this is being written David Cameron's Tory Government are pushing through yet another anti-trade union Bill – the Trade Unions Act 2015.

Outrages. One would expect the local museums to give the subject a high profile but only the Kelham Island Industrial Museum has a permanent display on the Outrages, which is well worth a visit. What has been written on the outrages has tended to vilify and condemn Sheffield trade unionists as murderous outlaws and be inclined to show the employers, the non-union and anti-union workers as being long suffering victims of their bullying; the masters were the 'good guys' and the trade unionists were the 'baddies'. As with most histories of conflict it is generally written by the victors and also generally bias. Although no winners came out of the Inquiry the employers had the media on their side and the immediate emphasis in the Sheffield press was on the guilt of those exposed, William Broadhead and the saw grinders in particular, and there was little debate about why honest working people were driven to criminal actions in defence of their right to earn a decent living. Social historians tend to limit their comment on the Outrages and as we have seen it was more than simply 'acts of violence against blacklegs in the cutlery trade, including the blowing up of a workman's house in October 1866' as Eric Hopkins relates in his history of the English working classes.[495] Sheffield trade unionists were painted as brutal criminals and that is how the history of the Sheffield Outrages has been traditionally handed down. But as we have seen, there is much more to the story and if we resist taking the moral high ground and consider the Outrages in the socio-economic context of the time, and objectively, we can have some sympathy for the 'baddies'.

Of course rattenings continued long after the Commissioners' Inquiry and unruly, sometimes violent

---

[495] Op. Cit. Hopkins, p.153

strikes continued to plague Sheffield's industrial relations. The use of gunpowder missiles subsided but shootings continued to be a problem for the local authorities. For example, in 1869 a dispute between the Tinsley Coal Company, owned by Benjamin Huntsman, and miners at the Manor Castle Colliery was the backdrop to shootings that resulted in two people being seriously injured. Trade union miners were locked out at the pit and non-union men were brought in. The likelihood of violent clashes between the two determined that a police escort was provided for the non-union men as they went into work at the pit. It transpired that some of these men carried firearms for their own protection. On the night of 10 July 1869 Joseph Jackson, the police officer escorting the men, and who was stationed at the Manor, had to leave them after apprehending a man for stealing a fawn. Jackson returned to Sheffield with the man in custody leaving the non-union miners to proceed the final quarter of a mile to the colliery gates unescorted. At this point some of the men readied their firearms, which included a six-barrel revolver and a blunderbuss. It wasn't long before the first incident occurred when a man by the name of Davis, who was reported as being 'in a state of liquor', let off a number of shots, one of which hit a woman named Sykes, who came close to death but eventually made a recovery. It isn't clear if this incident was connected to the dispute at the pit but the second incident involved a clash with union miners which resulted in a collier named John Nixon being shot in the thigh by Samuel Arblaster with a blunderbuss. Samuel's brother, Richard Arblaster, also fired a pistol in the disturbance and there were reports of other shots being fired by the union men.[496]

---

[496] *Rotherham Independent,* 31 March 1870

Before considering my own conclusion to the history of the Sheffield Outrages I invite the reader to mull over the thoughts of a couple of earlier writers. I have made a number of references to the chapter on the Outrages in John Derry's *The Story of Sheffield*. In his concluding remarks in this chapter he quotes Professor G I H Lloyd's summary on the Sheffield Outrages taken from his book, *The Cutlery Trades:*

'Broadly speaking, the result of the outrages inquiry was to vindicate trade-unionism in Sheffield, in the sense that the many grave crimes were shown to have been the work of a few clever and unscrupulous scoundrels such as Broadhead, and they were further shown to be utterly abhorrent to the great body of workers. It must also be remembered that trade-unionism in Sheffield, both before and since, has produced many leaders of the highest type, and that even at this unhappy epoch the principal leader of the local labour movement was not Broadhead but William Dronfield, whose work and whose character were never impugned, but, on the contrary, commanded universal respect and admiration.'[497]

This seems to sum things up objectively but Derry goes on to say:

'It is a sad story of wrong-doing and suffering and failure, which brought only discredit, with no gain, to those who defied the law; as all such violence must do in the end, whenever people try to terrorise men instead of convincing them.'[498]

---

[497] Op. Cit. Derry, p.153
[498] Ibid

Conclusion

I hope that I have shown that the history of the Sheffield Outrages deserves better than being a mere footnote in the city's history and that perhaps it was not altogether the negative saga as that which it has been portrayed. The myth of 19th century Sheffield trade unionists being a band of brutish rogues led by the saw grinders and their tyrannical leader, and that only death and destruction came of their fearful doings, is exposed. The orthodox and somewhat bias history of the Sheffield Outrages that has been handed down and swept under the Town Hall carpet omits a great deal of the actual events and presents us with only negative aspects and outcomes. The very title given to this series of events suggests something of a horror story, not the narrative of the prevailing conflict between working men and greedy industrial capitalists. But once we understand the dark, dirty and dangerous conditions that Sheffield's craftsmen worked under at this time and that the trade unions were their only means of defence against unemployment, dire poverty, the workhouse and an early grave; how, when unchecked by their trade unions, they were exploited beyond reasonable limits; and when we appreciate the inadequacies of their 'short and merry lives', we might at least consider both factions in the industrial struggle of the day as being equally outrageous. The use of violence to settle an argument, often under the influence of drink, was common practice at this time and arguments over trade issues were no different to any other. The Commissioners were aware of this and were anxious to ensure that the incidents they were investigating were relevant to the Inquiry and not the outcome of some personal quarrel.

In the main, trade unionists considered that the victims of rattening deserved all that they got, particularly those who deliberately worked against the unions, and few sympathised with those who got into arrears with their *'natty'*. The non-violent rattenings and threatening letters became routine forms of intimidation amongst the Sheffield trades and most rattenings were undertaken without the official sanction of the unions, principally because it wasn't needed. The threatening letters, which were generally sent by a union officer, although not always in an official capacity, gave the obnoxious member or defiant employer an opportunity to steer clear of conflict with the unions. And as damage was done to the property of employers when rattenings had occurred, the unions were honourable in paying compensation provided it wasn't construed as an admission of the union being responsible, as when William Broadhead sent 2s-6d to Moses Eadon & Co. for the damage that Abraham Green had done to their door. The violent outrages that occurred, including those that resulted in the unintended deaths of two people, one of them a totally innocent old lady, were committed by a very small minority within the trade union ranks and although not condoned, and despite large rewards being offered, no-one stepped forward to inform on the perpetrators. Such was the loyalty within the Sheffield trade union movement, although it was argued by some, especially the press, that the reluctance to inform on the perpetrators was out of fear for personal safety.

The orthodox history of the Sheffield Outrages underscores the role of William Broadhead, as did the press reports of the day. The fraction of Sheffield people who today are aware of this part of the city's history will no doubt also be aware of the role of William Broadhead but will they know about the other culpable union leaders such as Henry Skidmore, Joseph Barker and Michael Thompson? They may know of the roles of Samuel Crookes and maybe James Hallam but would they be able to tell us about Robert Renshaw who was just as much a killer as Crookes was? All of these men are high profile players in the history of the Sheffield Outrages but only Broadhead is centre stage and given the principal role of arch-villain. The emphasis on the Sheffield saw grinders also ignores the fact that outrages were undertaken in many other trades and that they stretched well beyond the Sheffield region, although most of the incidents investigated by the Commissioners were undertaken by grinders of one kind or another. Similar incidents occurred in other trades and in other parts of the country but Sheffield and the saw grinders were highlighted, not because the extent of the problem in the town was greater than elsewhere but more to do with the crusade of the local press, led by a determined William Leng, in promoting that perception. Of course the solution to ending the outrages was to eradicate the causal factors. If trade unions were legal entities and they had recourse in law to protect their funds, there would be no need to act outside of the law. There had for far too long been an imbalance in the rights of men and masters and redressing this disparity was William Broadhead's overriding objective. The Commissioners, and subsequently the government, also recognised that this inequality was at least partly to blame for the prevailing industrial confrontation but the employers, civic dignitaries and the press clearly didn't, or wouldn't.

The role of the employers in the story of the outrages is less defined than that of the unions and their leaders, yet some where high profile civic dignitaries, aldermen and magistrates. Why were they so seemingly tolerant of the trade unions' criminal tendencies? Joshua Tyzack for example, who was a magistrate as well as a merchant and manufacturer, didn't even report being shot at to the police. Was this due to a fear of being judged on his role in the prevailing local conflict between labour and industrial capital? In contrast magistrates like Wilson Overend were overtly anti-trade union and often overstepped the mark of their authority when ratteners came before them in court. However, Overend was a surgeon with no workers to exploit. The masters may have been portrayed as victims in the press but they were well aware of the reasons behind the attacks upon them and that should all of the facts in a case be made known, as they would inevitably be should it go to court, the general public's support would be with the trade unions, not the masters.

Although Robert Applegarth and the other members of the 'Junta' distanced the nation-wide trade union movement from the Sheffield Outrages, they nevertheless were able to use what had happened in Sheffield to add weight to their argument for legislation that would even the field in British industrial relations. Ultimately that argument was won as new rights for trade unions were gradually enacted by the government in response to Frederic Harrison's Report following the Royal Commissions. It is likely that these rights would have been won in the fullness of time irrespective of the Sheffield Outrages through reasoned argument and progressive governance but without the issue being brought to a head by the Inquiries, the fight would have been harder and trade union rights in law would have taken much longer to achieve.

Whilst we cannot approve of the actions of William Broadhead and his cohort we can accept them as being congruent of their time and at least recognise the effect that they had upon the development of trade unions and the progress made in British industrial relations since; the Sheffield Outrages were a catalyst for progress. Perhaps as we approach the 150th anniversary of the Royal Commission in 2017 someone at the Town Hall will take enough interest to organise a commemorative event, perhaps a joint venture between Sheffield City Council and Sheffield Trades Union Council; the local employers' federations may also be interested. As for commemorating the Sheffield Outrages with a permanent feature, a statue of William Broadhead across from the Cutlers' Hall may be a step too far for some but it would be appropriate to have a focal point in the city centre to inform tourists and to remind local people of these turbulent times and of the significance of the Sheffield Outrages, emphasising the positive changes that they brought about.

Bibliography

Bentley, David, *The Sheffield Hanged 1750-1864,* ALD Design & Print, 2002

Bentley, David, *The Sheffield Murders 1865-1965,* ALD Design & Print, 2003

Best, Geoffrey, *Mid-Victorian Britain 1851-75,* Fontana press, 1971

Briggs, Asa and Saville, John, (Eds), *Essays in Labour History,* Macmillan, 1967

Chesney, Kellow, *The Victorian Underworld,* Temple Smith, London, 1970

Coates, Ken and Topham, Tony, *Trade Unions in Britain,* Fontana Press, 1988

Derry, John, *The Story of Sheffield,* S.R. Publishers Limited, 1971

Dickens, Charles, *Bleak House,* Centennial Edition, Edito-Service S A, Geneva, originally published in 1853

Drewry, Mick, *Inundation - The History, the Times and the People of the Great Sheffield Flood of 1864, youbooks.co.uk, 2014*

Drinkall, Margaret, *Murder & Crime Sheffield,* The History Press, 2009

Drinkall, Margaret, *The Sheffield Book of Days,* The History Press, 2012

Evans, Eric J., *The Forging of the Modern State – Early Industrial Britain 1783-1870,* Longman, London and New York, 1996

Fraser, W Hamish, *A History of British Trade Unionism 1700-1998,* Macmillan Press Ltd, 1999

Gilmour, Ian, *Riot, Risings and Revolution – Governance and Violence in Eighteenth-century England,* Pimlico, 1992

Hart-Davis, Adam, *What the Victorians Did for Us,* Headline Book Publishing, 2001

Hey, David, *A History of Sheffield,* Carnegie Publishing, 1998

Hibbert, Christopher, *The English – A Social History 1066 – 1945,* Guild Publishing, London, 1987

Hopkins, Eric, *A Social History of the English Working Classes 1815-1945,* Hodder & Stoughton, 2004

Hunt, Tristram, *Building Jerusalem, The Rise and Fall of the Victorian City,* Phoenix, 2005

Laroff, Gary P, *Addis History and Carving Tool Imprint Overview,* 2006

Longmate, Norman, *Milestones in Working Class History,* BBC, 1975

Machan, Peter, *Outrage – The Story of William Broadhead and the Trade Union Scandals of Victorian Sheffield,* (No. 3 in a series of Tales of Victorian Sheffield), Alistair Lofthouse Design & Print

Mathers, Helen, and McIntosh, Tania, *Born in Sheffield – A History of the Women's Health Services 1864 – 2000,* Wharncliffe Books, 2000

Pelling, Henry, *A History of British Trade Unionism,* Penguin Books, 1992

Reade, Charles, *Put Yourself in His Place,* Chatto & Windus, Piccadilly, London, c.1870

Robertson, David, *Dictionary of Politics,* Penguin Books, 1993

Taylor, John (Ed), *The Illustrated Guide to Sheffield and the Surrounding District*, Pawson and Brailsford, Sheffield, 1879

The Sheffield Outrages – Report Presented to the Trades Unions Commissioners in 1867, Adams & Dart, 1971

Tholfsen, Trygve R, *Working Class Radicalism in Mid-Victorian England,* Croom Helm, London, 1976

Thompson, E.P., *The Making of the English Working Class,* Pelican Books, 1968

Thompson, F.M.L., *The Rise of Respectable Society – A Social History of Victorian Britain, 1830-1900,* Fontana Press, 1988

Vickers, J Edward, *A Popular History of Sheffield,* Applebaum Bookshop Ltd, Sheffield, 1987

Walton, Mary, *Sheffield Its Story and its Achievements,* The Sheffield Telegraph & Star Limited, 1948

Wright, Christopher, *The Working Class,* B. T. Batsford Ltd, London, 1972

Other sources:

Directory of Sheffield 1787

Dr. J C Hall, *The Trades of Sheffield as Influencing Life and Health – More Particularly File Cutters and Grinders,* Longman, Green and Co., London, read before the National Association for the Promotion of Social Science, 5 October 1865

Dr. J C Hall, *On The Prevention and treatment of the Sheffield Grinders' Disease,* Longman, Brown, Green, Longman & Roberts, 1857

History Today, Vol. 65, Issue 8, August 2015

Holland, G Calvert M.D., *The Mortality, Sufferings and Diseases of Grinders Part II – Pen-Blade Grinders,* Ridge and Jackson, 1842

Holland, G Calvert M.D., *Vital Statistics of Sheffield,* London, 1843

Johnson, M P, *The History of Grinders' Asthma in Sheffield*

Kelly's Post Office Directory of Sheffield 1854 and 1881

Leader, Robert, *The Local Register and Chronological Account of Occurrences and Facts Connected with the Town and Neighbourhood of Sheffield,* 1830 with continuations to 1857

Lightowler, Karen, *Sheffield Flood - The Aftermath,* www.lulu.com, 2011

Pollard, Sidney, *The Ethics of the Sheffield Outrages,* article in the *Transactions of the Hunter Archaeological Society,* 1954

Sheffield Hallam University, *Sheffield Flood Claims Archive,* www2.shu.ac.uk/sfca

Sheffield Independent, 16 October 1847

Slater's Directory, 1855

Sources for the Study of The Sheffield Outrages, Sheffield Libraries Archives and Information, www.sheffield.gov.uk/archives, 2011

The Concise Dictionary of National Biography, Volume I A-F, Volume II G-M, Volume III, Oxford University Press, 1994

The Rotherham Independent, 31 March 1870

The Spectator, 27 October 1866

The Sheffield Daily Telegraph, 12 & 14 October 1866

The Times, 29 June 1867

Tweedale, Geoffrey, *Addis: A Famous Name in Carving Tools,* www.wkfinetools.com, 2015

Whites General Directory 1841, 1845, 1849, 1854, 1855, 1856, 1857, 1862, 1871 and 1879

www.truecrimelibrary.com/Victorianhangings

http://freepages.history.rootsweb.ancestry.com/~calder dalecompanion/qq_105.html

www.penmorfa.com/bricks/england19.html

www.sheffielddiary.blogspot.com

www.sheffieldtuc.co.uk/history

www.straightrazorplace.com

www.youle.info/history/fh_material/making_of_sheffield